THE ROUGH GUIDE TO

THE GREAT LAKES & CHICAGO

First edition written by Andrea Bastien.

This book includes extractions from The Rough Guide to the USA written by Maria Edwards, Stephen Keeling, Todd Obolsky, Annelise Sorensen, Georgia Stephens and Greg Ward, updated and published in 2021 by Apa Publications Ltd. A big thank you to all the contributing authors of the Rough Guide to the USA.

ROUGH GUIDES

Contents

A NOTE TO READERS

At Rough Guides, we always strive to bring you the most up-to-date information. This book was produced during a period of continuing uncertainty caused by the Covid-19 pandemic, so please note that content is more subject to change than usual. We recommend checking the latest restrictions and official guidance.

Introduction to

The Great Lakes

No region better embodies both the endearing and perplexing attributes of the USA than the cities and natural sites of the Great Lakes region. Considered the third coast (and with more shoreline than either the Pacific or Atlantic coasts), the thousands of miles surrounding what makes up a whopping 21% of the Earth's freshwater are significant hubs of both industry and biodiversity. Most tourists are first drawn to the major cities lining lakes Michigan and Erie, each contributing their own rich, distinctive, and complicated takes on American history, industry, and culture. At the center of it all is Chicago, the de-facto capital of the region and the heart of the country itself. Away from the city centres you'll find natural wonders that run the gamut, from breathtaking cliffs to rolling dunes. To the northwest, Minnesota's northern passage and Michigan's Upper Peninsula offers a gateway to the most secluded and untouched wilderness in the region, and the best place in the country to view the Northern Lights (*aurora borealis*). Further inland, observe cities like Springfield, IL and Indianapolis, IN, more reminiscent of the out of the way hamlets of the Midwest than the hustle and bustle on the coasts. This is a region of outdoor sports, dining, music, politics – truly something for everyone can be found here. In essence, The Great Lakes represent the USA in all its flaws and all its glory - the American Dream for all of its attainability and volatility.

The crux of the Great Lakes region is that of world class experiences with working-class sensibilities. The cities and towns around the Great Lakes are home to icons as diverse as Michael Jordan, Madonna, Lebron James, Abraham Lincoln, Carl Sandburg, Frank Lloyd Wright, Oprah Winfrey and Walt Disney. From the floor of the first Ford factory to the 180th floor of the Willis (Sears) Tower, throughout history the Great Lakes have been the place of innovators and change-makers. With influential contributions to every genre of music, including blues, country, jazz, rock 'n' roll and hip-hop – many American musical innovations have taken place in urban hubs of Chicago, Detroit, Cleveland, and Minneapolis. The result is a region that acts almost as a mirror to the rest of the country, reflecting both the real and ideal nature of the United States in its most potent, concentrated form.

Across the region are enclaves of Irish Americans, Italian Americans, African Americans, Asian Americans, and Latinos from every Spanish speaking country in the world. The historical segregation in the major cities have resulted in distinctive multitudes of traditions and experiences that vary from neighborhood to neighbor, representing people of the world and every corner of American life. The duality of these places, to capture both the American Dream and the inequalities that weigh it down within the same square mile, is what gives the cities here such a bewildering quality. The contradictions of the wealthy industrialist and the weary workers; of affluent suburbs and struggling inner cities; of dense metropolises and desolate forests; simultaneously challenging and confirming our perceptions.

There are many ways to experience this region, with each location emphasizing a different food, culture, or connection to the lakes. What all citizens of this region share, from the Chicagoans in high rises to folks in the North woods of Wisconsin, is a deep rooted, defiant pride in their home, dedication to their communities, and an enthusiasm to share what William Faulkner would call their "own little postage stamp of native soil".

USA

N

CANADA

CENTRAL
STANDARD
TIME

EASTERN
STANDARD
TIME

MINNESOTA

Lake Superior

Lake
Huron

WISCONSIN

Minneapolis-
St Paul

Milwaukee

Madison

MICHIGAN

Lake Michigan

Detroit

IOWA

Des Moines

Chicago

Lake Erie

Cleveland

Montréal

MAINE

VERMONT

Portland

NEW
HAMPSHIRE

NEW
YORK

Boston

Cape
Cod

Toronto

Lake Ontario

Niagara
Falls

MASSACHUSETTS

RHODE
ISLAND

CONNECTICUT

PENNSYLVANIA

Philadelphia

New York City

Pittsburgh

NEW JERSEY

Atlantic City

DELAWARE

MARYLAND

ILLINOIS

INDIANA

OHIO

Cincinnati

WEST
VIRGINIA

WASHINGTON DC

maha

KANSAS

MISSOURI

Kansas
City

St Louis

KENTUCKY

Richmond

VIRGINIA

Outer Banks

Wichita

Nashville

Asheville

Durham

NORTH
CAROLINA

Jacksonville

OKLAHOMA

ARKANSAS

TENNESSEE

SOUTH
CAROLINA

Wilmington

Oklahoma
City

Little Rock

Memphis

Atlanta

Columbia

ATLANTIC
OCEAN

Birmingham

Charleston

Dallas

MISSISSIPPI

ALABAMA

GEORGIA

Savannah

LOUISIANA

ustin

Houston

New Orleans

Orlando

FLORIDA

Gulf of
Mexico

Miami

Feet	
9800	
6500	
3300	
1600	
700	
330	
0	

CUBA

Where to go

You do not have to traverse the entire Great Lakes region from east to west in order to appreciate its charms; to drive the coasts of Lakes Superior, Michigan, and Erie from Duluth, Minnesota to Cleveland, Ohio would take you 27 hours, and over 1,600 miles. Some cities, like Chicago and Milwaukee, are known for their reliable public transit, while others like Indianapolis and Detroit are notorious for the delays and disconnects of theirs. Generally, you'll need a **car** – that mandatory component of life in the USA.

The obvious place to start for most people is **Chicago** – with its colourful history and numerous skyscrapers to prove its status as the essential American metropolis. Located on the southeastern corner of Lake Michigan, here you will find magnificent architecture new and old, lively bars, sports arenas and music venues, fine dining and neighborhood deli counters, all surrounded by a sea of pizza places and hotdog stands. You could spend a week exploring downtown Chicago and its surrounding neighborhoods, enjoying summer bike rides along Lake Shore Drive or ice skating at Maggie Daley Park in winter. There are plenty of sites of culture and history to take in, from galleries and archives on the museum campus to the heritage of the buildings themselves. If the only place you can go in the Great Lakes region is Chicago, the city is certainly a full itinerary within itself. For history buffs, the state capital of Springfield offers immersion in everything Abraham Lincoln.

Due north of the Windy City along Lake Michigan are the big cities, college towns, and dairy farms of Wisconsin. Imbibe in the beer capital of Milwaukee, visit the country's largest farmer's market in the lively college town and state capital of Madison, and take in the sublime beauty of the Door Peninsula. Be sure to enjoy some cheese curds along the way!

Further east is Michigan, the birthplace of the automotive industry and one known as much for its deciduous forests. Pay a visit to the up and coming Detroit, a city witness to the rise and fall of industrial America now reinventing itself once more. Travel north along the coastline and take a ferry to Isle Royale National Park and the Upper Peninsula for isolated encounters with the region's natural beauty.

South of Michigan, seven hundred miles west, lie the **Great Lakes**, on the whole the country's most underappreciated region. Here lie dynamic cities like Chicago and a regenerating Cleveland, isolated and evocative lakeshores in Michigan and Minnesota, remote national parks such as Isle Royale and Voyageurs, and lively college towns such as Madison, Wisconsin.

When to go

The Great Lakes and Chicago region experiences the full range of seasons, from the stifling hot to the bitter cold. Winters can be abjectly cold, with temperatures below freezing and heavy snow making travel through even well-prepared cities difficult, and

causing intercity flights to be delayed and even cancelled. The cold season tends to last from late November to mid-March, but spring can be unpredictable and precipitous.

Tornadoes (or "twisters") are a frequent local phenomenon, tending to cut a narrow swathe of destruction in the wake of violent spring or summer thunderstorms. While they are less common in the more built-up parts of the Midwest, they have been known to touch down on major cities from time to time.

AVERAGE TEMPERATURE (°F) AND RAINFALL

To convert °F to °C, subtract 32 and multiply by 5/9

	Jan	Feb	Mar	Apr	May	Jun	Jul	Aug	Sep	Oct	Nov	Dec
ANN ARBOR, MI												
Max/min temp	31/19	34/20	46/28	59/39	70/49	79/59	83/63	81/61	73/53	61/43	48/33	36/24
Days of rain	6	5	7	9	10	10	11	10	9	8	7	7
CHICAGO												
Max/min temp	32/18	34/20	43/29	55/40	65/50	75/60	81/66	79/65	73/58	61/47	47/34	36/23
Days of rain	11	10	12	11	12	11	9	9	9	9	10	11
CLEVELAND, OH												
Max/min temp	36/22	39/24	47/31	60/41	71/51	80/61	84/65	82/64	76/57	63/47	51/37	40/23
Days of rain	17	15	15	15	12	11	9	9	10	12	14	16
DETROIT, MI												
Max/min temp	32/21	35/23	45/30	58/41	70/52	79/62	83/66	80/65	73/57	61/46	48/36	37/27
Days of rain	6	5	7	9	10	10	10	10	9	7	7	7
DULUTH, MN												
Max/min temp	23/8	27/11	37/22	49/34	61/43	70/52	77/60	75/59	66/51	53/40	39/27	26/14
Days of rain	3	2	5	7	10	12	11	11	9	7	5	4
INDIANAPOLIS, IN												
Max/min temp	36/23	41/26	52/35	64/45	74/55	82/64	85/67	83/65	77/58	65/47	52/37	40/27
Days of rain	7	6	9	11	12	12	12	10	8	8	8	8
MADISON, WI												
Max/min temp	28/14	32/17	45/28	59/39	70/49	79/59	82/63	80/61	72/53	59/42	45/30	32/19
Days of rain	4	4	6	9	11	11	11	11	9	7	6	5
MINNEAPOLIS-ST. PAUL												
Max/min temp	24/10	29/14	42/26	58/47	70/50	79/60	83/62	80/62	71/53	58/41	42/28	28/15
Days of rain	3	3	5	8	11	12	12	11	9	6	4	4
SPRINGFIELD												
Max/min temp	36/21	40/25	53/35	65/45	75/55	83/64	86/67	84/65	78/57	66/46	52/37	40/26
Days of rain	5	5	8	10	12	11	10	10	8	8	7	7

Author picks

Our hard-travelling authors have visited every corner of this vast, magnificent region and have picked out their personal highlights.

Literary landmarks The American Writers Museum (see page 51) is a must for any bibliophiles visiting the Great Lakes. Visit the Ernest Hemingway house in Oak Park, IL (see page 59) and the Kurt Vonnegut Museum & Library in Indianapolis (see page 72), for a fresh take on how their hometowns impacted their work. The region is also home to dozens of independent bookstores, from those clustered on 57th St in Hyde Park, Chicago (see page 60) and on Main Street in Ann Arbor, MI (see page 98), to the unique *Falling Rocks Café & Bookstore* in Munising, MI.

Best microbreweries Since the 1990s America has been experiencing a craft beer revolution. The environmentally conscious *Great Lakes Brewing, Cleveland*, OH, makes a selection of great beers (see page 82).

Classic diners Few American icons are so beloved as the roadside diner, where burgers, apple pie and strong coffee are often served 24/7. In Chicago, there's *Lou Mitchell's* (see page 64).

Top wildlife spots The Great Lakes are incredibly rich in wildlife, and reserves such as Boundary Waters in Minnesota (see page 120) hold wolves and white-tailed deer.

BREAKFAST IN LOU MITCHELL'S ON ROUTE 66

BALD EAGLE AT NEL'S LAKE

Our author recommendations don't end here. We've flagged up our favourite places – a perfectly sited hotel, an atmospheric café, a special restaurant – throughout the Guide, highlighted with the ★ symbol.

things not to miss

It's obviously not possible to see everything that the Great Lakes have to offer in one trip. What follows is a selective and subjective taste of the region's highlights: unforgettable cities, spectacular drives, magnificent parks, spirited celebrations and stunning natural phenomena. All highlights are colour-coded by chapter and have a page reference to take you straight into the Guide, where you can find out more.

1 CHICAGO RIVER BOAT TOURS, IL
See page 62

Take a boat tour on the Chicago River to soak up the Windy' City's diverse architectural and cultural heritage.

2 ISLE ROYALE NATIONAL PARK, MI
See page 105

Accessible only by ferry or boat, this one of a kind national park offers secluded adventures on a remote archipelago on Lake Superior. If you have the chance to go to Isle Royale, do not pass it up.

3 NORTH SHORE SCENIC DRIVE, MN
See page 120

Explore the north coast of Lake Superior from Duluth to the Canadian border, lined with dense forests and plunging cascades.

4 DETROIT, MI
See page 92

What was once a post-industrial dystopia is now a city on the rise. Explore one of America's most intriguing, edgy and creative cities.

5 ROCK AND ROLL HALL OF FAME, OH
See page 79

From rockabilly to Motown to punk – it's all here inside this absorbing museum.

6 VOYAGEURS NATIONAL PARK, MN
See page 121
With 218,055 acres of exposed rock ridges, cliffs, forests, wetlands, lakes, and streams, Voyageurs is a remote gem of vast northern wilderness for year-round exploration.

7 ABRAHAM LINCOLN SITES, IL
See page 68
Immerse yourself in all things Abraham Lincoln at the Illinois state capitol, now a virtual shrine to the great American president.

8 INDY 500, IN
See page 71
Hosted in Indianapolis every May since 1911, this is the premiere open wheel automobile racing event in the United States.

9 BASEBALL GAME AT WRIGLEY FIELD, IL
See page 59
There is no better place to enjoy America's favorite pastime than from the historic, ivy-clad baseball field on Chicago's north side.

10 PICTURED ROCKS NAT LAKESHORE, MI
See page 104
Multi-hued sandstone cliffs, spectacular sand dunes and picturesque waterfalls dot this remote corner of Michigan's Upper Peninsula.

10

11

12

13

14

15

Itineraries

The following itineraries span the entire length of this incredibly diverse region, from the earliest trading posts to the most modern cities, and miles of jaw-dropping coastline. Given the vast distances involved, you may not be able to cover everything, but even picking a few highlights will give you a deeper insight into the Great Lakes' natural and historic wonders.

CLASSIC LAKE MICHIGAN LOOP

This three-week tour strikes a balance between Lake Michigan's great cities and natural scenery, travelling through Illinois, Wisconsin, Michigan and Indiana. Can be taken in either direction.

❶ **Chicago, IL** America's third city boasts some serious skyscrapers, top museums, live blues, the Cubs and the Bears, and those deep-dish pizzas. See page 48

❷ **Indiana Dunes National Park, IN** Just one hour east of Chicago, find secluded, contemplative beaches and wetlands in one of the region's most accessible natial parks. See page 71

❸ **Grand Rapids, MI** Michigan's second largest city is known for its high quality microbreweries and being the home of former president Gerald Ford. See page 100

❹ **Sleeping Bear Dunes National Lakeshore, MI** The highlight of Michigan's northern coast features towering dunes, ample forests and precipitous 400ft drops. See page 101

❺ **Traverse City, MI** The Cherry Capital of the world at the top of the mitt offers a rustic downtown, sandy beaches, and plenty of activities on water and on land. See page 100

❻ **Petoskey and Harbor Springs, MI** Two affluent towns on the Little Traverse Bay marked by grand Victorian Houses, see where Ernest Hemingway spend his childhood summers. See page 101

❼ **Mackinac Island, MI** Take a ferry from Mackinaw City to witness historic sights and landmarks from the Great Lakes' maritime history. See page 103

❽ **Door County Coastal Byway, WI** Take a drive along the Door County Peninsula, including jaunts by the coastline towns of Sister Bay and Egg Harbor. See page 48

❾ **Milwaukee, WI** Perched on Lake Michigan just 90 miles north of Chicago, end your trip in the beer and motorcycle capital of the US. See page 106

THE NORTH SHORES PASSAGE

Only when you traverse the northern passage of the Great Lakes can you begin to appreciate how big – and rich in natural beauty – the

---

Create your own itinerary with Rough Guides. Whether you're after adventure or a family-friendly holiday, we have a trip for you, with all the activities you enjoy doing and the sights you want to see. All our trips are devised by local experts who get the most out of the destination. Visit **www.roughguides.com/trips** to chat with one of our travel agents.

Great Lakes are. Take three to four weeks to enjoy this trip around Lake Superior via Minnesota, Wisconsin, and the Upper Peninsula of Michigan. Make sure you have all the proper gear for roughing it in the backcountry.

❶ Duluth MN Perched at the Western extremity of Lake Superior, its busy harbor and downtown waterfront are a great starting point for any northern adventure. See page 119

❷ Voyageurs National Park Set along the border lakes between Minnesota and Canada, Voyageurs is like no other national park. Leave your car and venture out by boat to truly experience the area. See page 121

❸ Grand Portage National Monument, MN From this historic fur trading post, catch a ferry to Isle Royale National Park. See page 121

❹ Isle Royale National Park, MI Fifty miles out in Lake Superior, this is the most remote national park in the region, receiving under 15,000 visitors a year. See page 105

❺ North Shore Scenic Drive Follow the thickly forested Lake Superior shoreline for 150 miles northeast from Duluth to the US/Canadian border. See page 120

❻ Apostle Islands National Lakeshore, WI This stretch of shoreline and archipelago features breathtaking cliffs and stunning sea caves teaming with wildlife. See page 113

❼ Houghton and the Keweenaw Peninsula A scenic drive to the northernmost tip of the Upper Peninsula at Copper Bay. See page 105

❽ Marquette, MI The only real city on the Upper Peninsula, this low-key college town is the unofficial capital of the UP. See page 105

❾ Pictured Rocks National Park, MI Covering a 42 mile stretch of Lake Superior, this park features a splendid array of multicoloured cliffs, rolling dunes, and secluded sandy beaches. See page 104

GREAT LAKES CITIES & CAPITALS TOUR

Enjoy two or three weeks travelling through the heart of the Great Lakes region from hub to hub. Make sure to budget a few days in Chicago and the Twin Cities – both have large metropolitan areas with plenty to see.

❶ Detroit, MI There's much more to Motor City than its urban ruins; this is an exciting city emerging from the ashes of its troubled past. See page 92

❷ Cleveland, OH With the well-established Rock and Roll Hall of Fame and revamped Lake Erie waterfront, Cleveland can no longer be seen as "the mistake on the lake". See page 77

❸ Columbus, OH State capital and home to the Ohio State University, Ohio's largest city offers a vibrant nightlife and gorgeous architecture. See page 84

❹ Cincinnati, OH In the southeast corner of the state, Cincinnati is a dynamic commercial metropolis with a European flavor and a sense of the South. See page 87

❺ Indianapolis, IN Home of the Indy 500, this state capital also hosts other major sports downtown as well as intriguing museums and monuments. See page 71

❻ Springfield, IL The state capital of Illinois is now a virtual shrine to 16th US president Abraham Lincoln. See page 68

❼ Chicago, IL No trip to the Great Lakes would be complete without a stop in the largest and most central city in the region. See page 48

❽ Madison, WI The capital of Wisconsin also happens to be the most attractive college town in the USA, just a 2hr 30min drive northwest of Chicago. See page 110

❾ Minneapolis, MN More than half of all Minnesotans live around the Twin Cities, visit the Mall of America and Paisley Park, the estate of the late pop icon Prince. See page 113

CHICAGO DEEP DISH PIZZA

Basics

Getting there

Anyone travelling to the Great Lakes from abroad will most likely purchase a flight to O'Hare International Airport in Chicago, the most accessible international airport in the region. From there, you can either book a local flight to any of the other Great Lakes city hubs, or rent a car and take a scenic route from state to state.

In general, ticket prices are highest from July to September, and around Easter, Thanksgiving and Christmas. Fares drop during the shoulder seasons – April to June, and October – and even more so in low season, from November to March (excluding Easter, Christmas and New Year). Prices depend more on when Americans want to head overseas than on the demand from foreign visitors. Flying at weekends usually costs significantly more.

Flights from the UK and Ireland

Chicago is the only city in the Great Lakes region accessible by nonstop flights from the UK. Direct services (which may land once or twice on the way but are called direct if they keep the same flight number throughout their journey) fly from Britain to nearly every other major Great Lakes city.

Nonstop flights to Chicago from London take eight or nine hours. Following winds ensure that return flights take an hour or two less. One-stop direct flights to destinations beyond the East Coast add time to the journey but can work out cheaper than nonstop flights.

Four airlines run nonstop scheduled services to the USA from Ireland. Flights depart from both Dublin and Shannon airports, and the journey times are very similar to those from London.

As for fares, Britain remains one of the best places in Europe to obtain flight bargains, though prices vary widely. In low or shoulder season, you should be able to find an affordable return flight to Chicago, while high-season rates can more than double. These days the fares available on the airlines' own websites are

often just as good as those you'll find on more general travel websites. Be sure to check the airline's policy on flight cancellations, insurance, and changing your flights. Many airlines have improved their flexibility in altering flights in light of the unpredictable nature of the Covid-19 pandemic.

With an open-jaw ticket, you can fly into one city and out of another, though if you're renting a car remember that there's usually a high drop-off fee for returning a rental car in a different state than where you picked it up. An air pass can be a good idea if you want to see a lot of the country. These are available only to non-US residents, and must be bought before reaching the USA (see page 23).

Flights from Australia, New Zealand and South Africa

For passengers travelling from Australasia to the USA, the most expensive time to fly has traditionally been during the northern summer (mid-May to end Aug) and over the Christmas period (Dec to mid-Jan), with shoulder seasons covering March to mid-May and September, and the rest of the year counting as low season. Fares no longer vary as much across the year as they used to, however.

From New Zealand, the cost of flying from Auckland or Christchurch does vary slightly depending on the time of year. From South Africa (again, when travel restrictions are lifted), transatlantic flights from Cape Town or Johannesburg are not as expensive as they used to be, depending on the time of year.

Various add-on fares and air passes valid in the continental US are available with your main ticket, allowing you to fly to destinations across the States. These must be bought before you go.

AIRLINES

Aer Lingus Ⓦ aerlingus.com
Air Canada Ⓦ aircanada.com
AeroMexico Ⓦ aeromexico.com
Air Choice One Ⓦ airchoiceone.com
Air France Ⓦ airfrance.com
Air India Ⓦ airindia.com

A BETTER KIND OF TRAVEL

At Rough Guides we are passionately committed to travel. We believe it helps us understand the world we live in and the people we share it with – and of course tourism is vital to many developing economies. But the scale of modern tourism has also damaged some places irreparably, and climate change is accelerated by most forms of transport, especially flying. We encourage all our authors to consider the carbon footprint of the journeys they make in the course of researching our guides.

Air New Zealand Ⓦ airnewzealand.com
Alaska Airlines Ⓦ alaskaair.com
Alitalia Ⓦ alitalia.com
All Nippon Ⓦ .na.co.jp
American Airlines Ⓦ aa.com
Austrian Airlines Ⓦ austrian.com
Boutique Air Ⓦ boutiqueair.com
British Airways Ⓦ ba.com
Cape Air Ⓦ capeair.com
Cathay Pacific Airways Ⓦ cathaypacific.com
China Eastern Airlines Ⓦ us.ceair.com
Copa Airlines Ⓦ copaair.com
Delta Air Lines Ⓦ delta.com
EVA Air Ⓦ evaair.com
Emirates Ⓦ emirates.com
Ethiopian Airlines Ⓦ ethiopianairlines.com
Etihad Airways Ⓦ flights.Etihad.com
Finnair Ⓦ finnair.com
Frontier Airlines Ⓦ flyfrontier.com
Hainan Airlines Ⓦ hainanairlines.com
Iberian Airlines Ⓦ iberia.com
Icelandair Ⓦ icelandair.us
Interjet Airlines Ⓦ interjet.com
JAL (Japan Airlines) Ⓦ jal.com
JetBlue Ⓦ jetblue.com
KLM Ⓦ klm.com
Korean Air Ⓦ koreanair.com
LOT Polish Airlines Ⓦ lot.com
Lufthansa Ⓦ lufthansa.com
Norwegian Ⓦ norwegian.com
Qantas Airways Ⓦ qantas.com.au
Qatar Airways Ⓦ qatarairways.com
Royal Jordanian Ⓦ rj.com
SWISS Ⓦ swiss.com
Scandinavian Airlines (SAS) Ⓦ flysas.com
Southwest Ⓦ southwest.com
Spirit Airlines Ⓦ spirit.com
Sun Country Ⓦ suncountry.com
TAP Air Portugal Ⓦ flytap.com
Turkish Airlines Ⓦ turkishairlines.com
United Airlines Ⓦ united.com
VivaAerobus Ⓦ vivaaerobus.com
Volaris Airlines Ⓦ volaris.com

Getting around

Distances in the USA are so great that it's essential to plan in advance how you'll get from place to place. Amtrak provides a skeletal but often scenic rail service, and there are usually good bus links between the major cities. Even in rural areas, with advance planning, you can usually reach the main points of interest without too much trouble by using local buses and charter services.

That said, travel between cities is almost always easier if you have a car. Many worthwhile and memorable US destinations are far from the cities: even if a bus or train can take you to the general vicinity of one of the great national parks, for example, it would be of little use when it comes to enjoying the great outdoors.

By rail

Travelling on the national Amtrak network (Ⓦ amtrak. com) is rarely the fastest way to get around, though if you have the time, it can be a pleasant and relaxing experience. As you will note from our map (see page 22), the Amtrak system connects many of the major cities in the Great Lakes region, with Chicago serving as a connection. A number of small local train services connect stops on the Amtrak lines with towns and cities not on the main grid. Amtrak also runs the coordinated, but still limited, thruway bus service that connects some cities that their trains don't reach.

For any one specific journey, the train is usually more expensive than taking a Greyhound bus, or even a plane though special deals, especially in the off-peak seasons (Sept–May, excluding Christmas), can bring the cost of a coast-to-coast return trip down. Money-saving passes are also available (see page 23).

Even with a pass, you should always reserve as far in advance as possible; all passengers must have seats, and some trains are booked solid. Sleeping compartments are the most expensive, and they include three

---

HISTORIC RAILROADS

While Amtrak has a monopoly on long-distance rail travel, a number of historic or scenic railways, some steam-powered or running along narrow-gauge mining tracks, bring back the glory days of train travel. Many are purely tourist attractions, doing a full circuit through beautiful countryside in two or three hours, though some can drop you off in otherwise hard-to-reach wilderness areas. Fares vary widely according to the length of your trip. We've covered the most appealing options in the relevant Guide chapters.

PACKAGES AND TOURS

Although independent travel is usually cheaper, countless flight and accommodation packages allow you to bypass all the organizational hassles. A typical package from the UK might be a return flight plus mid-range hotel accommodation in downtown Chicago with the price doubling in peak periods.

Fly-drive deals, which give cut-rate car rental when a traveller buys a transatlantic ticket from an airline or tour operator, are always cheaper than renting on the spot, and give great value if you intend to do a lot of driving. They're readily available through general online booking agents such as Expedia and Travelocity, as well as through specific airlines. Several of the operators listed here also book accommodation for self-drive tours.

full meals, in addition to your seat fare, for one or two people. However, even standard Amtrak quarters are surprisingly spacious compared to aeroplane seats, and there are additional dining cars and lounge cars (with full bars and sometimes glass-domed 360° viewing compartments).

By bus

If you're travelling on your own and plan on making a lot of stops, buses are by far the cheapest way to get around. The main long-distance operator, Greyhound (Ⓦgreyhound.com, international customers without toll-free access can also call 214 849 8100; open 24/7), links all major cities and many towns. Out in the country, buses are fairly scarce, sometimes appearing only once a day, if at all. However, along the main highways, buses run around the clock to a full timetable, stopping only for meal breaks (almost always fast-food chains) and driver changeovers.

To avoid possible hassle, travellers should take care to sit as near to the driver as possible, and to arrive during daylight hours – many bus stations are in dodgy areas, at least in large cities. In many smaller places, the post office or a gas station doubles as the bus stop and ticket office. Reservations can be made in person at the station, online or on the toll-free number. Oddly they do not guarantee a seat, so it's wise to join the queue early – if a bus is full, you may have to wait for the next one, although Greyhound claims it will lay on an extra bus if more than ten people are left behind. For long hauls there are plenty of savings available – check the website's discounts page.

Other operators include Trailways (877 908 9330, Ⓦtrailways.com), whose regional divisions cover some parts of the country more comprehensively; and Megabus (877 462 6342; Ⓦus.megabus.com), whose low-cost service covers some Great Lakes cities.

By plane

Despite the presence of good-value discount airlines – most notably Southwest and JetBlue – air travel is a much less appealing way of getting around

PRE-TRIP PLANNING FOR OVERSEAS TRAVELLERS

AMTRAK PASSES

The USA Rail Pass covers the entire Amtrak network for the designated period, though you are restricted to a set number of individual journeys. Passes can be bought from the Amtrak website (Ⓦamtrak.com).

AIR PASSES

The main American airlines offer air passes for visitors who plan to fly a lot within the USA. These must be bought in advance and are often sold with the proviso that you cross the Atlantic with the same airline or group of airlines (such as Star Alliance or American Airlines). Each deal will involve the purchase of a certain number of flights, air miles or coupons. Other plans entitle foreign travellers to discounts on regular US domestic fares, again with the proviso that you buy the ticket before you leave home. Check with the individual airlines to see what they offer and the overall range of prices.

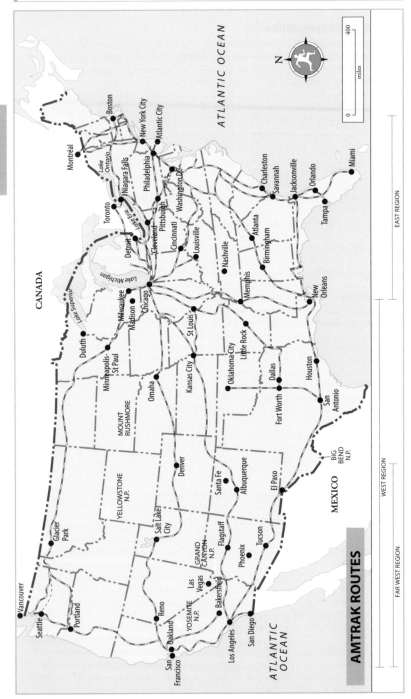

AMTRAK ROUTES

DRIVING FOR FOREIGNERS

Foreign nationals from English-speaking countries can drive in the USA using their full domestic driving licences (International Driving Permits are not always regarded as sufficient). Fly-drive deals are good value if you want to rent a car (see above), though you can save up to fifty percent simply by booking in advance with a major firm. If you choose not to pay until you arrive, be sure you take a written confirmation of the price with you. Remember that it's safer not to drive right after a long transatlantic flight – and that most standard rental cars have automatic transmissions.

the country than it used to be. With air fuel costs escalating even faster than gas costs, and airlines cutting routes, the days of using jet travel as a spur to vacation adventuring are long gone. To get any kind of break on price, you'll have to reserve well ahead of time (at least three weeks), and preferably not embark in the high season. One silver lining of the global pandemic is that many airlines have improved their booking flexibility in response to Covid-19, so there is less risk in booking flights far in advance. In those examples where flying can make sense for short local hops, we mention such options wherever appropriate throughout this Guide. Otherwise, phone the airlines or visit their websites to find out routes and schedules.

By car

For many, the concept of cruising down the highway, preferably in a convertible with the radio blasting, is one of the main reasons to set out on a tour of the USA. The romantic images of countless road movies are not far from the truth, though you don't have to embark on a wild spree of drinking, drugs and sex to enjoy driving across America. Apart from anything else, a car makes it possible to choose your own itinerary and to explore the astonishing wide-open landscapes that may well provide your most enduring memories of the country.

Driving in the cities, on the other hand, is not exactly fun, and can be hair-raising. Yet in larger places a car is by far the most convenient way to make your way around, especially as public transport tends to be spotty outside the major cities. Many urban areas, especially in the West, have grown up since cars were invented. As such, they sprawl for so many miles that your hotel may be on the other side of a freeway that cannot be crossed on foot.

Renting a car

To rent a car, you must have held your licence for at least one year. Drivers under 25 may encounter problems and have to pay higher than normal insurance premiums. Rental companies expect customers to have a credit card; if you don't, they may let you leave a cash deposit (at least $500), but don't count on it. All the major rental companies have outlets at the main airports but it can often be cheaper to rent from a city branch. Reservations are handled centrally, so the best way to shop around is either online, or by calling their national toll-free numbers. Potential variations are endless; certain cities and states are consistently cheaper than others, while individual travellers may be eligible for corporate, frequent-flier or AAA discounts. In low season you may find a tiny car (a "subcompact") for as little as $185 per week, but a typical budget rate would be more like $35–40 per day or around $245 per week, including taxes. You can get some good deals from strictly local operators, though it can be risky as well. Make reading up on such inexpensive vendors part of your pre-trip planning.

Even between the major operators, who tend to be more epensive than the local competition, there can be a big difference in the quality of cars. Industry leaders like Alamo, Hertz and Avis tend to have newer, lower-mileage cars and more reliable breakdown services. Always be sure to get unlimited mileage and remember that leaving a rental car in a different city from the one where you rented it can incur a sometimes significant drop-off charge.

Small print and insurance

When you rent a car, read the small print carefully for details on Collision Damage Waiver (CDW), sometimes called Liability Damage Waiver (LDW). This form of insurance specifically covers the car that you are driving yourself – you are in any case insured for damage to other vehicles. It can add substantially to the total cost, but without it you're liable for every scratch to the car – even those that aren't your fault. Increasing numbers of states are requiring that this insurance be included in the weekly rental rate and are regulating the amounts charged to cut down on rental-car company profiteering. Some credit card companies offer automatic CDW coverage to customers using their card; contact your issuing

HITCHHIKING

Hitchhiking in the United States is generally a bad idea, especially for women, making you a potential victim both inside (you never know who you're travelling with) and outside the car, as the odd fatality may occur from hitchers getting a little too close to the highway lanes. At a minimum, in the many states where the practice is illegal, you can expect a steep fine from the police and, on occasion, an overnight stay in the local jail. The practice is still fairly common, however, in more remote rural areas with little or no public transport.

company for details. Alternatively, European residents can cover themselves against such costs with a reasonably priced annual policy from Insurance4Car-Hire (Ⓦinsurance4carhire.com).

The American Automobile Association, or AAA (800 222 4357, Ⓦaaa.com), provides free maps and assistance to its members and to members of affiliated associations overseas, such as the British AA and RAC. If you break down in a rented car, call one of these services if you have towing coverage, or the emergency number pinned to the dashboard.

CAR RENTAL AGENCIES

Alamo USA 800 462 5266, Ⓦ alamo.com
Avis USA 800 230 4898, Ⓦ avis.com
Budget USA 800 527 0700, Ⓦ budget.com
Dollar USA 800 800 3665, Ⓦ dollar.com
Enterprise USA 800 261 7331, Ⓦ enterprise.com
Hertz USA 800 654 3131, Ⓦ hertz.com
National USA 800 227 7368, Ⓦ nationalcar.com
Thrifty USA & Canada 800 847 4389, Ⓦ thrifty.com

Cycling

Cycling is another realistic mode of transport. An increasing number of big cities have bicycle lanes and local buses equipped to carry bikes (strapped to the outside), while in country areas, roads have wide shoulders and fewer passing motorists. Unless you plan to cycle a lot and take your own bike, however, it's not especially cheap. Bikes can be rented for $20–50 per day, or at discounted weekly rates, from outlets that are usually found close to beaches, university campuses and good cycling areas. Local visitor centres have details.

The national non-profit Adventure Cycling Association, based in Missoula Montana (Ⓦadventurecycling.org), publishes maps of several lengthy routes, detailing campgrounds, motels, restaurants, bike shops and places of interest. Many individual states issue their own cycling guides; contact the state tourist offices (see page 43). Before setting out on a long-distance cycling trip, you'll need a good-quality, multispeed bike, panniers, tools and spares, maps,

padded shorts and a helmet (legally required in many states and localities). Plan a route that avoids interstate highways (on which cycling is unpleasant and usually illegal) and sticks to well-maintained, paved rural roads. Of problems you'll encounter, the main one is traffic: RVs, huge eighteen-wheelers and logging trucks can create intense backdraughts capable of pulling you out into the middle of the road.

Backroads Bicycle Tours (Ⓦbackroads.com), and the HI-USA hostelling group (see page 28) arrange multi-day cycle tours, with camping or stays in country inns; where appropriate we've also mentioned local firms that offer this.

Greyhound, Amtrak and major airlines will carry passengers' bikes – dismantled and packed into a box – for a small fee.

Accommodation

The cost of accommodation is significant for any traveller exploring the Great Lakes, especially in the cities, but wherever you travel, you're almost certain to find a good-quality, reasonably priced motel or hotel. If you're prepared to pay a little extra, wonderful historic hotels and lodges can offer truly memorable experiences.

The four price codes used in the Guide (see box) are based on a standard double room in high season – including breakfast – though substantial discounts are available at slack times Unsurprisingly, the sky's the limit for luxury hotels, where exclusive suites can easily run into four figures. Many hotels will set up a third single

ACCOMMODATION PRICE CODES

$̲ under 75
$̲$̲ 75-149
$̲$̲$̲ 150-200
$̲$̲$̲$̲ Over 200

bed for an extra fee, reducing costs for three people sharing. For lone travellers, on the other hand, a "single room" is usually a double at a slightly reduced rate at best. A dorm bed in a hostel is the most economical option per night, but standards of cleanliness and security can be low, and for groups of two or more the saving compared to a motel is often minimal. In certain parts of the USA, camping makes a cheap – and exhilarating – alternative. Alternative methods of finding a room online are through wairbnb.com and the free hosting site Ⓦcouchsurfing.org.

Wherever you stay, you'll be expected to pay in advance, at least for the first night and perhaps for further nights, too. Most hotels ask for a credit card imprint when you arrive, but many still accept cash for the actual payment. Reservations – essential in busy areas in summer – are held only until 6pm, unless you've said you'll be arriving late. Note that some cities – probably the ones you most want to visit – tack on a hotel tax that can raise the total tax for accommodation to as much as fifteen percent.

Note that as well as the local numbers we give in the Guide, many hotels have free phone numbers (found on their websites), which you can use within the USA.

Hotels and motels

The term "hotels" refers to most accommodation in the Guide. Motels, or "motor hotels", tend to be found beside the main roads away from city centres, and are thus much more accessible to drivers. Budget hotels or motels can be pretty basic, but in general standards of comfort are uniform – each room comes with a double bed (often two), a TV, phone and usually a portable coffeemaker, plus an attached bathroom. For an increase in price, the room and its fittings simply get bigger and include more amenities, and there may be a swimming pool and added amenities such as irons and ironing boards, or premium cable TV (HBO, Showtime, etc). Almost all hotels and motels now offer wi-fi, albeit of varying quality and sometimes in the lobby only.

The least expensive properties tend to be family-run, independent "mom 'n' pop" motels, but these are rarer nowadays, in the big urban areas at least. When you're driving along the main interstates there's a lot to be said for paying a few dollars more to stay in motels belonging to the national chains. These range from the ever-reliable and cheap Super 8 and Motel 6 through to the mid-range Days Inn and La Quinta up to the more commodious Holiday Inn Express and Hampton Inn.

During off-peak periods, many motels and hotels struggle to fill their rooms, so it's worth bargaining to get a few dollars off the asking price, especially at independent establishments. Staying in the same place for more than one night may bring further reductions. Also, look for discount coupons, especially in the free magazines distributed by local visitor centres and welcome centres near the borders between states. These can offer amazing value – but read the small print first. Online rates are also usually cheaper, sometimes considerably so.

Few budget hotels or motels bother to compete with the ubiquitous diners by offering full breakfasts, although most will provide free self-service coffee, pastries and if you are lucky, fruit or cereal, collectively referred to as "continental breakfast".

B&Bs

Staying in a B&B is a popular, sometimes luxurious, alternative to conventional hotels. Some B&Bs consist of no more than a couple of furnished rooms in someone's home, and even the larger establishments tend to have fewer than ten rooms, sometimes without TV or phone, but often laden with potpourri, chintzy cushions and an assertively precious Victorian atmosphere. If this cosy, twee setting appeals to you, there's a range of choices throughout the region, but keep a few things in mind. For one, you may not be an anonymous guest, as you would in a chain hotel, but may be expected to chat with the host and other guests, especially during breakfast. Also, some B&Bs enforce curfews, and take a dim view of guests stumbling in after midnight after an evening's partying. The only way to know the policy for certain is to check each B&B's policy online – there's often a lengthy list of do's and don'ts.

The price you pay for a B&B – which varies for a double room – always includes breakfast (sometimes a buffet on a sideboard, but more often a full-blown cooked meal). The crucial determining factor is whether each room has an en suite bathroom; most B&Bs provide private bath facilities, although that can damage the authenticity of a fine old house. At the top end of the spectrum, the distinction between a "boutique hotel" and a "bed-and-breakfast inn" may amount to no more than that the B&B is owned by a private individual rather than a chain. In many areas, B&Bs have united to form central booking agencies, making it much easier to find a room at short notice; we've given contact information for these where appropriate.

Historic hotels and lodges

Throughout the country many towns still have historic hotels, whether dating from the arrival of the railroads or from the heyday of Route 66 in the 1940s and 1950s. So long as you accept that not all will have up-to-date facilities to match their period charm, these can make wonderfully ambient places to spend a night or two. Those that are exceptionally well preserved or restored may charge more per room than a typical rate for a not overly luxurious but atmospheric, antique-furnished room.

In addition, several national parks feature long-established and architecturally distinguished hotels, traditionally known as lodges, that can be real bargains, thanks to federally controlled rates. The only drawback is that all rooms tend to be reserved far in advance. Among the best in the region are the Rock Harbor Lodge in Isle Royale National Park, see page 106 and Voyageurs Park Lodge at Lake Kabetogama in Voyageur's National Park, see page 121.

Hostels

Hostel-type accommodation is not as plentiful in the USA as it is in Europe, but provision for backpackers and low-budget travellers does exist. Unless you're travelling alone, most hostels cost about the same as motels; stay in them only if you prefer their youthful ambience, energy and sociability. Many are not accessible on public transport, or convenient for sightseeing in the towns and cities, let alone in rural areas.

These days, most hostels are independent, with no affiliation to the HI-USA (Hostelling-International-USA; http://hiusa.org) network. Many are no more than converted motels, where the "dorms" consist of a couple of sets of bunk beds in a musty room, which is also let out as a private unit on demand. Most expect guests to bring sheets or sleeping bags. Rates start low for a dorm bed and increase slightly for a double room, with prices in the major cities at the higher end. Those few hostels that do belong to HI-USA tend to impose curfews and limit daytime access hours, and segregate dormitories by sex.

Food and drink

Every state in the Great Lakes region offers its own specialties, and regional cuisines are distinctive and delicious. In addition, international food turns up regularly – not only in the big cities, but also in more unexpected places. Somali restaurants are plentiful in the Minneapolis-St. Paul area, and eastern European meats and pastries can be found in the historic town of Cleveland.

In the Guide, restaurants are given one of four price codes, based on the average price of two courses and an alcoholic drink for two people. In the big cities, you can pretty much eat whatever you want, whenever you want, thanks to the ubiquity of restaurants, 24-hour diners, and bars and street carts selling food well into the night. Also, along all the highways and on virtually every town's main street, restaurants, fast-food joints and cafés try to outdo one another with bargains and special offers. Whatever you eat and wherever you eat it, service is usually prompt, friendly and attentive – thanks in large part to the institution of tipping. Waiters depend on tips for the bulk of their earnings; twenty percent is the standard rate, with anything less sure to be seen as an insult.

Great Lakes cuisine

It is perfectly possible to create a fabulous Great Lakes road-trip itinerary by tracking the region's cuisines, which blend locally available ingredients with traditional dishes and techniques of local ethnic groups. Broadly, steaks and other cuts of beef are prominent in the Midwest, and each city has their own take on the classic burger. Fresh quality seafood and freshwater fish can be found along the Great Lakes, particularly in major cities. Be aware, however, that the farther you get from the major cities and lakeshores, the more likely it becomes that seafood is flown in and frozen.

Southern cooking, or soul food, is widely available in Great Lakes cities – everything from grits to collard greens, from crispy fried chicken to creamy baked macaroni and cheese. Barbecue is also very popular in Chicago, offering anything from dry-rub ribs to sweetly smoky barbecue. On the other end of the spectrum, new American cuisine applies the same principles to different regional food, generally presenting healthier versions of local favourites. The state of Wisconsin is regionally known for their farm-to-table fresh dairy and produce, and farmer's markets can be found in cities, towns, and roadsides across the Great Lakes when the weather is fair.

Finally, there are also regional variations on American staples. You can get plain old burgers and hot dogs anywhere, but for a truly American experi-

EATING PRICE CODES

$ under 25
$$ 25-49
$$$ 50-75
$$$$ over 75

VEGETARIAN EATING

In the big US cities at least, being a vegetarian – or even a vegan – presents few problems. However, don't be too surprised in rural areas if you find yourself restricted to a diet of eggs, grilled-cheese sandwiches and limp salads. Be aware, most soul food cafés or barbeque joints offer great-value vegetable plates (four different veggies, including potatoes), but many dishes will be cooked with pork fat, so ask before tucking in.

ence, try a Jucy Lucy in Minnesota, which includes a hamburger patty with a melted cheddar cheese centre, or a horseshoe in Springfield, an open-faced burger served on thick toast and topped with French fries.. Regardless of where you go, you can find a good range of authentic diners where the buns are fresh, the patties are large, handcrafted and tasty, and the dressings and condiments are inspired.

Other cuisines

In the cities, in particular, where centuries of settlement have created distinctive local neighbourhoods, each community offers its own take on the cuisine of its homeland. Chicago has its Chinatown, its Jewish delis, its Italian restaurants, and its taco trucks. Mexican food is so common it might as well be an indigenous cuisine.

Italian food is widely available, too; the top-shelf restaurants in major cities tend to focus on the northern end of the boot, while the tomato-heavy, gut-busting portions associated with southern Italian cooking are usually confined to more affordable, old school family restaurants.. Pizza restaurants occupy a similar range from high-end gourmet places to cheap and tasty dives – New Yorkers and Chicagoans can argue for days over which of their respective cities makes the best kind, either Gotham's shingle-flat "slices" or the Windy City's overstuffed wedges that actually resemble slices of meat pie (see page 43).

When it comes to Asian eating, Indian cuisine is usually better in the cities, though there are increasing exceptions as the resident population grows. When found in the Chinatown neighbourhoods of major cities Chinese cooking will be top-notch, and often inexpensive – beware, though, of the dismal-tasting "chop suey" and "chow mein" joints in the suburbs and small towns. Japanese, once the preserve of the coasts and sophisticated cities, has become widely popular, with sushi restaurants in all price ranges and chain teriyaki joints out on the freeways. Thai and Vietnamese restaurants, meanwhile, provide some of the best and cheapest ethnic food available, sometimes in diners mixing the two, and occasionally in the form of "fusion"

cooking with other Asian cuisines (or "pan-Asian", as it's widely known).

Drink

While Chicago is the consummate boozing town in the region – filled with tales of famous, plastered authors indulging in famously bad behaviour – but almost anywhere you shouldn't have to search very hard for a comfortable place to drink. The Great Lakes are peppered with college towns, each with their designated watering holes and youthful drinking traditions. You need to be 21 years old to buy and consume alcohol in the USA, and it's likely you'll be asked for ID if you look under 30.

"Blue laws" – archaic statutes that restrict when, where and under what conditions alcohol can be purchased – are held by many states, and prohibit the sale of alcohol on Sundays; on the extreme end of the scale, some counties (known as "dry") don't allow any alcohol, ever. Minnesota restricts the alcohol content in beer to just 3.2 percent, almost half the usual strength. Rest assured, though, that in a few of the more liberal parts of the region alcohol can be bought 24/7, except on Sundays, but can be serviced in bars between 8am until 4am the next day, seven days a week.

Note that if a bar is advertising a happy hour on "rail drinks" or "well drinks", these are cocktails made from the liquors and mixers the bar has to hand (as opposed to top-shelf, higher-quality brands).

Beer

The most popular American beers may be the fizzy, insipid lagers from national brands, but there is no lack of alternatives. The craze for craft beer breweries started in northern California several decades ago, and has spread like wildfire in the Great Lakes region since. Major hubs in this region include Chicago, Cleveland, OH, and Milwaukee, WI, and even the smaller towns have their own share of decent handcrafted beers.

In Chicago look for locally made Goose Island and its mix of mainstream and alternative brews. In Wisconsin, check out the top-notch offerings of

Milwaukee's historic Pabst Brewery, or visit the small town of New Glarus, where the New Glarus Brewing Company makes delicious beers only sold in the state of Wisconsin. Elsewhere, Indiana's best beverages come from Three Floyds Brewing, and Pete's Wicked Ales in Minnesota can be found throughout the USA. Indeed, craft breweries have undergone an explosion in most parts of the country in recent years and brewpubs can now be found in virtually every sizeable US city and college town. Almost all serve a wide range of good-value, hearty food to help soak up the drink. For more on craft beers, see Ⓦ craftbeer.com.

Wine

The Great Lakes regions are not exactly famous for their wines. Still, there are plenty of gorgeous and locally known wineries in the region. Hubs include Traverse City, Michigan and Geneva and Galena, Illinois. Many tourists take "wine-tasting" jags in these areas, where you can sip (or slurp) at sites ranging from down-home country farms with tractors and hayrides to upper-crust estates thick with modern art and folks in designer wear. Beyond this, a broad variety of towns across the Great Lakes have established wineries, typically of varying quality, though there are always a few standouts in each state that may merit a taste while you're on your journey. You'll find details of tours and tastings throughout the Guide.

Festivals

In addition to the main public holidays, there is a diverse multitude of engaging local events in the Great Lakes: arts-and-crafts shows, county fairs, ethnic celebrations, music festivals, rodeos, sandcastle-building competitions, chilli cookoffs and countless others.

Certain festivities, such as Lollapalooza in Chicago or the Indianapolis 500, are well worth planning your holiday around but obviously other people will have the same idea, so visiting during these times requires an extra amount of advance effort, not to mention money. Halloween (Oct 31) is also immensely popular. No longer just the domain of masked kids running around the streets banging on doors and demanding "trick or treat", in some bigger cities Halloween has evolved into a massive celebration. Thanksgiving Day, on the fourth Thursday in November, is more sedate. Relatives return to the nest to share a meal (traditionally, roast turkey and stuffing, cranberry sauce, and all manner of delicious pies) and give thanks for

family and friends. Ostensibly, the holiday recalls the first harvest of the Pilgrims in Massachusetts, though Thanksgiving was a national holiday before anyone thought to make that connection.

Annual festivals and events

For further details of the festivals and events listed below, including more precise dates, see the relevant page of the Guide (where covered) or access their websites. The state tourist boards (see page 43) can provide more complete calendars for each area.

JANUARY

Winter Carnival St Paul, MN (into Feb) Ⓦ wintercarnival.com. See page 119.

FEBRUARY

Chinatown Lunar New Year Parade Chicago, IL Ⓦ ccc-foundation.org/lunar-new-year-parade/

MARCH

Dying of the Chicago River/St. Patrick's Day Parade Chicago, IL Ⓦ chicagostpatricksdayparade.org/
Restaurant Week Chicago IL (into April) Ⓦ choosechicago.com/chicago-restaurant-week/
Ann Arbor Film Festival Ann Arbor, MI Ⓦ aafilmfest.org
Minneapolis Home and Garden Show Minneapolis, MN Ⓦ homeandgardenshow.com/

MAY

Indianapolis 500 Indianapolis, IN Ⓦ indy500.com. See page 71.

JUNE

Summerfest Milwaukee, WI (into July) Ⓦ summerfest.com
Pride Festival and Parade Chicago IL Ⓦ northalsted.com/pridefest/
Chicago Blues Festival Chicago IL Ⓦ chicago.gov/city/en/depts/dca/supp_info/chicago_blues_festival.html
Electric Forest Festival Rothbury, MI Ⓦ electricforestfestival.com

JULY

Lollapalooza Chicago, IL Ⓦ lollapalooza.com/
Taste of Chicago Ⓦ chicago.gov/city/en/depts/dca/supp_info/taste_of_chicago.html
Pierogi Fest Whiting, IN Ⓦ pierogifest.net
National Cherry Festival Traverse City, MI Ⓦ cherryfestival.org. See page 101.

AUGUST

Chicago Air and Water Show IL Ⓦ chicago.gov/city/en/depts/dca/supp_info/chicago_air_and_watershow.html
Windy City Smokeout Chicago IL Ⓦ windycitysmokeout.com/

Minnesota State Fair Minneapolis-St. Paul, MN (runs through Labor Day Weekend) Ⓦ mnstatefair.org/
Indiana State Fair Indianapolis, IN (through August) Ⓦ indianastatefair.com
Chicago Jazz Festival Chicago, IL (into September) Ⓦ chicago.gov/city/en/depts/dca/supp_info/chicago_jazz_festival.html
Quad Cities Hot Air Balloon Fest East Moline, IL Ⓦ quadcitiesballoonfestival.com
Uptown Air Fair Minneapolis, MN Ⓦ uptownminneapolis.com/events/uptown-art-fair/

SEPTEMBER

Oktoberfest Zinzinnati Cincinnati, OH Ⓦ oktoberfestzinzinnati.com
Pitchfork Musical Festival Chicago IL Ⓦ pitchforkmusicfestival.com/
Warrens Cranberry Festival Warrens, WI Ⓦ cranfest.com
Detroit International Jazz Festival Detroit, MI Ⓦ detroitjazzfest.com.
Geneva's Festival of the Vine Geneva, IL Ⓦ genevachamber.com/festival-of-the-vine.php
Oktoberfest La Crosse, WI (into October) Ⓦ oktoberfstusa.com

NOVEMBER

Christkindlmarket Chicago IL (and other GL Locations – runs until New Year's) Ⓦ christkindlmarket.com

The outdoors

Coated by dense forests thick foliage and bountiful freshwater streams, the Great Lakes region is blessed with fabulous backcountry and wilderness areas. Protected forest preserves and wildlife can be found within an hour's drive of Chicago, and Lake Michigan is bordered by two of the rarest, most remote national parks in the country.

National parks and monuments

The National Park Service administers both national parks and national monuments. Its rangers do a superb job of providing information and advice to visitors, maintaining trails and organizing such activities as free guided hikes and campfire talks.

In principle, a national park preserves an area of outstanding natural beauty, encompassing a wide range of terrain and prime examples of particular landforms and wildlife. A national monument is usually much smaller, focusing perhaps on just one archeological site or geological phenomenon, such as Abraham Lincoln's childhood home. Altogether, the

MAIN ATTRACTIONS IN NATIONAL PARKS

The Park Service website, Ⓦ nps.gov, details the main attractions of the national parks, plus opening hours, the best times to visit, admission fees, hiking trails and visitor facilities.

national park system comprises around four hundred units, including national seashores, lakeshores, battlefields and other historic sites. The Great Lakes region contains four national parks, four national lakeshores and several national monuments and historic sites.

While national parks tend to be perfect places to hike – almost all have extensive trail networks – most are far too large to tour entirely on foot. Even in those rare cases where you can use public transport to reach a park, you'll almost certainly need some sort of vehicle to explore it once you're there. Voyageurs National Park in northern Minnesota is howling wilderness, with virtually no roads or facilities for tourists – you're on your own.

Most parks and monuments charge admission fees, which cover a vehicle and all its occupants for up to a week. For anyone on a touring vacation, it may well make more sense to buy the Inter-agency Annual Pass, also known as the "America the Beautiful Pass". Sold at all federal parks and monuments, or online at Ⓦ store.usgs.gov, this grants unrestricted access for a year to the bearer, and any accompanying passengers in the same vehicle, to all national parks and monuments, as well as sites managed by such agencies as the US Fish and Wildlife Service, the Forest Service and the BLM (Bureau of Land Management). It does not, however, cover or reduce additional fees like charges for camping in official park campgrounds, or permits for backcountry hiking or rafting.

Two further passes, obtainable at any park or online, grant free access for life to all national parks and monuments, again to the holder and any accompanying passengers, and also provide a fifty-percent discount on camping fees. The Senior Pass is available to any US citizen or permanent resident aged 62 or older for a one-time fee, while the Access Pass is issued free to blind or permanently disabled US citizens or permanent residents, with a processing fee. While hotel-style lodges are found only in major parks, every park or monument tends to have at least one well-organized campground. Often, a cluster of motels can be found not far outside the park boundaries. With appropriate permits – subject to restrictions in popular parks – backpackers can also

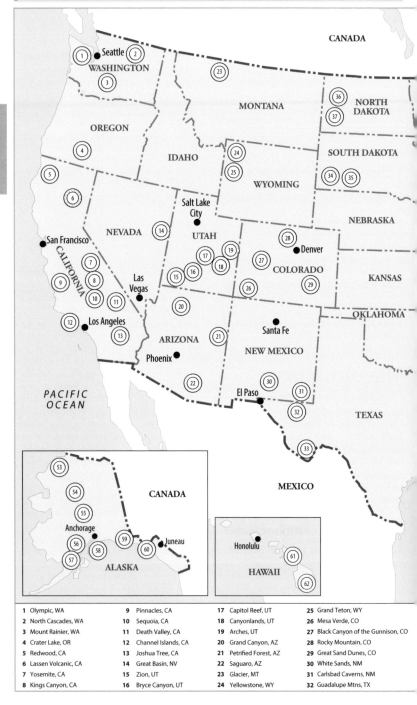

1 Olympic, WA	**9** Pinnacles, CA	**17** Capitol Reef, UT	**25** Grand Teton, WY
2 North Cascades, WA	**10** Sequoia, CA	**18** Canyonlands, UT	**26** Mesa Verde, CO
3 Mount Rainier, WA	**11** Death Valley, CA	**19** Arches, UT	**27** Black Canyon of the Gunnison, CO
4 Crater Lake, OR	**12** Channel Islands, CA	**20** Grand Canyon, AZ	**28** Rocky Mountain, CO
5 Redwood, CA	**13** Joshua Tree, CA	**21** Petrified Forest, AZ	**29** Great Sand Dunes, CO
6 Lassen Volcanic, CA	**14** Great Basin, NV	**22** Saguaro, AZ	**30** White Sands, NM
7 Yosemite, CA	**15** Zion, UT	**23** Glacier, MT	**31** Carlsbad Caverns, NM
8 Kings Canyon, CA	**16** Bryce Canyon, UT	**24** Yellowstone, WY	**32** Guadalupe Mtns, TX

US NATIONAL PARKS

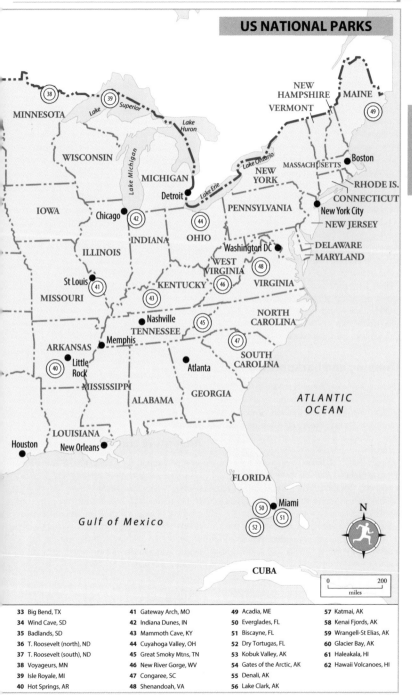

33 Big Bend, TX	**41** Gateway Arch, MO	**49** Acadia, ME	**57** Katmai, AK
34 Wind Cave, SD	**42** Indiana Dunes, IN	**50** Everglades, FL	**58** Kenai Fjords, AK
35 Badlands, SD	**43** Mammoth Cave, KY	**51** Biscayne, FL	**59** Wrangell-St Elias, AK
36 T. Roosevelt (north), ND	**44** Cuyahoga Valley, OH	**52** Dry Tortugas, FL	**60** Glacier Bay, AK
37 T. Roosevelt (south), ND	**45** Great Smoky Mtns, TN	**53** Kobuk Valley, AK	**61** Haleakala, HI
38 Voyageurs, MN	**46** New River Gorge, WV	**54** Gates of the Arctic, AK	**62** Hawaii Volcanoes, HI
39 Isle Royale, MI	**47** Congaree, SC	**55** Denali, AK	
40 Hot Springs, AR	**48** Shenandoah, VA	**56** Lake Clark, AK	

usually camp in the backcountry (a general term for areas inaccessible by road).

Other public lands

National parks and monuments are often surrounded by tracts of national forest – also federally administered but much less protected. These too usually hold appealing rural campgrounds but, in the words of the slogan, each is a "Land of Many Uses", and usually allows logging and other land-based industry (thankfully, more often ski resorts than strip mines).

Other government departments administer wildlife refuges, national scenic rivers, recreation areas and the like. The Bureau of Land Management (BLM) has the largest holdings of all, most of it open rangeland, but also including some enticingly out-of-the-way reaches. Environmentalist groups engage in endless running battles with developers, ranchers and the extracting industries over uses – or alleged misuses – of federal lands.

While state parks and state monuments, administered by individual states, preserve sites of more limited, local significance, many are explicitly intended for recreational use, and thus hold better campgrounds than their federal equivalents.

Camping and backpacking

The ideal way to see the great outdoors – especially if you're on a low budget – is to tour by car and camp in state and federal campgrounds. Typical public campgrounds range in price from free (usually when there's no water available, which may be seasonal) on up. Fees at the generally less scenic commercial campgrounds – abundant near major towns, and often resembling open-air hotels, complete with shops and restaurants are comparable. If you're camping in high season, either reserve in advance or avoid the most popular areas.

Backcountry camping in the national parks is usually free, by permit only. Before you set off on anything more than a half-day hike, and whenever you're headed for anywhere at all isolated, be sure to inform a ranger of your plans, and ask about weather conditions and specific local tips. Carry sufficient food and drink to cover emergencies, as well as all the necessary equipment and maps. Check whether fires are permitted; even if they are, try to use a camp stove in preference to local materials. In wilderness areas, try to camp on previously used sites. Where there are no toilets, bury human waste at least six inches into the ground and 100ft from the nearest water supply and campground.

Health issues

Backpackers should never drink from rivers and streams; you never know what acts people – or animals – have performed further upstream. Giardia – a water-borne bacteria that causes an intestinal disease characterized by chronic diarrhoea, abdominal cramps, fatigue and weight loss – is a serious problem. Water that doesn't come from a tap should be boiled for at least five minutes or cleansed with an iodine-based purifier or a giardia-rated filter.

Hiking at lower elevations should present few problems, though near water mosquitoes can drive you crazy; Avon Skin-so-Soft or anything containing DEET are fairly reliable repellents. Ticks – tiny beetles that plunge their heads into your skin and swell up – are another hazard. They sometimes leave their heads inside, causing blood clots or infections, so get advice from a ranger if you've been bitten. One species of tick causes Lyme Disease, a serious condition that can even affect the brain. Nightly inspections of your skin are strongly recommended.

Beware, too, of poison oak, which grows throughout the west, usually among oak trees. Its leaves come in groups of three (the middle one on a short stem) and are distinguished by prominent veins and shiny surfaces. If you come into contact with it, wash your skin (with soap and cold water) and clothes as soon as possible – and don't scratch. In serious cases, hospital emergency rooms can give antihistamine or adrenaline shots. A comparable curse is poison ivy, found throughout the country. For both plants, remember the sage advice, "Leaves of three, let it be".

Adventure travel

The opportunities for adventure travel in the Great Lakes are all but endless, whether your tastes run towards whitewater rafting down the rivers of Michigan, mountain biking Great Plains bike trails, canoeing around the Lake Erie Islands, horseback riding in Mackinac Island or rock climbing the walls of Devils Lake, Wisconsin. Throughout the text we recommend guides, outfitters and local adventure-tour operators.

Skiing

While less well-known and mountainous than the slopes of Aspen and Vail, downhill ski resorts can be found all over the Great Lakes region. The closest resorts to Chicago are Alpine Valley Resort, two hours north in Wisconsin, and Bittersweet Resort in Michigan, two and a half hours away. Expect to pay per day for lift tickets and equipment rentals.

A cheaper alternative is cross-country skiing, or ski touring. Backcountry ski lodges dot northern Michigan and Wisconsin. They offer a range of rustic accommodation, equipment rental and lessons, renting skis, boots and poles out per day, or offering an all-inclusive weekend tour.

Wildlife

Watch out for bears, deer, moose, mountain lions and rattlesnakes in the backcountry, and consider the effect your presence can have on their environment.

Other than in a national park, you're highly unlikely to encounter a bear. Even there, it's rare to stumble across one in the wilderness. If you do, don't run, just back away slowly. Most fundamentally, it will be after your food, which should be stored in airtight containers when camping. Ideally, hang both food and garbage from a high but slender branch some distance from your camp. Never attempt to feed bears, and never get between a mother and her young. Young animals are cute; their irate mothers are not.

Snakes and creepy-crawlies

Though the backcountry is home to a wide assortment of poisonous creatures, these are rarely aggressive towards humans. To avoid trouble, observe obvious precautions. Don't attempt to handle wildlife; keep your eyes open as you walk, and watch where you put your hands when scrambling over obstacles; shake out shoes, clothing and bedding before use; and back off if you do spot a creature, giving it room to escape.

If you are bitten or stung, current medical thinking rejects the concept of cutting yourself open and attempting to suck out the venom. Whether snake, scorpion or spider is responsible, apply a cold compress to the wound, constrict the area with a tourniquet to prevent the spread of venom, drink lots of water and bring your temperature down by resting in a shady area. Stay as calm as possible and seek medical help immediately.

Sports

As well as being good fun, catching a baseball game at Chicago's Wrigley Field on a summer afternoon or joining the screaming throngs at a college football game can give visitors an unforgettable insight into a town and its people. Professional teams almost always put on the most spectacular shows, but big games between college rivals, Minor League baseball games and even Friday night high-school football games provide an easy and enjoyable way to get on intimate terms with a place.

Specific details for the most important teams in all the sports are given in the various city accounts in this Guide. They can also be found through the Major League websites: Wmlb.com (baseball); Wnba.com (basketball); Wnfl.com (football); Wnhl.com (ice hockey); and Wmlssoccer.com (soccer).

Major spectator sports

Baseball, because the Major League teams play so many games (162 in the regular season, usually at least five a week from April to September, plus the October playoffs), is probably the easiest sport to catch when travelling. The ballparks in the Midwest are great places to spend time, from ivy-clad Wrigley Field to Great American Ballpark in Cincinnati, home to the Cincinnati Reds and baseball's first national franchise. It's also among the cheapest sports to watch and tickets are usually easy to come by.

Pro football, the American variety, is quite the opposite. Tickets are exorbitantly expensive and almost impossible to obtain (if the team is any good), and most games are played in huge, fortress-like stadiums far out in the suburbs; you'll do better in a bar to watch it on TV. College football is a whole lot better and more exciting, with chanting crowds, cheerleaders and cheaper tickets, which can be hard to obtain in football-crazed college towns in parts of the Midwest. Although New Year's Day games such as the Rose Bowl or the Orange Bowl are all but impossible to see live, big games featuring local rivalries or Notre Dame vs anybody are not to be missed if you're anywhere nearby.

Basketball also brings out intense emotions. The protracted pro playoffs run well into June. The month-long college playoff tournament, called "March Madness", is acclaimed by many as the nation's most exciting sports extravaganza, taking place at venues spread across the country in many small to mid-sized towns.

Ice hockey, usually referred to simply as hockey, was long the preserve of Canada and cities in the Great Lakes. Tickets, particularly for successful teams, are hard to get and not cheap.

Other sports

Soccer remains much more popular as a participant sport, especially for kids, than a spectator one, but

COLLEGE FOOTBALL IN THE GREAT LAKES

For college campuses across the region, fall is synonymous with football season. With no minor national league, the college level is considered the second tier of the sport in the US; and it was originally at the college level where the sport first gained popularity. Even in places with professional teams, college football is still revered, and game day is widely celebrated in cities and colleges towns across the region. The following list includes the major college teams in each state and where they play their home games:

ILLINOIS

Northwestern University Ryan Field 1301 S. Central St, Evanston (30 minutes north of downtown Chicago); Ⓦ nusports.com

University of Illinois-Urbana Champaign University of Illinois Memorial Stadium 1402 S 1st St, Champaign (2 hrs from Chicago, 1hr30mins from Springfield); Ⓦ fightingillini.com

INDIANA

Indiana University Indiana University Memorial Stadium 701 E 17th St, Bloomington; Ⓦ iuhoosiers.com
Purdue University Ross-Ade Stadium, John R Wooden Dr, West Lafayette (1 hr form Indianapolis, 2 hrs from Chicago); Ⓦ purduesports.com/sports/football

University of Notre Dame Notre Dame Stadium 2010 Moose Krause Cir, Notre Dame, IN (1hr 40 min from Chicago); Ⓦ undcom

MICHIGAN

Michigan State University Spartan Stadium, 325 W Shaw Ln, East Lansing (1hr from Grand Rapids and Ann Arbor); Ⓦ msuspartans.com/sports/football

University of Michigan Ann Arbor Michigan Stadium, 1201 S Main St, Ann Arbor; Ⓦ mgoblue.com/sports/football

MINNESOTA

University of Minnesota-Twin Cities Huntington Bank Stadium, 420 23rd Ave SE, Minneapolis; Ⓦ gophersports.com/sports/football

OHIO

The Ohio State University Ohio Stadium, 411 Woody Hayes Dr, Columbus; Ⓦ ohiostatebuckeyes.com

WISCONSIN

University of Wisconsin-Madison Camp Randall Stadium, 1440 Monroe St, Madison; Ⓦ uwbadgers.com/sports/football

Tickets can be purchased in advance but are often available day of as well. Plenty of merriment can be had without a ticket, too. Around each of these campuses, you'll find scores of people tailgating in parking lots, fields, and backyards around the football stadiums. At tailgates, you'll see people drinking, grilling out and playing corn hole (a game that involves throwing bean bags into a hole on a wooden board). Be sure to consult the local ordinances on public consumption of alcohol, or you could receive a citation. For later in the season when the weather starts to turn, warm up and watch the game from a bar near the campus. Bars and pubs known for being a great gameday destination will be highlighted where they appear in the Guide.

the following for American soccer teams is on the rise nationally. Soccer enthusiasts can catch a Chicago Fire, or female Chicago Red Stars game, at Soldier Field from February to October. Those Americans who are avid soccer fans usually follow foreign matches like England's Premier League, rather than their home-grown talent. The good news for international travellers is that any decent-sized city will have one or two pubs where you can catch games from England, various European countries or Latin America; check out ⓦ livesoccertv.com for a list of such establishments and match schedules.

Golf, once the province of moneyed businessmen, has attracted a wider following in recent decades due to the rise of celebrity golfers such as Tiger Woods and the construction of numerous municipal and public courses. You'll have your best access at these. Private golf courses have varying standards for allowing non-members to play (check their websites) and steeper fees.

The other sporting events that attract national interest involve four legs or four wheels. The Kentucky Derby, held in Louisville on the first Saturday in May is the biggest date on the horse-racing calendar, with satellite celebrations held at racetracks across the Great Lakes. Also in May, the NASCAR Indianapolis 500, the world's largest motor-racing event, fills that city with visitors throughout the month, with practice sessions and carnival events building up to the big race. In the winter months, dog sled racing can be enjoyed in parts of Ohio, Minnesota, and Michigan's Upper Peninsula.

Travel essentials

Costs

When it comes to average costs for travelling expenses, much depends on where you've chosen to go. A road trip around the backroads of Indiana and Ohio won't cost you much in accommodation, dining or souvenir-buying, although the amount spent on gas will add up – this varies from state to state, but at the time of writing the average price was between $3and $4 per gallon. By contrast, getting around a city such as Chicago or Minneapolis will be relatively cheap, but you'll pay much more for your hotel, meals, sightseeing and shopping. Most items you buy will be subject to some form of state – not federal – sales tax, anywhere from less than five percent to more than seven percent, depending on the state. In addition, varying from state to state, some counties and cities may add on another point or two to that rate.

Unless you're camping or staying in a hostel, accommodation will be your greatest expense while in the USA. A detailed breakdown is given in the Accommodation section, but you can reckon on at least $50–100 per day, based on sharing, double that if travelling solo. Unlike accommodation, prices for good food don't automatically take a bite out of your wallet, and you can indulge anywhere from the lowliest (but still scrumptious) burger shack to the choicest restaurant helmed by a celebrity chef. You can get by on as little as $30 a day, but realistically you should aim for more like $60.

Where it exists, and where it is useful (which tends to be only in the larger cities), public transport is usually affordable, with many cities offering good-value travel passes. Renting a car, at $175–250 per week, is a far more efficient way to explore the broader part of the country, and, for a group of two or more, it could well work out cheaper. Drivers staying in larger hotels in the cities should factor in the increasing trend towards charging even for self-parking; this daily fee may well be just a few dollars less than that for valet parking.

Tipping

In the USA, waiters and others in the service industry earn less than the minimum hourly wage, and therefore rely on tips to make up the majority of their income. Waiting staff expect tips of at least twenty percent, and up to twenty-five percent for very good service. When sitting at a bar, you should leave at least a dollar per round for the barkeeper; more if the round is more than two drinks. Hotel porters and bellhops should receive at least $2 per piece of luggage, more if it has been lugged up several flights of stairs. About fifteen percent should be added to taxi fares, rounded up to the nearest 50¢ or dollar.

Crime and personal safety

No one could pretend that America is crime-free, although away from the urban centres crime is often remarkably low. Even the lawless reputations of Chicago and Detroit are far in excess of the truth and most parts of these cities, by day at least, are safe; at night, however, some areas are completely off-limits. All the major tourist areas and the main nightlife zones in cities are invariably brightly lit and well policed. By planning carefully and taking good care of your possessions, you should, generally speaking, have few problems.

Car crime

Crimes committed against tourists driving rented cars aren't as common as they once were, but it still pays to be cautious. In major urban areas, any car you rent should have nothing on it – such as a particular licence plate – that makes it easy to spot as a rental car. When driving, under no circumstances should you stop in any unlit or seemingly deserted urban area – and especially not if someone is waving you down and suggesting that there is something wrong with your car. Similarly, if you are accidentally rammed by the driver behind you, do not stop immediately,

MARIJUANA AND OTHER DRUGS

Over recent years, the legalization of marijuana for recreational purposes has been introduced in a number of states. In Illinois and Michigan marijuana is completely legal for medical and recreational use. Pot, as it is commonly referred to in America, is now on sale at licensed shops in these states, though there are no Amsterdam-style coffeeshops anywhere as of yet. Rules as to whether only local residents can buy it and how much vary from state to state; smoking in public is usually still illegal.

Paradoxically, the substance is still illegal at the federal level but this has not been creating problems in the above states. Ohio and Minnesota allow the usage of medical marijuana but only with a license. These states have decriminalized marijuana, meaning if you are found in possession you will be fined but not criminally charged. Note that in states where pot is still illegal, like Indiana and Wisconsin, you can be prosecuted even if you have bought it legally elsewhere, so it's wise not to take it across state lines in such cases. Also note that all other recreational drugs remain illegal at both state and federal level, so even simple possession can get you into serious trouble.

but proceed on to the nearest well-lit, busy area and call 911 for assistance. Hide any valuables out of sight, preferably locked in the trunk or in the glove compartment, and never leave your car running or unlocked, even when filling up at a gas station.

Electricity

Electricity runs on 110V AC. All plugs are two-pronged and rather insubstantial. Some travel plug adapters don't fit American sockets.

Entry requirements

At the time of writing, the citizens of several countries were not permitted to enter the US, due to measures to limit the spread of Covid-19. The situation may remain subject to specific restrictions for some time to come, and testing or proof of a negative Covid test may be required, even after the border has reopened. For the latest information, consult Ⓦ https://travel. state.gov/content/travel/en/international-travel.html.

Temporary restrictions aside, citizens of 35 countries – including the UK, Ireland, Australia, New Zealand and most Western European countries – can enter under the Visa Waiver Program if visiting the United States for a period of less than ninety days. To obtain authorization, you must apply online for ESTA (Electronic System for Travel Authorization) approval before setting off. This is a straightforward process – simply go to the ESTA website (Ⓦ esta.cbp.dhs.gov), fill in your info and wait a very short while (sometimes just minutes, but it's best to leave at least 72hr before travelling to make sure) for them to provide you with an authorization number. You will not generally be asked to produce that number at your port of entry, but it is as well to

keep a copy just in case, especially in times of high-security alerts – you will be denied entry if you don't have one. This ESTA authorization is valid for up to two years (or until your passport expires, whichever comes first) and costs $14, payable by credit card when applying. When you arrive at your port of entry you will be asked to confirm that your trip has an end date, that you have an onward ticket and that you have adequate funds to cover your stay. The customs official may also ask you for your address while in the USA; the hotel you are staying at on your first night will suffice. Each traveller must also undergo the US-VISIT process at immigration, where both index fingers are digitally scanned and a digital head shot is also taken for file.

Prospective visitors from parts of the world not mentioned above require a valid passport and a non-immigrant visitor's visa for a maximum ninety-day stay. How you'll obtain a visa depends on what country you're in and your status when you apply; check Ⓦ travel.state.gov. Whatever your nationality, visas are not issued to convicted felons and anybody who owns up to being a communist, fascist, drug dealer or guilty of genocide (fair enough, perhaps). On arrival, the date stamped on your passport is the latest you're legally allowed to stay. The Department of Homeland Security (DHS) has toughened its stance on anyone violating this rule, so even overstaying by a few days can result in a protracted interrogation from officials. Overstaying may also cause you to be turned away next time you try to enter the USA. To get an extension before your time is up, apply at the nearest Department of Homeland Security office, whose address will be under the Federal Government Offices listings at the front of the phone book. INS officials will assume that you're working in the USA illegally, and it's up to you to convince them otherwise by providing evidence of ample finances. If you can, bring along an upstanding American citizen to vouch for you. You'll also have to explain why you didn't plan for the extra time initially.

FOREIGN EMBASSIES IN THE USA

Australia 1601 Massachusetts Ave NW, Washington DC 20036, 202 797 3000, ⓦ usa.embassy.gov.au

Canada 501 Pennsylvania Ave NW, Washington DC 20001, 202 682 1740, ⓦ international.gc.ca

Ireland 2234 Massachusetts Ave NW, Washington DC 20008, 202 462 3939, ⓦ dfa.ie/irish-embassy/usa

New Zealand 37 Observatory Circle NW, Washington DC 20008, 202 328 4800, ⓦ mfat.govt.nz

South Africa 3051 Massachusetts Ave NW, Washington DC 20008, 202 232 4400, ⓦ saembasy.org

UK 3100 Massachusetts Ave NW, Washington DC 20008, 202 588 6500, ⓦ ukinusa.fco.gov.uk

FOREIGN CONSULATES IN CHICAGO

Australia 123 N Wacker Dr, Chicago IL 60606, 312 419 1480, ⓦ chicago.consulate.gov.au

Canada Two Prudential Plaza, Suite 2400, 180 N Stetson Ave, Chicago IL 60611, 844 880 6519, ⓦ international.gc.ca

Ireland 1 E Wacker Dr, Suite 1820, Chicago IL 60611, 312 337 2700, ⓦ dfa.ie/irish-consulate/chicago/

New Zealand 1223 Oakwood Ln, Glenview IL 60025, 312 953 4251, ⓦ mfat.govt.nz

South Africa 200 S Michigan Ave, Suite 600, Chicago 60604, 312 939 7929, ⓦ saembassy.org

UK 625 N Michigan Ave, Suite 2200, Chicago IL 60611, 312 970 3800, ⓦ ukinusa.fco.gov.uk

Health

If you have a serious accident while in the USA, emergency medical services will get to you quickly and charge you later. For emergencies or ambulances, dial 911, the nationwide emergency number.

Should you need to see a doctor, consult the Yellow Pages telephone directory under "Clinics" or "Physicians and Surgeons" or search for one online. The basic consultation fee is payable in advance or at the end of your appointment, and usually start at $150. Tests, X-rays etc are additional costs and can quickly add up. Medications aren't cheap either – keep all your receipts for later claims on your insurance policy.

Foreign visitors should bear in mind that many pills available over the counter at home – most codeine-based painkillers, for example – require a prescription in the USA. Local brand names can be confusing; ask for advice at the pharmacy in any drugstore.

In general, inoculations aren't required for entry to the USA, though be sure to check the latest COVID regulations (See below).

Covid-19

The global Covid-19 pandemic impacted the US from early 2020 and by February 2022, it had claimed the lives of 918,000 Americans, the highest number in the world by some margin, and a total that was still climbing at time of writing. More positively, the US's vaccination programme to protect citizens from future infections was well underway, with 200 million vaccine shots given before President Biden's 100th day in office, doubling his original pledge made.

Visitors should check what health precautions are necessary at both federal and state level, in particular with regards to mask-wearing and social distancing.

MEDICAL RESOURCES FOR TRAVELLERS

CDC ⓦ cdc.gov/travel. Official US government travel health site.
International Society for Travel Medicine ⓦ istm.org. Full listing of travel health clinics.

Insurance

In view of the high cost of medical care in the USA, all travellers visiting from overseas should be sure to buy some form of travel insurance. American and Canadian citizens should check whether they are already covered – some homeowners' or renters' policies are valid on holiday, and credit cards such

ROUGH GUIDES TRAVEL INSURANCE

Rough Guides has teamed up with WorldNomads.com to offer great travel insurance deals. Policies are available to residents of over 150 countries, with cover for a wide range of adventure sports, 24hr emergency assistance, high levels of medical and evacuation cover and a stream of travel safety information. Roughguides.com users can take advantage of their policies online 24/7, from anywhere in the world – even if you're already travelling. And since plans often change when you're on the road, you can extend your policy and even claim online. Roughguides.com users who buy travel insurance with WorldNomads.com can also leave a positive footprint and donate to a community development project. For more information go to ⓦ roughguides.com/travel-insurance.

OPENING HOURS AND PUBLIC HOLIDAYS

The traditional summer holiday period runs between the weekends of Memorial Day, the last Monday in May, and Labor Day, the first Monday in September. Many parks, attractions and visitor centres operate longer hours or only open during this period and we denote such cases as "summer" throughout the Guide. Otherwise, specific months of opening are given.

Government offices (including post offices) and banks will be closed on the following national public holidays:

Jan 1 New Year's Day
Third Mon in Jan Martin Luther King, Jr's Birthday
Third Mon in Feb Presidents' Day
Last Mon in May Memorial Day
June 14 Juneteenth
July 4 Independence Day
First Mon in Sept Labor Day
Second Mon in Oct Columbus Day
Nov 11 Veterans' Day
Fourth Thurs in Nov Thanksgiving Day
Dec 25 Christmas Day

as American Express often include some medical or other insurance, while most Canadians are covered for medical mishaps overseas by their provincial health plans. If you only need trip cancellation/interruption coverage (to supplement your existing plan), this is generally available at a cost of about six percent of the trip value.

Internet

Almost all hotels and many coffeeshops and restaurants offer free wi-fi for guests, though some upmarket hotels charge for access. As a result, cybercafés, where you can use a terminal in the establishment and pay per hour, are increasingly uncommon. Nearly all public libraries provide free internet access, but often there's a wait and machine time is limited.

LGBTQ travellers

The LGBTQ scene in America is huge, albeit heavily concentrated in the major cities. In Chicago, gay men and women make up almost 8% of the city's total population and enjoy the kind of visibility and influence those in other places can only dream about. LGBTQ public officials and police officers are no longer a novelty. Resources, facilities and organizations are endless.

Virtually every major city has a predominantly LGBTQ area and we've tried to give an overview of local resources, bars and clubs in each large urban area. In the rural heartland, however, life can look more like the Fifties – members of the LGBTQ community still can face oppression, persecution, and even violence. LGBTQ travellers need to be aware of their surroundings in order to avoid hassles and possible aggression.

National publications are available from any good bookstore. Bob Damron in San Francisco (Ⓦdamron. com) produces the best and sells them at a discount online. These include the Men's Travel Guide, a pocket-sized yearbook listing hotels, bars, clubs and resources for gay men; the Women's Traveller, which provides similar listings for lesbians; the Damron City Guide, which details lodging and entertainment in major cities; and Damron Accommodations, with 1000 accommodation listings for LGBTQ travellers worldwide.

Gayellow Pages in New York (Ⓦgayellowpages.com) publishes a useful directory of businesses in the USA and Canada, plus regional directories for New England, New York and the South. The Advocate, based in Los Angeles (Ⓦadvocate.com) is a bimonthly national LGBTQ news magazine, with features, general info and classified ads. Finally, the International Gay & Lesbian Travel Association in Fort Lauderdale, FL (Ⓦiglta.org), is a comprehensive, invaluable source for LGBTQ travellers.

Mail

Post offices are usually open Monday to Friday from 8.30am to 5.30pm, and Saturday from 9am to 12.30pm, and there are blue mailboxes on many street corners. Airmail between the USA and Europe may take a week.

In the USA, the last line of the address includes the city or town and an abbreviation denoting the state ("IL" for Illinois; "MN" for Minnesota, for example).

The last line also includes a five-digit number – the zip code – denoting the local post office. It is very important to include this, though the additional four digits that you will sometimes see appended are not essential. You can check zip codes on the US Postal Service website, at Ⓦusps.com.

Rules on sending parcels are very rigid: packages must be in special containers bought from post offices and sealed according to their instructions. To send anything out of the country, you'll need a green customs declaration form from a post office.

Maps

The free road maps distributed by each state through its tourist offices and welcome centres are usually fine for general driving and route planning.

Though most travellers now use GPS devices – which are available at all car rental offices – Rand McNally still produces maps for each state, bound together in the Rand McNally Road Atlas, and you're apt to find even cheaper state and regional maps at practically any gas station along the major highways. In Chicago, Volume's Bookcafe at Water Tower Place (Ⓦvolumes.com) has a wide variety of maps available. Britain's best source for maps is Stanfords, at 7 Mercer Walk, London WC2H 9FA (Ⓦstanfords.co.uk), and 29 Corn St, Bristol BS1 1HT; it also has a mail-order service.

The American Automobile Association, or AAA ("Triple A"; 800 222 4357, Ⓦaaa.com) provides free maps and assistance to its members, as well as to British members of the AA and RAC. Call the main number to get the location of a branch near you; bring your membership card or at least a copy of your membership number.

If you're after really detailed maps that go far beyond the usual fold-out, try Thomas Guides (Ⓦmapbooks4u.com). Highly detailed park, wilderness and topographical maps are available through the Bureau of Land Management for the West (Ⓦblm.gov) and for the entire country through the Forest Service (Ⓦfs.fed.us/maps). The best supplier of detailed, large-format map books for travel through the American backcountry is Benchmark Maps (Ⓦbenchmarkmaps.com), whose elegantly designed depictions are easy to follow and make even the most remote dirt roads look appealing.

Money

The US dollar comes in $1, $2, $5, $10, $20, $50 and $100 denominations. One dollar comprises one hundred cents, made up of combinations of one-cent pennies, five-cent nickels, ten-cent dimes and 25-cent

---

CALLING HOME FROM THE USA

For country codes not listed below, dial 0 for the operator, consult any phone directory or log onto Ⓦcountrycallingcodes.com.
Australia 011 + 61 + area code minus its initial zero.
New Zealand 011 + 64 + area code minus its initial zero.
Republic of Ireland 011 + 353 + area code minus its initial zero.
South Africa 011 + 27 + area code.
UK 011 + 44 + area code minus its initial zero.

---

quarters. You can check current exchange rates at Ⓦx-rates.com.

Bank hours generally run from 9am to 5pm Monday to Thursday, and until 6pm on Friday; the big bank names are Wells Fargo, US Bank, Chase, and Bank of America. With an ATM card, you'll be able to withdraw cash just about anywhere, though you'll be charged $2–5 per transaction for using a different bank's network. International Bank Charles Schwab, while not having any brick and mortar locations, has offices globally and charges no international or ATM fees. Foreign cash-dispensing cards linked to international networks, such as Plus or Cirrus, are also widely accepted – ask your home bank or credit card company which branches you can use. To find the location of the nearest ATM, check online with AmEx (Ⓦnetwork.americanexpress.com); Mastercard (Ⓦmastercard.us); Accel (Ⓦaccelnetwork.com); or Plus (Ⓦusa.visa.com).

Credit and debit cards are the most widely accepted form of payment at major hotels, restaurants and retailers, even though a few smaller or older merchants still do not accept them. You'll be asked to show some plastic when renting a car, bike or other such item, or to start a "tab" at hotels for incidental charges; in any case, you can always pay the bill in cash when you return the item or check out of your room.

Phones

The USA currently has well over one hundred area codes – three-digit numbers that must precede the seven-figure number if you're calling from abroad (following the 001 international access code) or from a different area code, in which case you prefix the ten digits with a 1. It can get confusing, especially as certain cities have several different area codes within their boundaries; for clarity, in this Guide,

CLOTHING AND SHOE SIZES

WOMEN'S CLOTHING

American	4	6	8	10	12	14	16	18
British	6	8	10	12	14	16	18	20
Continental	34	36	38	40	42	44	46	48

WOMEN'S SHOES

American	5	6	7	8	9	10	11
British	3	4	5	6	7	8	9
Continental	36	37	38	39	40	41	42

MEN'S SHIRTS

American	14	15	15.5	16	16.5	17	17.5	18
British	14	15	15.5	16	16.5	17	17.5	18
Continental	36	38	39	41	42	43	44	45

MEN'S SHOES

American	7	7.5	8	8.5	9	9.5	10	10.5	11	11.5
British	6	7	7.5	8	8.5	9	9.5	10	11	12
Continental	39	40	41	42	42.5	43	44	44	45	46

MEN'S SUITS

American	34	36	38	40	42	44	46	48
British	34	36	38	40	42	44	46	48
Continental	44	46	48	50	52	54	56	58

we've included the local area codes in all telephone numbers. Note that some cities require you to dial all ten digits, even when calling within the same code. Numbers that start with the digits 800 – or increasingly commonly 888, 877 and 866 – are toll-free, but these can only be called from within the USA itself; most hotels and many companies have a toll-free number that can easily be found on their websites.

Unless you can organize to do all your calling online via Skype (⑩ skype.com), Zoom (⑩ zoom.us), or Google Meet (⑩ meet.google.com), the cheapest way to make long-distance and international calls is to buy a prepaid phonecard, commonly found in newsagents or grocery stores, especially in urban areas. These are cheaper than the similar cards issued by the big phone companies, such as AT&T, that are usually on sale in pharmacy outlets and chain stores, and will charge only a few cents per minute to call from the USA to most European and other western countries. Such cards can be used from any touchpad phone but there is usually a surcharge for using them from a payphone (which, in any case, are increasingly rare). You can also usually arrange with your local telecom provider to have a charge card account with free phone access in the USA, so that any calls you make are billed to your home. This may be convenient, but it's more expensive than using prepaid cards.

If you are planning to take your mobile phone (more often called a cell phone in America) from outside the USA, you'll need to check with your service provider whether it will work in the country: you will need a tri-band or quad-band phone that is enabled for international calls. Using your phone from home will probably incur hefty roaming charges for making calls and charge you extra for incoming calls, as the people calling you will be paying the usual rate. Depending on the length of your stay, it might make sense to rent a phone or buy a compatible prepaid SIM card from a US provider; check ⑩ triptel.com or ⑩ telestial.com. Alternatively, you could pick up an inexpensive pay-as-you-go phone from one of the major electrical shops.

Senior travellers

Anyone aged over 62 (with appropriate ID) can enjoy a vast range of discounts in the USA. Both Amtrak and Greyhound offer (smallish) percentage reductions on fares to older passengers, and any US citizen or permanent resident aged 62 or over is entitled to free admission for life to all national parks, monuments and historic sites using a Senior Pass (issued for a one-time fee). This free admission applies to all accompanying travellers in the same vehicle and also gives a fifty-percent reduction on park user fees, such as camping charges.

For discounts on accommodation, group tours and vehicle rental, US residents aged 50 or over should consider joining the AARP (American Association of Retired Persons; Ⓦaarp.org) for an annual fee, or a multi-year deal; the website also offers lots of good travel tips and features. Road Scholar (Ⓦroadscholar. org) runs an extensive network of educational and activity programmes for people over 60 throughout the USA, at prices in line with those of commercial tours.

Shopping

The Great Lakes have some of the greatest shopping opportunities in the world – from the luxury-lined blocks of the Magnificent Mile in Chicago =to the local markets found in cities both big and small, offering everything from fruit and vegetables to handmade local crafts.

When buying clothing and accessories, international visitors will need to convert their sizes into American equivalents (see box). For almost all purchases, state taxes will be applied (see page 37).

Time

The Great Lakes region covers two time zones. The Eastern zone, covering Ohio, Michigan, and almost all of Indiana is five hours behind Greenwich Mean Time (GMT), so 3pm London time is 10am in Cincinnati. The Central zone, covering Wisconsin, Illinois, Northwestern Indiana, and Minnesota, is an hour behind the east (10am in Cincinnati is 9am in Chicago). Most states in the US puts their clocks forward one hour to daylight saving time on the second Sunday in March and turn them back on the first Sunday in November.

Tourist information

Each state has its own tourist office (see box). These offer prospective visitors a colossal range of free maps, leaflets and brochures on attractions from overlooked wonders to the usual tourist traps. You can either contact the offices before you set off, or, as you travel around the country, look for the state-run "welcome centres", usually along main highways close to the state borders. In heavily visited states, these often have piles of discount coupons for cut-price

accommodation and food. In addition, visitor centres in most towns and cities – often known as the "Convention and Visitors Bureau", or CVB, and listed throughout this Guide – provide details on the area, as do local Chambers of Commerce in almost any town of any size.

Travelling with children

Children under 2 years old go free on domestic flights and for ten percent of the adult fare on international flights – though that doesn't mean they get a seat, let alone frequent-flier miles. Kids aged between 2 and 14 are usually entitled to full price tickets, although some country-specific discounts may apply for international flights. Discounts for trains are better: children under 2 years old go free as long as they do not need their own seat, and children up to age 12 receive 50 percent off full fare. Bus fare is similar to air travel – children over 2 and adults pay the same fare.

Car-rental companies usually provide kids' car seats – which are required by law for children under the age of 4 – for an additional fee per day. You would, however, be advised to check, or bring your own; they are not always available. Recreational vehicles (RVs) are a particularly good option for families. Even the cheapest motel will offer inexpensive two-double bed rooms as a matter of course, which is a relief for non-US travellers used to paying a premium for a "family room", or having to pay for two rooms.

Virtually all tourist attractions offer reduced rates for kids. Most large cities have natural history museums or aquariums, and quite a few also have hands-on children's museums; in addition, most state and national parks organize children's activities. All the national restaurant chains provide highchairs and special kids' menus; and the trend for more upmarket family-friendly restaurants to provide crayons with which to draw on paper tablecloths is still going strong.

For a database of kids' attractions, events and activities all over the USA, check the useful site ⓦnickelodeonparents.com.

Travellers with disabilities

By international standards, the USA is exceptionally accommodating for travellers with mobility concerns or other physical disabilities. By law, all public buildings, including hotels and restaurants, must be wheelchair accessible and provide suitable toilet facilities. Most street corners have dropped curbs (less so in rural areas), and most public transport systems include subway stations with elevators and buses that "kneel" to let passengers in wheelchairs board.

Getting around

The Americans with Disabilities Act (1990) obliges all air carriers to make the majority of their services accessible to travellers with disabilities, and airlines will usually let attendants of more severely disabled people accompany them at no extra charge.

Almost every Amtrak train includes one or more coaches with accommodation for handicapped passengers. Guide dogs travel free and may accompany blind, deaf or disabled passengers. Be sure to give 24 hours' notice. Hearing-impaired passengers can get information on 800 523 6590 (TTY/TDD).

Greyhound, however, has its challenges. Buses are not equipped with lifts for wheelchairs, though staff will assist with boarding (intercity carriers are required by law to do this), and the "Helping Hand" policy offers two-for-the-price-of-one tickets to passengers unable to travel alone (carry a doctor's certificate). The American Public Transportation Association, in Washington DC (202 496 4800, ⓦapta.com), provides information about the accessibility of public transport in cities.

The American Automobile Association (contact ⓦhttp://aaa.com for phone number access for each state) produces the Handicapped Driver's Mobility Guide, while the larger car-rental companies provide cars with hand controls at no extra charge, though only on their full-sized (i.e. most expensive) models; reserve well in advance.

Resources

Most state tourism offices provide information for disabled travellers (see page 43). In addition, SATH, the Society for Accessible Travel and Hospitality, in New York (ⓦsath.org), is a not-for-profit travel-industry group of travel agents, tour operators, hotel and airline management, and people with disabilities. They pass on any enquiry to the appropriate member, though you should allow plenty of time for a response. Mobility International USA, in Eugene, OR (ⓦmiusa.org), offers travel tips and operates exchange programmes for disabled people; it also serves as a national information centre on disability.

The "America the Beautiful Access Pass", issued without charge to permanently disabled or blind US citizens, gives free lifetime admission to all national parks. It can only be obtained in person at a federal area where an entrance fee is charged; you'll have to show proof of permanent disability, or that you are eligible for receiving benefits under federal law.

Women travellers

A woman travelling alone in America is not usually made to feel conspicuous, or liable to attract unwelcome attention. Cities can feel a lot safer than you might expect from recurrent media images of demented urban jungles, though particular care must be taken at night: walking through unlit, empty streets is never a good idea, and, if there's no bus service, take a taxi.

In the major urban centres, if you stick to the better parts of town, going into bars and clubs alone should pose few problems: there's generally a pretty healthy attitude toward women who do so, and your privacy will be respected.

However, small towns may lack the same liberal or indifferent attitude toward lone women travellers. People seem to jump immediately to the conclusion that your car has broken down, or that you've suffered some strange misfortune. If your vehicle does break down on heavily travelled roads, wait in the car for a police or highway patrol car to arrive. If you don't already have one, you should also rent a mobile phone with your car, for a small charge.

Women should never hitchhike in the USA. Similarly, you should never pick up anyone who's trying to hitchhike. If someone is waving you down on the road, ostensibly to get help with a broken-down vehicle, just drive on by or call the highway patrol to help them.

Avoid travelling at night by public transport – deserted bus stations, if not actually threatening, will do little to make you feel secure. Where possible, team up with a fellow traveller. On Greyhound buses, sit near the driver.

In the event it becomes necessary, all major towns have rape counselling services; if not, the local sheriff's office will arrange for you to get help and counselling, and, if necessary, get you home. The National Organization for Women (202 628 8669, ⓦnow.org) has branches listed in local phone directories and on its website, and can provide information on rape crisis centres and counselling services.

Working in the USA

Permission to work in the USA can only be granted by the Immigration and Naturalization Service in the USA itself. Contact your local embassy or consulate for advice on current regulations, but be warned that unless you have relatives or a prospective employer in the USA to sponsor you, your chances are at best slim. Students have the best chance of prolonging their stay, while a number of volunteer and work programmes allow you to experience the country less like a tourist and more like a resident.

STUDY, VOLUNTEER AND WORK PROGRAMMES

American Field Service Intercultural Programs Ⓦ afs.org, Ⓦ afs.org.au, Ⓦ afs.org.nz, Ⓦ afs.org.za. Global UN-recognized organization running summer student exchange programmes to foster international understanding.

American Institute for Foreign Study Ⓦ aifs.com. Language study and cultural immersion, as well as au pair and Camp America programmes.

BUNAC (British Universities North America Club) Ⓦ bunac.org. Working holidays in the USA for international students and young people.

Camp America Ⓦ campamerica.co.uk. Well-known company that places young people as counsellors or support staff in US summer camps, for a minimum of nine weeks.

Council on International Educational Exchange (CIEE) Ⓦ ciee.org. Leading NGO offering study programmes and volunteer projects around the world.

Earthwatch Institute Ⓦ earthwatch.org. Long-established international charity with environmental and archeological research projects worldwide.

Go Overseas Ⓦ gooverseas.com. Specializes in gap year programmes and internships around the world, including a good number of opportunities in the USA.

The Great Lakes & Chicago

ROCK & ROLL HALL OF FAME, CLEVELAND, OH

1 The Great Lakes

The five interconnected Great Lakes (Superior, Ontario, Michigan, Erie and Huron) form the largest body of fresh water in the world, a vast inland sea that is impossible to appreciate from the shore. Though it's a region of dense birch, cedar and spruce forests and rich in natural wonders – Lake Superior and the northern reaches of Lake Michigan offer stunning rocky peninsulas, craggy cliffs, pine-covered islands, mammoth dunes and deserted beaches – it's cities such as Chicago, Cleveland, Detroit and Minneapolis that stand out most, along with complex histories that encompass Native American heroes such as Tecumseh, French fur traders, industrial giants such as Ford and towering skyscrapers.

Once heavily populated by Native American tribes, including the Ojibwe (Chippewa), Ontario, Miami and Potawatomi, the lakes became a focus for French fur-trading posts in the seventeenth century. In 1787 the newly independent United States formally organized the **Northwest Territory**, and a series of one-sided treaties beginning in 1795, backed up by brutal military campaigns, forced out the Native Americans. Settlers poured in, and the remaining tribes were forcibly removed from the region in the 1830s. One by one, states were carved out of the Northwest Territory: **Ohio** (1803), **Indiana** (1816), **Illinois** (1818), **Michigan** (1837), **Wisconsin** (1848) and **Minnesota** (1858). By the early twentieth century the Great Lakes region was one of the richest in the nation, thanks to a concentration of workers in industries like steel, oil, lumber, cattle processing and finally automobiles. Recession in the 1970s and deindustrialization in the 1980s ravaged the regional economy and gave the area the unpleasant title of "**Rust Belt**". Since then, cities such as **Cincinnati**, **Cleveland** and even **Detroit** have revived their fortunes to some degree. Today the older, more industrial states of the Great Lakes region are often considered "traditional" **Midwest**, in contrast to the vast farmland states of the Great Plains, though it is the latter that are increasingly much further to the right in terms of politics and religion.

Chicago

Studded with a bewitching ensemble of skyscrapers that rise up from Lake Michigan, **CHICAGO** is one of the great American cities, forever linked with the gangsters of Al Capone, the blues of Muddy Waters and the gravity-defying dunks of Michael Jordan. Its bike-friendly lakefront and jaw-dropping skyline (featuring the 110-storey **Willis**

GREAT REGIONAL DRIVES

Ohio route, OH Drive from Cleveland west along the shore of Lake Erie on Rte-3 to Sandusky, then south on rural Rte-4 to Columbus and on to Cincinnati via scenic Rte-3.

North Shore Scenic Drive, MN Jump on Hwy-61 in Duluth to follow a trail of tiny shoreline towns along the coast of Lake Superior. The fall foliage is top-notch and there are seven state parks along the way.

Door County Coastal Byway, WI North of Milwaukee, this road takes motorists along the Door County Peninsula, and includes jaunts by the rocky coastline and the towns of Sister Bay and Egg Harbor.

Rockford to Galena, IL Take US-20 west from Rockford, Illinois out to Galena. In a state that is quite flat, the rolling hills and valleys along this route make for some rather fine vistas.

PICTURED ROCKS NATIONAL LAKESHORE, MICHIGAN

Highlights

❶ Chicago River boat tours, IL Take a boat tour on the Chicago River to soak up the Windy City's diverse architectural and cultural heritage. See page 62

❷ Abraham Lincoln sites, Springfield, IL Learn about America's greatest president at his adopted hometown and final resting place. See page 68

❸ Rock & Roll Hall of Fame and Museum, Cleveland, OH From rockabilly to Motown to punk – it's all here inside this absorbing museum. See page 79

❹ Detroit, MI What was once a post-industrial dystopia is now a city on the rise. Explore one of America's most intriguing, edgy and creative cities. See page 92

❺ Pictured Rocks National Lakeshore, MI Multihued sandstone cliffs, spectacular sand dunes and picturesque waterfalls dot this remote corner of Michigan's Upper Peninsula. See page 104

❻ Taliesin, WI The home and studios of Frank Lloyd Wright offer a unique insight into the mind of the nation's most controversial architect. See page 112

❼ North Shore Scenic Drive, MN Explore the north coast of Lake Superior from Duluth to the Canadian border, lined with dense forests and plunging cascades. See page 120

HIGHLIGHTS ARE MARKED ON THE MAP ON PAGE 50

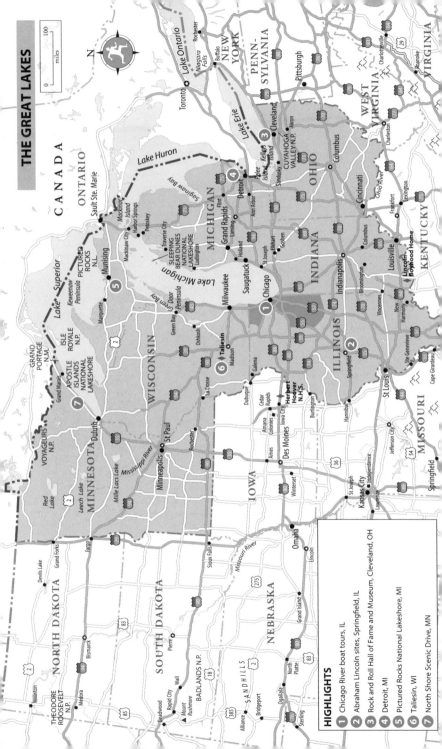

THE GREAT LAKES

HIGHLIGHTS

1. Chicago River boat tours, IL
2. Abraham Lincoln sites, Springfield, IL
3. Rock and Roll Hall of Fame and Museum, Cleveland, OH
4. Detroit, MI
5. Pictured Rocks National Lakeshore, MI
6. Taliesin, WI
7. North Shore Scenic Drive, MN

1

Tower), best viewed from the boats on the Chicago River, are perhaps its most memorable features – despite some world-class museums, it's Chicago's icons and their legacies that intrigue most visitors, from the Blues Brothers to its gut-busting deep-dish pizzas.

Founded in the 1830s, the city was virtually destroyed in the **Great Chicago Fire** of 1871, an event that sparked a building boom that has never really ended. Hosting the **World's Fair Columbian Exposition** in 1893 announced Chicago's arrival on the global stage, marking an era of unprecedented growth, industrialization, and the organization of industrial workers. Its steady growth since then has been a stormy affair, often blighted by the reign of historically corrupt "machine politics" resulting in some of the most segregated communities in the nation. Today it's a vast, sprawling conglomerate of distinctive neighbourhoods ranging from Polish to Mexican, from Korean to Greek. Despite recent improvements, the **South side of Chicago** is still grappling with high levels of poverty and one of the highest murder rates in the US – disproportionately affecting the African American population (see page 66). Visitors are rarely affected however, and most of the areas of interest are safe, friendly and host everything from inventive theatre to live music and festivals such as **Lollapalooza** (every July in Grant Park).

Downtown Chicago and The Loop

Downtown Chicago offers a masterclass in **modern architecture** with buildings that range from the prototype skyscrapers of the 1890s to Mies van der Rohe's "less is more" modernist masterpieces, and one of the tallest buildings in the world, the quarter-of-a-mile-high **Willis Tower**. Downtown covers several neighbourhoods and has long since expanded beyond **the Loop**, its traditional heart, so called because it's circled by the elevated tracks of the CTA "L" trains.

Chicago Cultural Center

78 E Washington St • Every day 10am–5pm, 1hr tours Thurs & Fri 1.15pm • Free ⓦ chicago.gov/city/en/depts/dca/supp_info/chicago_culturalcenterbuildingtours.html

Completed in 1897 as the original Chicago Public Library, the **Chicago Cultural Center** is a magnificent Beaux Arts palace filled primarily with temporary exhibitions of **Contemporary art**. The Washington Street Lobby is a dazzling space adorned with mosaics and Carrara marble, while the third-floor **Preston Bradley Hall** features the world's largest stained-glass Tiffany dome (38ft in diameter). Tiffany also supervised the design of the fourth-floor Sidney R. Yates Gallery, a monumental hall inspired by the Doge's Palace in Venice.

American Writers Museum

180 N Michigan Ave • Thurs–Mon 10am–5pm • charge • ⓦ americanwritersmuseum.org

Seeing as the city is home to some of America's most iconic authors, it's fitting that the first ever **American Writers Museum** opened in Chicago in 2017. Interactive exhibits include the "Mind of a Writer Gallery", offering insights into how writers think and work; special displays on children's literature; and galleries on American writers (featuring 100 authors) and Chicago wordsmiths – from poets Gwendolyn Brooks and Carl Sandburg (*Chicago Poems*), to authors Nelson Algren (*City on the Make*), Saul Bellow, Sandra Cisneros (*The*

CHICAGO'S CITYPASS

For significant **discounts** at five of the city's major tourist and cultural attractions – Skydeck Chicago (Willis Tower), the Field Museum, Shedd Aquarium, Adler Planetarium and the Museum of Science and Industry – you can purchase a **CityPass**. Valid for nine consecutive days, it lets you skip most queues and save money. Passes are sold at each of the attractions, or via the website (ⓦ citypass.com/chicago).

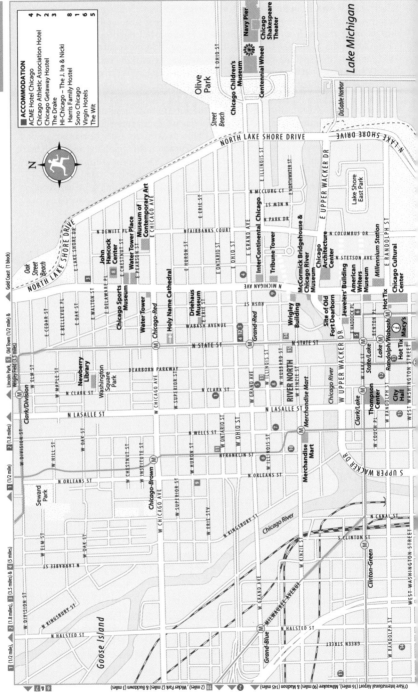

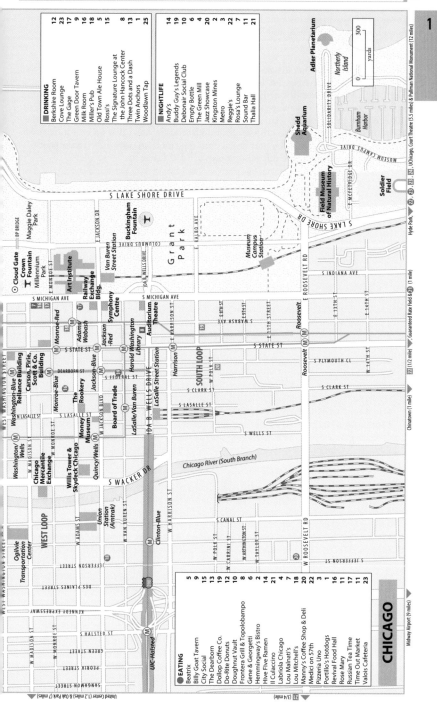

CHICAGO

● EATING

Beatrix	5
Billy Goat Tavern	9
City Social	15
The Dearborn	13
Dollop Coffee Co.	19
Do-Rite Donuts	12
Doughnut Vault	10
Frontera Grill & Topolobampo	8
Gene & Georgetti	6
Hemmingway's Bistro	2
Hive Five Ramen	14
Il Culaccino	4
Labriola Chicago	7
Lou Malnati's	18
Lou Mitchell's	3
Manny's Coffee Shop & Deli	22
Medici on 57th	1
Pizzeria Uno	16
Portillo's Hotdogs	11
Revival Food Hall	17
Rose Mary	11
Russian Tea Time	11
Time Out Market	23
Valois Cafeteria	

■ DRINKING

Berkshire Room	12
Cove Lounge	23
The Gage	17
Green Door Tavern	9
Milk Room	16
Miller's Pub	18
Old Town Ale House	5
Rossi's	15
The Signature Lounge at the John Hancock Center	8
Three Dots and a Dash	13
Twin Anchors	1
Woodlawn Tap	25

■ NIGHTLIFE

Andy's	14
Buddy Guy's Legends	19
Debonair Social Club	10
The Green Mill	6
Empty Bottle	4
Jazz Showcase	20
Kingston Mines	2
Metro	3
Reggie's	22
Rosa's Lounge	7
Sound Bar	11
Thalia Hall	21

House on Mango Street), Lorraine Hansberry (*A Raisin in the Sun*), Upton Sinclair (*The Jungle*), Iceberg Slim (*Pimp*) and Richard Wright (*Native Son*).

Willis Tower
233 S Wacker Drive, at Adams St · **Skydeck Chicago** Daily: March–Sept 9am–10pm; Oct–Feb Sun–Thurs 9am–8pm, Fri & Sat 9am-10pm · charge (included with Citypass) · ⓦ theskydeck.com

The 1451ft **Willis Tower** (formerly the Sears Tower) was the tallest building in the world from 1973 to 1998. It's so huge that it has more than one hundred elevators – some of these ascend, in little more than a minute, from the ground-level shopping mall to the 103rd-floor **Skydeck Chicago** (1353ft) for mind-bending views that on a clear day take in four states. Visitors can also peer down onto the city from one of the vertiginous glass boxes that hang off the side (also known as "The Ledge").

CHICAGO'S ARCHITECTURAL WONDERS

Chicago is jam-packed with historic skyscrapers, theatres and landmark buildings, and the best way to see them is on a river cruise or Architecture Foundation walking tour (see page 62). The following masterpieces can be seen on a 2–3hr walking tour starting at the Foundation's headquarters, the **Chicago Architecture Center**: a two-floor museum with illuminating exhibits and an excellent 3D scale model of Chicago (111 East Wacker Drive, daily 10am–4pm; charge, admission included with Foundation tours).

Auditorium Theatre 50 E Ida B Wells Dr, ⓦ auditoriumtheatre.org. This fortress-like beauty was completed in 1889 (designed by Dankmar Adler and the legendary Louis Sullivan, Chicago's father of the skyscraper), and now hosts performances by the Joffrey Ballet. Tours vary depending on the season and daily show times, earliest tours at 1PM last tours at 6 PM, charge.

The Rookery 209 S LaSalle St. Built in 1888 by Burnham & Root, with a Moorish-Gothic exterior. The airy lobby, decked out with Italian marble and gold leaf during a major 1905 remodelling by Frank Lloyd Wright, is open to the public, but to see the spiral cantilever staircase up close you must take a guided tour (Mon–Fri 10am–1pm, charge; ask at ShopWright inside, or visit ⓦ flwright.org/visit/rookery).

Carson, Pirie, Scott & Co Building 1 S State St. This 1899 Louis Sullivan-designed building (now a branch of Target), boasts a magnificent ironwork facade that blends botanic and geometric forms in an intuitive version of Art Moderne. Open 24 hours.

Reliance Building 1 W Washington St. Looking up at the proud facade of this small skyscraper you'd be forgiven for thinking it dates from the Art Deco Thirties, but it was in fact completed way back in 1895 by Charles Atwood on a base by Burnham & Root (it's now the *Staypineapple The Loop Chicago* hotel).

Macy's 111 N State St. The gorgeous spherical bronze clocks suspended from the corners of this department store were immortalized in a Norman Rockwell *Saturday Evening Post* cover in 1945; the building was another Burnham project originally completed in the 1890s for Marshall Field. Pop in to see the elaborate Tiffany ceiling, which is made up of more than one million pieces of iridescent glass. Mon–Sat 10am–8pm, Sun 11am–7pm.

Jewelers' Building 35 E Wacker Drive. This elegant Beaux Arts, 522ft terracotta-clad building was completed in 1927 (designed by Burnham protégés Joachim Giæver and Frederick P. Dinkelberg) and is capped on the seventeenth floor by a domed rotunda that once housed Al Capone's favourite speakeasy. It's slated to reopen as a boutique hotel.

Wrigley Building 400 N Michigan Ave. The white terracotta, wedding-cake colossus was completed for the Chicago-based chewing-gum magnate in 1924 (Wrigley moved out in 2012).

Tribune Tower 435 N Michigan Ave. Completed in 1925 and topped by flying buttresses and Gothic detailing inspired by Rouen's cathedral. It still houses the editorial offices of Chicago's morning newspaper. Look closely at the walls either side of the entrance and you'll see embedded chunks of historic buildings – from China, the Parthenon, Westminster Cathedral and even Dublin's General Post Office of 1916 fame – "borrowed" from around the world by *Tribune* staffers. The lobby really seems like a Gothic cathedral, adorned with famous quotes defending the freedom of the press and a giant topographical map of North America.

InterContinental Chicago 505 N Michigan Ave. This Art Deco gem was completed in 1929, originally as the home of the Medinah Athletic Club. Its Indiana limestone facade is decorated with a giant frieze in Assyrian style and adorned with carvings of three Sumerian warriors.

The Chicago River

1

Broad, double-decked Wacker Drive, parallel to the **Chicago River**, was designed as a sophisticated promenade, lined by benches and obelisk-shaped lanterns, by Daniel Burnham in 1909. Just below Wacker Drive, the **Riverwalk** runs along the south bank for several pleasant blocks. The direction of the river itself was reversed in 1900 using a series of locks, in an engineering project more extensive than the digging of the Panama Canal. As a result, rather than letting its sewage and industrial waste flow east into Lake Michigan, Chicago now sends it all south into the Corn Belt.

McCormick Bridgehouse & Chicago River Museum

99 Riverwalk • Mid May to early Nov Mon–Thurs 10am–5pm, Fri–Mon 10am–5pm • charge, ages 5 and under free • Ⓦ bridgehousemuseum.org

The tiny **McCormick Bridgehouse & Chicago River Museum** lies on the riverside, just below the Michigan Avenue/DuSable Bridge, with absorbing exhibits on the river and its many bascule drawbridges within a five-story bridgehouse. Up on the entrance to the bridge itself is a small plaque marking the spot of **Fort Dearborn**, founded in 1803; the expressive mural carved into the bridge entrance pillar commemorates its destruction and the massacre of its inhabitants by the Potawatomi in 1812.

Millennium Park and around

201 E Randolph St • Daily 8am–9pm • Free • Ⓦ maggiedaleypark.com

Thanks to a highly ambitious renovation project, **Millennium Park** is now a showcase for public art, landscape design and performing arts that overshadows its older southern neighbour, **Grant Park**. Its centrepiece is a stunning, seamless, stainless-steel sculpture officially titled **Cloud Gate** by British-based artist Anish Kapoor, universally known as "The Bean". Inspired by liquid mercury, it invites viewers to walk around, beside and even underneath it to enjoy spectacular and endlessly intriguing reflections of both the city and the sky above. Nearby, **Crown Fountain** by Jaume Plensa consists of two 50ft, glass-brick towers set either side of a black granite plaza; giant video images of the faces of ordinary Chicagoans play across them both. Further back, the **Jay Pritzker Pavilion** (focus of the annual **Chicago Blues Festival**) is a striking open-air auditorium designed by renowned-architect Frank Gehry, who used mighty swirls and flourishes of steel to improve its acoustics – Gehry's **BP Bridge** is an equally stunning, silvery pathway that snakes its way from here across Columbus Drive to **Maggie Daley Park** (daily 6am– 11pm; free; Ⓦ maggiedaleypark.com). The newest addition to the waterfront, this park is sprinkled with fun activities such as a climbing wall, mini golf, play areas for kids, an ice-skating ribbon, tennis courts. Hours, rates, and availability changed based on the season and day. Check online before visiting to see what's currently available.

The Art Institute of Chicago

111 S Michigan Ave • Thurs–Mon 11am–5pm, Thurs till 8pm • charge (included with Citypass) • Ⓦ artic.edu

The **Art Institute of Chicago** ranks as one of the world's greatest art museums. Completed in 1893 for the World's Fair, the original galleries have been greatly expanded over the years, most recently with an extension by Renzo Piano completed in 2009. With thousands of works ranging from ancient Greece and China to Impressionist gems and Andy Warhol, expect to spend at least half a day here. Most visitors head straight upstairs to the Impressionist section, but make time for the quirky but mesmerizing **Thorne Miniature Rooms** on the **Lower Level**, tiny but precise replicas of famous interiors from thirteenth-century Europe to 1930s America.

First Level

The sprawling **First Level** contains a trove of multicultural art going back thousands of years, beginning with a vast ensemble of African, Native American and Asian artefacts, ceramics, statuary and screen paintings. Highlights of the Indian Arts of Americas gallery (136) include the ornate carved stone used for the coronation of the Aztec ruler Moctezuma II on July 15, 1503. Beyond the McKinlock Court Garden (used as an open-air café in summer) is Chagall's stunning stained-glass *America Windows* and the reconstructed Art Moderne trading room of the Chicago Stock Exchange, designed by Louis Sullivan in 1893 and preserved here in the 1970s.

Second Level

The real showstoppers reside on the **Second Level**, beginning with an exceptional collection of Renoir paintings (201), and a whole room dedicated to Degas (226). Monet's landscapes feature in gallery 240, along with Seurat's immediately familiar Pointillist *Sunday Afternoon on La Grande Jatte*, regarded by many critics as the most successful Post-Impressionist painting ever. Monet's *Haystacks* captured in various lights, plus some of his classic *Water Lilies*, hold court in 243. Gallery 242 is dedicated to Toulouse-Lautrec (*At the Moulin Rouge*), while Gauguin, Van Gogh and Pissarro feature in 241 and 246. Beyond these masterworks, other highlights include the pitchfork-holding farmer of Grant Wood's oft-parodied *American Gothic* (263), which he painted as a student at the Art Institute school, and sold to the museum for $300 in 1930; El Greco's startling *Assumption of the Virgin* (211), which painter Mary Cassatt persuaded the Institute to buy; Edward Hopper's lonely *Nighthawks* (262), purchased for $3000 soon after its completion in 1942; and Jules Breton's inspirational *Song of the Lark* (222), much admired by Eleanor Roosevelt and (years later) actor Bill Murray. Earlier work from Rembrandt (213), Rubens (208), Tintoretto (206) and Botticelli (*Virgin & Child* in 204) is also worth seeking out. Highlights of the modern and contemporary art galleries include several works by Georgia O'Keeffe (265), David Hockney's slightly creepy but perceptive *American Collectors* (297) and Warhol's iconic *Liz* (292).

Third Level

The modern and contemporary art on the **Third Level** includes Henri Matisse's monumental *Bathers by a River* and Pablo Picasso's melancholy *Old Guitarist* (both 391), one of the definitive masterpieces of his Blue Period. There's also a tortured, tuxedoed self-portrait that was Max Beckmann's last Berlin painting before fleeing the Nazis (392); Picasso's *Red Armchair* (394) and *Nude under a Pine Tree* (398); and Chagall's challenging *White Crucifixion* (395), depicting a definitively Jewish Jesus.

Field Museum of Natural History

1200 S Lake Shore Drive, at Roosevelt Rd · Daily 9am–5pm; last entry 4pm · charge (included in Citypass), discount for ages 3-11, plus extra for temporary exhibitions and 3D movies · Ⓦ fieldmuseum.org

The extensive and engaging **Field Museum of Natural History** occupies a huge, marble-clad, Daniel Burnham-designed Greek temple in the southern half of **Grant Park** (known as the Museum Campus). It's quite an erratic museum, in which the exhibits vary enormously in their age and sophistication. There's a hall of stupendous dinosaurs, including "Sue", the most complete *T.rex* fossil ever found, Egyptian tombs – the entire burial chamber of the son of a Fifth Dynasty pharaoh was brought here in 1908 – and some fascinating displays on the islands of the Pacific. Best of all for young kids is the "Underground Adventure", a simulated environment that "shrinks" visitors to a hundredth of their normal size and propels them into a world of giant animatronic spiders and crayfish.

Shedd Aquarium

1200 S Lake Shore Drive · Mid-June to Aug daily 9am–6pm; Sept to mid-June Tues–Fri 9am–5pm, Sat-Mon & holidays 9am–6pm; tickets required in advance, arrive early to beat the long queues and school groups · charge (included in Citypass), discount for ages 3-11 · Ⓦ sheddaquarium.org

On the shores of Lake Michigan, the **Shedd Aquarium** proclaims itself the largest indoor aquarium in the world. The 1920s structure is rather old-fashioned, but the light-hearted displays are informative and entertaining. The central exhibit, a 90,000-gallon recreation of a coral reef, complete with eels, sea turtles and thousands of tropical fish, is surrounded by more than a hundred smaller habitats. Highlights include the **Wild Reef** exhibit, featuring floor-to-ceiling living reefs, tropical fish, sharks and rays. The **Oceanarium** provides an enormous contrast, with its modern lakeview home for marine mammals such as Pacific white-sided dolphins and beluga whales.

Adler Planetarium

1300 S Lake Shore Drive • open daily 9am–4pm (set to reopen March 4, 2022) • charge (included in Citypass), plus extra for Sky Show & Atwood Sphere experience • ⓦ adlerplanetarium.org

Looking like a heavily stylized temple, the Art Deco **Adler Planetarium** opens with the exhibit "Our Solar System", which includes interactive stations displaying moon rocks and a fantastical globe that simulates the wayward motions of clouds on various gas-filled planets like Jupiter and Saturn. The real highlight however is the **Sky Theater**, where the unmissable "Cosmic Wonder" (five daily) show probes the cosmos through remarkable images of the Crab Nebula, star formations and Orion the Hunter. You can also visit (for an extra fee) the 1913 **Atwood Sphere**, Chicago's oldest planetarium.

The Magnificent Mile

When the Michigan Avenue Bridge was built over the Chicago River in 1920, the warehouse district along its north bank quickly changed into one of the city's most upmarket quarters, now known as the **Magnificent Mile** ("Mag Mile"), famed for its fashionable shops and department stores such as Neiman-Marcus and Tiffany & Co. Throughout the Roaring Twenties one glitzy tower after another appeared along Michigan Avenue, including the wedding-cake colossus of the **Wrigley Building**, and the **Tribune Tower**. It's still Chicago's prime **shopping district**, though most of the shops are enclosed within multistorey shopping malls. The oldest of these – and still the best – is **Water Tower Place**, 835 N Michigan Ave, with more than a hundred stores on seven floors, plus a bustling food court. Opposite at 806 N Michigan Ave, the **Historic Water Tower**, a whimsically Gothic stone castle topped by a 100ft tower, was built in 1869 and is one of the very few structures to have survived the Great Fire. Inside the Water Tower is the tiny **City Gallery** of rotating photographic exhibits by Chicago-based artists (currently closed due to COVID-19).

Driehaus Museum

40 E Erie St • Fri & Sat 10am–5pm, Sun noon–5pm • charge • ⓦ driehausmuseum.org

Housed in the elegant 1883 Nickerson Mansion, two blocks west of Mag Mile, the **Driehaus Museum** hosts travelling decorative arts exhibitions, as well as providing tours of its gorgeous Gilded Age interiors and collection of work by Louis Comfort Tiffany (including a stained-glass dome).

Museum of Contemporary Art

220 E Chicago Ave • Wed–Sun 10am–5pm, Tues 10am–9pm • Suggested donation • ⓦ mcachicago.org

The **Museum of Contemporary Art**, one block east of the Historic Water Tower, is a spare space that holds revolving exhibits of photography, video and installation works on everything from "selfies" and cartoons to the influential African American artist Kerry James Marshall.

Chicago Sports Museum

835 N Michigan Ave (Water Tower Place) • Mon–Fri 11.30am–7pm, Sat 11:30am–8pm, Sun 12am–6pm • charge • ⓦ chicagosportsmuseum.com

1

Chicago is one of America's great sporting cities, a legacy explored at the entertaining **Chicago Sports Museum** inside Water Tower Place. Interactive displays allow you to hit baseballs, throw (American) footballs, shoot baskets and drive cars at the Chicago Speedway. Exhibits include Michael Jordan's Chicago Bulls' jersey, and the largest collection of Chicago Cubs World Series memorabilia anywhere – the team won in 2016.

John Hancock Center

875 N Michigan Ave • **360 Chicago** Mon–Thurs 9am–9pm, Fri & Sat 9am–11pm, closed on Sundays, last entry 1hr before closing • charge • ⊛ 360chicago.com

While the Tribune Tower anchors its southern end, the Mag Mile's northern reaches are dominated by the cross-braced steel **John Hancock Center** (1128ft), completed in 1968 by local architects Skidmore, Owings and Merrill. Though it's about 325ft shorter than the Willis Tower, the 360-degree panorama on a clear day from its 94th-floor **360 Chicago** observatory (1030ft) is unforgettable. It also features TILT, an enclosed moving platform that literally tilts you out over Michigan Avenue. It's worth pointing out that taking the elevator to the swanky *Signature Lounge* on the 96th floor (see page 66) costs nothing, and you can use that extra money to buy a cocktail of your choice.

Gold Coast

As its name suggests, the **Gold Coast**, stretching north from the Magnificent Mile along the lakeshore, is one of Chicago's wealthiest and most desirable neighbourhoods. This residential district is primarily notable for **Oak Street Beach** (open from 6 am-11pm, but swimming permitted only when life-guards are on duty, 11am–7pm), the city's most central (and style-conscious) strand. It's accessible via a walkway under Lake Shore Drive, across from the *Drake Hotel*.

Navy Pier

600 E Grand Ave • Sun–Thurs 11am–7pm, Fri & Sat 11am–9pm • ⊛ navypier.com

Built in 1916, **Navy Pier** reopened in 1995 as a shopping and entertainment complex that hums with people in the summer, when the promenade provides stunning views across the city and Lake Michigan. Other than trawling its bars and cafés, taking a boat tour, checking out the **IMAX theatre** and giant **Centennial Wheel** or seeing a show at the **Shakespeare Theater** (⊛ chicagoshakes.com), there's a couple of worthwhile museums here. Three floors are taken up by the imaginative interactive exhibits of the **Chicago Children's Museum** (Fri–Sun 10am–5pm; charge; ⊛ chicagochildrensmuseum.org).

CHICAGO SPECTATOR SPORTS

Chicagoans are, for better or worse, loyally supportive of their teams. The **Bulls** basketball team, helmed by Michael Jordan, was winner of six NBA championships in the 1990s (⊛ nba. com/bulls), but has had little success in the post-Jordan era. They play in the modern United Center, 1901 W Madison St, as do hockey's **Blackhawks**, winners of the Stanley Cup six times, most recently in 2015 (⊛ nhl.com/blackhawks). The **Bears** football team (⊛ chicagobears.com) won the Superbowl in 1985 but have never repeated that feat – they can be seen at Soldier Field, 425 E McFetridge Drive, at the south end of Grant Park. As for baseball, the **Cubs**, based at Wrigley Field (⊛ mlb.com/cubs), broke one of the longest droughts in sports history in 2016 by winning the World Series for the first time since 1908. Their rivals the **White Sox** – Barack Obama's favourite team – won the World Series in 2005. They play at Guaranteed Rate Field, at 333 W 35th St (⊛ mlb.com/whitesox).

Lincoln Park

N Lake Shore Drive • Daily 6am–11pm

1

In summer, Chicago's largest green space, **Lincoln Park**, provides a much-needed respite from the gridded pavements of the rest of the city. Set aside as the city cemetery in 1842, it was gradually converted to a park from the 1870s (the ornate 1858 **Couch Family Mausoleum** is the only remnant of its earlier function). It's packed with leafy nooks and crannies, monuments and sculptures, and has a couple of friendly, family-oriented **beaches** at the eastern ends of North and Fullerton avenues.

Near the small **Lincoln Park Zoo** at the heart of the park (10am–5pm daily; free, ⓦlpzoo.org), renowned for its menagerie of African apes and curious red pandas, you can rent paddleboats or bikes. If the weather's bad, head for the pleasantly humid **Lincoln Park Conservancy**, 2391 N Stockton Drive (Wed–Sun 10am–3pm; free; ⓦlincolnparkconservancy.org), a giant greenhouse built in the 1890s, or the **Peggy Notebaert Nature Museum** (Thurs–Mon 10am–4pm; charge; ⓦnaturemuseum.org), with family-friendly exhibits on the local environment and wildlife.

Chicago History Museum

1601 N Clark St • Tues–Sat 9.30am–4.30pm, Sun noon–5pm • charge • ⓦchicagohistory.org

Bone up on Chicago's complex and stormy past at the **Chicago History Museum**, at the south end of Lincoln Park, with comprehensive displays on regional and national history in its permanent exhibition, "Chicago: Crossroads of America", featuring everything from the Great Fire of 1871 to the 1968 Democratic National Convention.

Wrigley Field

1060 W Addison St, at N Clark • Tours (75–90min) run May–Sept daily (every 30min–1hr 9am–5pm) • charge • ⓦmlb.com/cubs • Red Line via Addison Station

Six miles northwest of downtown, **Wrigley Field** is the ivy-covered 1920s stadium of baseball's much-loved Cubs. It's one of the best places to get a real feel for the game – it still has a hand-operated scoreboard and the best "frosty malts" in the city. There are few more pleasant and relaxing ways to spend an afternoon than drinking beer, eating hot dogs and watching a ballgame in the sunshine, among the Cubs' faithful.

Oak Park

Visitor office 1010 Lake St • ⓦvisitoakpark.com • Take the Green Line west to the Oak Park stop

Nine miles west of the Loop, the affluent and well-designed nineteenth-century suburb of **Oak Park** is best known for its links to two of America's most celebrated artists: Nobel Prize-winning author **Ernest Hemingway** and legendary architect **Frank Lloyd Wright**.

Ernest Hemingway's Birthplace Museum

339 N Oak Park Ave • Fri & Sun 1–5pm, Sat 10am–5pm • charge • ⓦhemingwaybirthplace.com

Ernest Hemingway was born in Oak Park in 1899, growing up in an upper middle-class family with two working parents, unusual at the time. His **birthplace**, where he lived until the age of 6, is a beautifully preserved 1890 Queen Anne-style townhouse, accessible via enlightening guided tours that run throughout the day. The museum hopes to build a new **Hemingway Center for Writing & Research**, at the back of the house, in the coming years.

Frank Lloyd Wright Home and Studio

951 Chicago Ave, at Forest • Guided 1hr tours daily 10am–4pm, 10am–3pm daily in January and February • charge • ⓦflwright.org

In 1889, a decade before Hemingway's birth, an ambitious young architect named **Frank Lloyd Wright** arrived in Oak Park, which he used for the next twenty years as a testing ground for his innovative design theories. The small, brown-shingled **Frank**

1

Lloyd Wright Home and Studio, remodelled repeatedly, shows all his hallmarks, years ahead of their time: large fireplaces to symbolize the heart of the home and family; free-flowing, open-plan rooms; and the visual linking of interior and exterior spaces. The furniture of the kitchen and dining rooms is Wright's own design; he added a two-storey studio in 1898, with a mezzanine drafting area suspended by chains from the roof beams. You can only see the house and studio on a guided tour – try to make a reservation in advance. Lengthier, **self-guided audio walking tours** take in the dozen other Wright-designed houses within a two-block radius.

Unity Temple

875 Lake St • Tours (guided 45–60min, or self-guided with audio) Mon–Thurs 10am–5pm, Fri 10am–4pm, Sat 9am–noon • charge • ⓦ unitytemple.org

Frank Lloyd Wright's ideal of an "organic architecture", in which all aspects of the design derive from a single unifying concept – quite at odds with the fussy "gingerbread" style popular at the time – is exemplified by the **Unity Temple**, completed in 1908. Still used as a Unitarian Universalist church, it's open for tours (reserve in advance).

Hyde Park

Take the Metra train to 55th–56th–57th Street Station

Six miles south of the Loop, **Hyde Park**, the most attractive and sophisticated South Side neighbourhood, is home to the principal campus of the **University of Chicago** and several enticing museums. Hyde Park is also slated to be the location of the **Obama Presidential Center** (due to open by 2022), an innovative tower structure in Jackson Park (see ⓦ obama.org/the-center). The Obamas bought their home on South Greenwood Avenue (a $2 million Georgian Revival mansion) in Hyde Park in 2005, and retain close links with the area.

Museum of Science and Industry and Jackson Park

5700 S Lake Shore Drive, at 57th St • Daily 9.30am–4pm • charge • ⓦ msichicago.org

At the north end of **Jackson Park**, the cavernous **Museum of Science and Industry** is aimed squarely at families, with interactive computer displays that explore subjects such as the inner workings of the brain and heart, exhibits including a captured German U-boat (additional charge for tours), a trip down a replica coal mine (additional charge), and a giant Omnimax movie dome (additional charge).

The museum is housed in what was the Palace of Fine Arts during the **1893 World's Columbian Exposition** – Jackson Park is where most of the fairgrounds were located, but the only site remaining is the **Osaka Garden**, designed in classical Japanese style. A replica of the original Statue of the Republic still stands in the park (6401 S Stony Island Ave), where it was installed in 1918 after the original caught fire.

University of Chicago

5801 S Ellis Ave • ⓦ uchicago.edu • **Rockefeller Chapel** 5850 S Woodlawn Ave, at 59th St • Mon–Fri 8am–2pm, Sun service 11 • Free • ⓦ rockefeller.uchicago.edu

Established in 1890 thanks to a donation from oil magnate John D. Rockefeller, the **University of Chicago** (UChicago), gives a college-town atmosphere to much of Hyde Park, with bookshops and cafés along **East 57th Street** in close proximity to its attractive campus. Perhaps best known for the **Chicago School of Economics** (it boasts twelve Nobel laureates in economics alone), this is where **Milton Friedman** and friends devised the policies that influenced Ronald Reagan and Margaret Thatcher in the 1980s. Highlights on campus include the massive Collegiate gothic pile of the **Rockefeller Chapel** completed in 1928, its cavernous interior well worth a peek. Tours take in the tower and 72-bell carillon.

THE PULLMAN EMPIRE

Industrialist and railroad mogul George Pullman built the town of Pullman in the 1880s to house the workers of the Pullman Palace Car Company. At first, it was considered a model community, with comfortable living conditions and indoor plumbing, gas, and sewers in each rowhouse. At the time, most workers were living in densely populated tenement buildings or older, run-down walkups.

During a recession in 1893, the company laid off workers and cut wages without decreasing the rent of the workers who lived in Pullman. 4,000 Pullman workers went on strike in May 1894, led by the American Railway Union, then headed by Eugene V. Debs. By the end of June over 100,000 workers across the country had walked off the job in solidarity, shutting down much of the nation's freight and passenger trains. The strike lasted for 2 months, ending with intervention by the US military and 30 dead.

George Pullman was also known for hiring formerly enslaved African Americans as porters on his sleeping cars following the Civil War. The Pullman porters were crucial to social advancement of African Americans, and the Brotherhood of Sleeping Car Porters, formed in 1925, was the first all-black union. Former Pullman porters include Thurgood Marshall and Malcolm X.

The community was incorporated into Chicago following Pullman's death, and the rowhouses were eventually sold to the workers who lived there. Pullman Park was designated a national monument in 2015 by President Obama.

Robie House

5757 S Woodlawn Ave • Tours (50min) Thurs–Mon 9.30am–4pm • charge for guided tour and self-guided audio • ⓦ flwright.org

Located on the UChicago campus, Frank Lloyd Wright's Prairie-style **Robie House** was completed in 1910, designated a U.S. National Historic Landmark in 1971, and is acknowledged today as one of the masterpieces of twentieth-century architecture and interior design. Reserve in advance the illuminating guided tours or take the self-guided audio walking tour (around 30min).

DuSable Museum of African American History

740 E 56th Place • Wed–Sun 11am–4pm (last admission 3:30pm) • charge • ⓦ dusablemuseum.org

Until the **DuSable Museum of African American History** moves into its impressive new premises across the street (the Roundhouse, a former horse stable designed by Daniel Burnham, slated to open by 2022), its enlightening and important collection of art and artefacts will be exhibited in these rather cramped quarters (on the western edge of the UChicago campus). Opened in 1961, it is the nation's oldest independent African American museum. The main display chronicles the African American experience from slavery to the Black Panthers (local leader **Fred Hampton** was killed by Chicago police in 1969), Civil Rights and Obama.

Pullman National Monument

610 E. 111th St • open daily 9am–5pm • south via I-94 expressway • free • ⓦ nps.gov/pull/index

Located 15 miles south of the city centre in the notorious South side of the city, the Pullman National Monument (see page 66) is often overlooked by visitors. But for anyone interested in the national labor movement or African American history the Pullman monument is a must.

ARRIVAL AND DEPARTURE   CHICAGO

BY PLANE

O'Hare International Airport Chicago's O'Hare International Airport (ⓦ flychicago.com/ohare) is 17 miles northwest of downtown. It is connected to the city centre by 24hr CTA (Blue Line) trains (around 45min). Taxis to downtown from O'Hare usually take 30min–1hr, and Ubers

1

are also available

Midway Airport Smaller than O'Hare and primarily used by domestic airlines, Midway (⬤flychicago.com/midway) is 11 miles southwest of downtown, and you can take one of CTA's Midway (Orange Line) trains from right outside the terminal (30min). The journey time into town is about 20–40min.

Airport shuttles Another option is the Go Airport Express bus and van service between the airports and downtown hotels ⬤airportexpress.com).

BY BUS

Greyhound and a number of regional bus companies pull into the large 24hr bus station at 630 W Harrison St (☎312 408 5800, ⬤greyhound.com), three blocks southwest of Union Station. Megabus drops off and picks up at W Polk St, between S Canal St and S Clinton St (near Union Station). Destinations (Greyhound) Cincinnati (6 daily, 6hr-10hr); Cleveland (2 daily, 7hr 45min-8hr 25min); Detroit (4 daily;

5hr 35min–6hr 20min); Indianapolis (9 daily; 3hr 25min–4hr 20min); Madison (2 daily; 4hr 10min–4hr 25min); Milwaukee (7 daily; 1hr 45min–2hr 40min); Minneapolis (2 daily, 10hr 20min-12hr 15min); Springfield (1 daily; 5hr). Minneapolis (2 daily, 10hr 20min-12hr 15min).

Destinations (Megabus) Madison (2 daily, 3hr 35min-3hr 50min); Rockford (1 daily, 2hr 10min); Minneapolis (1 daily, 9hr 40min); St. Paul (1 daily, 9 hrs)

BY TRAIN

Chicago is the hub of the Amtrak rail system, and almost every cross-country route passes through Union Station, west of the Loop at Canal and Adams streets.

Destinations Cleveland (1-3 daily; 6–7hr); Cincinnati (1 daily, 8hr 32min); Detroit (5 daily; 5hr 20min-5hr 45min); Indianapolis (5 daily, 4hr 15min-5hr); Madison (7 daily; 3hr 35min-4hr 20 min); Milwaukee (7 daily; 1hr 30min); Minneapolis (2 daily, 7hr 48min); Springfield (7 daily; 3hr 15 min); St. Paul (5 daily, 7hr 48 min-9hr 20 min).

GETTING AROUND

The **Chicago Transit Authority** (CTA; ⬤transitchicago. com) operates a system of elevated trains 24hr a day. Pick up a CTA system map, available at most subway stations and visitor centres, or from CTA headquarters west of the Chicago River at 567 W Lake St.

Bus and L train fares and passes CTA riders will need to buy a Ventra Card (available in all "L" stations) and add value to it, or a single-ride ticket. Passes good for one, three, or seven days of unlimited rides on both buses and the "L" are sold at O'Hare and Midway airports as well as Union Station, the visitor centre and other locations. The "L" Rapid transit trains run every 5–15min during the day and every 15min– 1hr all night. Lines are colour-coded and denoted by route rather than destination.

By bus CTA buses run every 5–15min during rush hours and every 8–20min at other times.

By commuter train Metra trains (⬤metrarail.com) run from various points downtown to and from the suburbs and outlying areas, including Oak Park and Hyde Park.

By taxi Chicago taxis can be hailed anytime in the Loop and other central neighbourhoods; otherwise call Yellow Cab (☎312 829 4222) or Checker Taxi (☎312 243 2537). If you have a smartphone, Lyft (⬤lyft.com) and Uber (⬤uber. com) have a major presence in Chicago.

By bike Divvy Bikes (⬤divvybikes.com), Chicago's bike-share scheme, offers visitors 24hr passes at kiosk stations throughout the city that provide unlimited free 3hr rides.

CHICAGO GUIDED TOURS

The best **guided tours** of Chicago are those offered by the **Chicago Architecture Foundation**, 111 E Wacker Drive (Fri-Mon 10am–4pm; ⬤architecture.org). Expert guides point out the city's many architectural treasures and explain their role in Chicago's history and development. In addition to the famous River Boat Tours (see bookmark), they also offer excellent walking tours and evening boat tours. Superb Architecture River Cruises along the Chicago River leave from 112 E Wacker Drive, opposite the Chicago Architecture Center (90min; late April to early June Mon–Fri 6 daily, Sat & Sun 8 daily; early June to Sept Mon–Fri 10 daily, Sat & Sun 13 daily; Oct Mon–Fri 6 daily, Sat & Sun 11 daily; Nov Mon–Fri 3 daily, Sat & Sun 6 daily; charge).

For a free and personalized tour, the **Chicago Greeter** (⬤chicagogreeter.com) "Greeter Visits" tours leave from the lobby of the Chicago Cultural Center – you must set up a tour ten business days before your arrival on the website. Alternately, just show up and take advantage of the "Instagreeter" programme; the 1hr tours are led by a trained greeter, with the "Loop InstaGreeter" available year round (Fri–Mon 10.30am–2.30pm). Millennium Park tours run late May to early Oct daily at 11.30pm (also from Chicago Cultural Center).

1

INFORMATION

Visitor centre 72 E. Randolph St (Mon–Sat 9:30am–6pm, Sun 10am–5pm, ⓦ choosechicago.com), with free brochures, multilingual maps and complimentary concierge services.

ACCOMMODATION   SEE MAP PAGE 52

Most central accommodation is oriented toward business and convention trade rather than tourism, but there are still plenty of moderately priced rooms in and around the Loop. Note, however, that a room tax of 17.4 percent is added to all bills, while overnight parking can cost as much as $50–70 at a fancy hotel. Airbnb offers well over 300 properties in Chicago, with rates as low as $30/night.

★ **ACME Hotel Chicago** 15 E Ohio St, ⓦ acmehotelcompany.com. Hip hotel where compact rooms feature splashy modern art, smart TVs, Apple docks, mega-fast wi-fi and free morning coffee delivery. Guests also get free Apple watches and wi-fi hotspots to carry around during their stay. $$$$

Chicago Athletic Association Hotel 12 S Michigan Ave, ⓦ chicagoathletichotel.com. Not a sports club but another slick boutique conversion of an 1890s Venetian Gothic landmark, with stylish rooms, antique-inspired furnishings, rooftop bar and a branch of *Shake Shack* on the premises. $$$$

Chicago Getaway Hostel 616 W Arlington Place, ⓦ getawayhostel.com. Easy-going hostel close to loads of good bars and eats on nearby Clark St. Oh yes, they also have free guitars for general use. Open 24hr, with free continental breakfast, stylish mixed dorms and private doubles, some with bathrooms. $

The Drake 140 E Walton Place, ⓦ thedrakehotel.com. Chicago's society hotel, just off the Magnificent Mile, has been modernized without sacrificing its sedate charms, and its well-appointed rooms have jacuzzis. You can always just pop in for a drink at the elegant *Coq d'Or*, which also features piano singalongs. $$$$

★ **HI-Chicago – The J. Ira & Nicki Harris Family Hostel** 24 E Ida B Wells Drive, ⓦ hiusa.org/hostels/illinois/chicago/chicago. Huge, very central hostel complete with a games room, luggage storage and laundry facilities. Open 24hr, with full kitchen and free continental breakfast. As well as female and male dorms, there are semi-private rooms with shared living room. No parking (public lots nearby). $$ Dorms $, private room $$$

Sono Chicago 1428 N Cleveland Ave, ⓦ thesonochicago.com. Boutique bed and breakfast in Old Town with an elegant, all-white colour scheme and stellar views of the Chicago skyline from the rooftop deck – plus free parking. $$$$

★ **Virgin Hotels** 203 N Wabash Ave, ⓦ virginhotels.com. The hip brand has branched out into the hotel business and this sleek boutique, with red-and-white colour scheme, compact but stylish rooms and rainforest showers certainly delivers. Rooms come equipped with fridge crammed with intriguing snacks, there's excellent free wi-fi everywhere, and a generous menu of free drinks 7–8pm daily – also free rides in the hotel's Tesla car (within a one-mile radius). $$$$

The Wit 201 N State St, ⓦ thewithotel.com. Contemporary Chicago hotel design calls for expansive glass exteriors, and the *Wit* does not disappoint. The rooms have soaking tubs, marine- and pastel-coloured interiors, and floor-to-ceiling windows. $$$$

EATING   SEE MAP PAGE 52

When it comes to eating, downtown Chicago (The Loop) and the surrounding neighbourhoods – West Loop, South Loop and River North – offer everything from contemporary award-winners to traditional hot-dog joints. Chicago is especially known for its messy **Italian beef sandwich** (thinly sliced beef simmered in a jus and served on an Italian roll with sweet peppers), Chicago-style beef hot dog (laden with tomatoes, onions, celery salt, hot peppers and pickle) and the Maxwell Street Polish, a kielbasa hot dog, topped with grilled onions, yellow mustard and hot peppers. Then there's deep-dish pizza, developed in 1943 at Pizzeria Uno (see page 65). For sweet fans there's Garrett Popcorn Shops (ⓦ garrettpopcorn.com), founded here in 1949, with branches all over the city.

THE LOOP

City Social 120 N LaSalle, Floor 1, ⓦ citysocialchicago.com. A common destination for the after-work crowd, this new American bar and restaurant has rotating beers on draft, prompt service, and a menu full of surprises. $$

The Dearborn 145 N Dearborn St, ⓦ thedearborntavern.com. Classy gastropub in the heart of downtown, with contemporary American food from burgers and fried chicken to creative pastas and seafood (such as wild Alaskan halibut with crab salad) They also offer brunch on the weekends from 10am–2:30pm. $$$$

Dollop Coffee Co. 343 S Dearborn St, ⓦ dollopcoffee.com. Chicago-based chain of coffee roasters who serve locally made coffee fare along with a relaxed, welcoming ambiance and displays of local art. Several locations across the city. $

Do-Rite Donuts 233 S Wacker Dr, ⓦ doritedonuts.com. Small chain doughnut shop with some fine offerings, include pistachio-Meyer lemon, vanilla bean and the outstanding Boston crème. They close when they sell out, so come early. $

1

CRASH COURSE IN CHICAGO PIZZA

While travelers often view pizza in the US as the polarizing New York slice versus Chicago deep dish, the truth is that the Great Lakes, and Chicago in particular, serve up an astounding variety of takes on the classic cheese, sauce, and dough combination.

Local Chicagoans will tell you the most commonly consumed pizza is served tavern-style, a pie made on a cracker-thin crust cut into squares to be shared. These pizzas are a much lighter fare than the traditional deep dish, prepared more quickly, and relatively inexpensive. While the traditional triangle slice is harder to come by, there are still many places in the city that serve something close to a New York slice on the cheap, for a grab and go pizza encounter.

Regarding the infamous "deep dish", even this phrase conjures up numerous iterations: Lou Malnati's famous deep dish is considered a pan pizza, with the thin wall of butter crust containing the oozing cheese and fresh tomato sauce contained within. Giordano's and Pizzeria Uno, however, serve a stuffed crust deep dish pizza, in which the crust is significantly higher and thicker, containing a centre of cheese and sauce, as if the ends of the pizza were rolled up. These are just the two extremes of deep dish; the rest fall somewhere in between in terms of thickness and heartiness. If going out for deep dish, make sure to order it as soon as possible after being seated, or be ready to wait. A deep-dish pizza can take anywhere from 45 minutes to over an hour to cook fully.

Chicago also offers both traditional and quirky takes on Neapolitan pizza, closer to those traditionally served in Italy, as well as Sicilian-style pizza (medium thick, flat crust with fresh tomatoes for sauce), and even a pizza pot pie, located at Chicago Pizza Oven Grinder Company in the Lincoln Park neighbourhood.

Across the Great Lakes, you'll find even more variations on pizza and "deep dish", including the mile-high hearty Detroit pan pizza, and medium-thick Cleveland style pizza, both identified by a rectangular shape. When visiting Chicago and the Great Lakes, make sure you don't limit yourself to the pizza possibilities. Don't get deep-dish tunnel vision!

★ **Revival Food Hall** 125 S Clark St, ⓦ revivalfoodhall. com. Chicago has several food halls, but this is one of the most central and most enticing (though it's closed at the weekend), with 15 fast-casual stalls featuring Chicago's favourite vendors. $$

Russian Tea Time 77 E Adams St, at Michigan Ave, ⓦ russianteatime.com. This Midwestern nod to New York's exclusive *Russian Tea Room* offers a (pricey) sampling of authentic fare from the former Soviet empire. $$$$

THE WEST LOOP

High Five Ramen 112 N Green St, ⓦ highfiveramen. com. Hip ramen joint, with steaming bowls of noodles served *tonkotsu*-style (made with a rich and creamy pork broth), with a variety of spice levels (from tongue-tingling to face-numbing). $$

Lou Mitchell's 565 W Jackson Ave, at Clinton St, ⓦ loumitchellsrestaurant.com. Near Union Station, *Lou's* has been around since 1923, serving terrific omelettes, waffles, and hash browns all day long. Try the pecan-laden cookies. $

★ **Rose Mary** 932 W Fulton St. Top Chef winner Joe Flamm opened this small plates, Italian-Croatian fusion in April 2020, and it has been the fuss around town ever since. Book well in advance, reservations fill up 3 months out. $$$$

★ **Time Out Market** 916 W Fulton St. Housed in a 50,000 square foot warehouse, this foodie hub hosts 24 of the city's best bars and restaurants, a demo kitchen, live music, a rooftop terrace and an outdoor patio. $$-$$$

SOUTH LOOP

Il Culaccino 2134 S Indiana Ave, ⓦ ilculaccino.com. Upscale Italian restaurant with fresh seafood and pasta, a full wine bar, and a shaded patio for a midscale price. An opportunity to try authentic Italian classics, as well as uniquely Chicago Italian-American standards. $$$

★ **Manny's Coffee Shop & Deli** 1141 S Jefferson St, ⓦ mannysdeli.com. Oldest and best Jewish deli/diner in the city, with strong coffee, traditional corned beef and pastrami sandwiches and matzo ball soup. $$

RIVER NORTH

Beatrix 519 N Clark St (located in Aloft Chicago Downtown River North), ⓦ beatrixrestaurants.com/ beatrix/river-north. Equal parts 1960s modish airline terminal and contemporary casual. Stand-outs include freshly squeezed juices, a warm pot roast sandwich, and the chili and chocolate-glazed salmon.

★ **Billy Goat Tavern** 430 N Michigan Ave, at Hubbard St, ⓦ billygoattavern.com. This legendary journalists' haunt serves the "cheezborgers" made famous by John Belushi's *SNL* comedy skit (Bill Murray was also a regular). Founder Billy Sianis was famed for bringing his goat to Cubs games (his ban in 1945 is said to be the reason they didn't win the World Series until 2016). Founded in 1934, the tavern moved to this underground spot in 1964 (it's below Michigan Ave). $\overline{\underline{555}}$

★ **Doughnut Vault** 401 N Franklin St, ⓦ doughnutvault.com. Tiny hole in the wall, with some outdoor seating, selling wildly popular old-fashioned buttermilk doughnuts, a crumbly delight, plus huge glazed doughnuts, in flavours such as chestnut. $\overline{\underline{5}}$

Frontera Grill & Topolobampo 445 N Clark St, at Illinois, ⓦ rickbayless.com. Wildly imaginative Mexican food from celebrity chef Rick Bayless: *Frontera Grill* is crowded and boisterous; *Topolobampo* is more refined and pricier (dinner set menus only). The front door and bar are shared between the two and going here for margaritas is a great way to start or finish the evening. $\overline{\underline{55}}$

Gene & Georgetti 500 N Franklin St, ⓦ geneandgeorgetti.com. Old school Italian steakhouse originally opened in 1941, this River North staple is the go-to lunch spot for countless characters throughout Chicago's history. $\overline{\underline{5555}}$

★ **Labriola Chicago** 535 N Michigan Ave, Floor 1, ⓦ labriolacafe.com. Lively Italian restaurant located on the River Walk, offering artisan, thin crust and deep-dish pizza (made with their signature caramelized crust). Great weekend deals and happy hour specials as well. $\overline{\underline{555}}$

Lou Malnati's 439 N Wells St, ⓦ loumalnatis.com. The most well-known and easily accessible place to try deep-dish pizza; pies topped with a fresh, sweet tomato sauce, a crispy crust and fresh mozzarella cheese; they also have killer desserts. $\overline{\underline{555}}$

Pizzeria Uno 29 E Ohio St, at Wabash Ave, ⓦ pizzeriaunodue.com. The original outlet of the chain that put Chicago deep-dish pizza on the map , set in an old nineteenth-century mansion. $\overline{\underline{555}}$

★ **Portillo's Hotdogs** 100 W Ontario St, ⓦ portillos. com. One-stop shop for all the Chicago classics, like Italian beef and hotdogs, with locations all over the city and suburbs. $\overline{\underline{55}}$

HYDE PARK

Medici on 57th 1327 E 57th St, ⓦ medici57.com. Hyde Park institution close to the University of Chicago, serving up a mix of salads, pizza and quality hamburgers. Next door is its in-house bakery, which is a solid choice for pain au chocolat and the like. $\overline{\underline{55}}$

★ **Valois Cafeteria** 1518 E 53rd St, ⓦ valoisrestaurant. com. In the "downtown" area of Hyde Park, the Obamas' local favourite is a fabulous deal, with huge breakfast plates and hot sandwiches (think slabs of beef on bread, slathered in gravy and mash). Line up with a tray and choose your food before you sit down. Cash only. $\overline{\underline{5}}$

OAK PARK

Hemmingway's Bistro 211 N Oak Park Ave, ⓦ hemmingwaysbistro.com. Best French restaurant in Chicago's suburbs, conveniently close to Oak Park museums, serving all the classics (coq au vin, bouillabaisse and duck à l'orange). $\overline{\underline{555}}$

DRINKING

SEE MAP PAGE 52

Chicago is a consummate boozer's town, but as with restaurants, the most popular bars are spread all across the neighbourhoods of Chicago, such as Wicker Park and Bucktown, just a few miles from the Loop (Chicago's craft-brew scene is also thriving beyond the centre, see ⓦ illinoisbeer.com) – Halsted Street between Belmont and Addison (5 miles north of the Loop) is known as Boystown for its LGBTQ bars and clubs. The following listings focus mainly on the downtown neighbourhoods, as well as Old Town, just southwest of Lincoln Park.

THE LOOP

The Gage 24 S Michigan Ave, ⓦ thegagechicago.com. Posh restaurant and popular after-work bar with outdoor street seating, a wide selection of cocktails, wines by the glass and bar snacks (think Scotch eggs and fried pickles). $\overline{\underline{555}}$

★ **Milk Room** 12 S Michigan Ave (Chicago Athletic Association Hotel), ⓦ lsdatcaa.com/milk-room. Helmed by one of the city's best-loved mixologists (Paul McGee), this is currently Chicago's trend-setting cocktail bar. The catch? You have to pay in advance to reserve one of the eight stools for a 2hr seating. If you manage it (and can afford the extortionate tab), expect to sample some of the best concoctions of your life. $\overline{\underline{5555}}$

Miller's Pub 134 S Wabash Ave, ⓦ millerspub.com. Downtown institution since 1935, offering craft brews and decent food at the long wooden counter or in cosy booths. $\overline{\underline{55}}$

RIVER NORTH

Berkshire Room 15 E Ohio St, ⓦ theberkshireroom. com. Sleek lounge in the trendy *ACME Hotel*, serving craft cocktails including "I'm the Money" (gin, vermouth, grapefruit and ginger) and "barrel-finished" bourbon specials such as the Double Barrel Manhattan (most cocktails). $\overline{\underline{555}}$

★ **Green Door Tavern** 678 N Orleans St, ⓦ greendoorchicago.com. In an unlikely spot near the galleries of River North, this historic joint (open since 1921; the wood-frame building dates from 1872) is chock-full of Chicago memorabilia: some pure kitsch, others genuine

1

antiques. Drink at the long bar or settle into a cosy back room to sample home-style cooking. $\overline{$$}$

Rossi's 412 N State St, ☎312 644 5775. Amid the sleek modern new buildings of River North, *Rossi's* is a low-down liquor store with a dive bar, great jukebox and lots of local colour. Grab a beer from the fridge and enjoy. $\overline{$}$

★**The Signature Lounge at the John Hancock Center** 875 N Michigan Ave, ⓦsignatureroom.com. Sensational views await on the 96th floor of the John Hancock Center, where this cocktail bar also offers an extensive wine list, beers and snack menu from oysters to duck nachos. $\overline{$$$$}$

Three Dots and a Dash 435 N Clark St, ⓦthreedotschicago.com. The worst kept secret in River North, this tiki bar has quality craft cocktails and a crash course in rum available in the Bamboo Room. Enter through the alley East on Clark St between Hubbard and Illinois. $\overline{$$$}$

OLD TOWN

★**Old Town Ale House** 219 W North Ave,

ⓦtheoldtownalehouse.com. An eclectic crowd of scruffy regulars and yuppies mingle in this convivial 1950s dive bar, complete with a pinball machine and a library of paperbacks. Cash only. $\overline{$$}$

Twin Anchors 1655 N Sedgwick St, at North Ave, ⓦtwinanchorsribs.com. You'll wait for a seat in this neighbourhood spot, famed for its BBQ ribs (and for being a favourite of Frank Sinatra), but the interesting clientele and 1950s-style bar make it worthwhile. $\overline{$$}$

HYDE PARK

Cove Lounge 1750 E 55th St, ☎773 684 1013. Classic Hyde Park dive bar (Kurt Vonnegut once supped here), with legendary jukebox, Obama mural, drink specials every night and bottles of Karlovačko beer all the way from Croatia. $\overline{$}$

★**Woodlawn Tap** 1172 E 55th St, at Woodlawn Ave, ☎773 643 5516. Near UChicago in Hyde Park, this place features cheap cold beer and conversation that alternates between Chicago politics and Plato. Jazz on Sunday evenings. Cash only. $\overline{$}$

NIGHTLIFE SEE MAP PAGE 52

For entertainment listings, pick up free weeklies including the excellent *Chicago Reader* (available Wed & Thurs afternoons plus online at ⓦchicagoreader.com), the *New City* (ⓦnewcity.com) or the LGBTQ *Windy City Times* (ⓦwindycitymediagroup.com). *Time Out Chicago* (online

only; ⓦtimeout.com/chicago) has good arts, music, theatre and movie listings.

CLUBS

Debonair Social Club 1575 N Milwaukee Ave, Wicker

SWEET HOME CHICAGO

Chicago has nurtured many of America's musical legends. The unofficial city anthem, *Sweet Home Chicago* is a blues classic first recorded by Robert Johnson in 1936 but popularized by the **Blues Brothers** (aka Dan Aykroyd and John Belushi), whose movie in 1980 was filmed in Chicago (see page 65). The city is celebrated as the birthplace of **Muddy Waters'** urban **blues** and where numerous blues artists made their mark; Howlin' Wolf, Willie Dixon, Magic Slim, Buddy Guy, Bo Diddley and Corky Siegel among them. The South Side is the adopted home of the blues and of **Chess Records**, the Chicago label that signed Muddy Waters, Chuck Berry and many other early R&B and jazz pioneers. Founded by Leonard and Phil Chess in 1950, the label famously hosted the Rolling Stones for sessions in the 1960s, before closing in 1972.

The city remains proud of its blues traditions (the **Chicago Blues Festival**, held every June in Millennium Park, is the largest free blues festival in the world), but has a history of innovation in many other genres. **Jazz** arrived here in the 1920s via New Orleans' musicians King Oliver, Jelly Roll Morton and Louis Armstrong. A distinctive "Chicago style" of jazz developed, with **Benny Goodman** perhaps the best known of the local stars. The **Chicago Jazz Festival** still takes place every Labor Day weekend (early Sept). In the early 1980s, a local DJ working at The Warehouse dance club named **Frankie Knuckles** pioneered what became known as **house music**, a genre of dance music that still dominates nightclubs worldwide. Keith Farley, Steve "Silk" Hurley, Paul Johnson, Lil' Louis and Joe Smooth were all part of the Chicago scene (the **Chicago House Music Festival** takes place every May).Currently, **Chicago hip-hop** is enjoying a revival with artists such as Chance the Rapper, Chief Keef, Lupe Fiasco, Noname, Smino and Saba leading the local scene (Kanye West and Common also hail from Chicago).Blues fan can check out the former home of Chess Records at 2120 S Michigan Ave, now **Willie Dixon's Blues Heaven** (ⓦbluesheaven.com).

DISCOUNTED THEATRE TICKETS

Hot Tix (⊛ hottix.org) sells half-price tickets to a wide variety of Chicago theatre productions for the current week as well as future performances. Buy them online or at Hot Tix booths across from the Chicago Cultural Center at 72 E Randolph St, and in stores at Block 37 at 108 N State St.

Park, ⊛ debonairsocialclub.com. Café, club and art space that hosts the long-running Neo new wave and 80s nights on Thursdays, as well as a variety of live music, big Saturday club nights and masquerade and cabaret parties.

Reggie's 2015 S State St, South Loop ⊛ reggieslive. com. Bar and grill, live rock and indie venue plus record store under one roof.

Sound Bar 226 W Ontario St, River North, ⊛ sound-bar. com. Cavernous River North nightclub featuring nine bars, minimalist decor and floor to ceiling video projection. Hosts all the major touring DJs.

BLUES

★ **Buddy Guy's Legends** 700 S Wabash Ave, ⊛ buddyguy.com. South Loop club owned by veteran bluesman Buddy Guy, with great acoustics, atmosphere and the very best local and national acts.

Kingston Mines 2548 N Halsted St (Lincoln Park), ⊛ kingstonmines.com. Top-notch local and national acts on two stages play to an up-for-it, partying crowd.

★ **Rosa's Lounge** 3420 W Armitage Ave (Logan Square), ⊛ rosaslounge.com. Run by Mama Rosa and her son Tony Mangiullo since 1984, this West Side club is undoubtedly the friendliest blues joint around. For real aficionados.

JAZZ

Andy's 11 E Hubbard St, ⊛ andysjazzclub.com. Very popular with the after-work crowd; informal with moderate prices. Cover $10–15.

★ **The Green Mill** 4802 N Broadway (Uptown), ⊛ greenmilljazz.com. One of the best – and most beautiful – rooms for local and national talent, including the fabulous pianist Patricia Barber and slam poetry innovator Marc Smith. Located six miles north of the Loop.

Jazz Showcase 806 S Plymouth Court, ⊛ jazzshowcase. com. A classy, dressed-up room that hosts premier jazz by top names. Cover $20–25.

ROCK

★ **Empty Bottle** 1035 N Western Ave (West Town), ⊛ emptybottle.com. Loud hole-in-the-wall club where you might hear just about anything: experimental jazz, alternative rock, hip-hop, house, dub and progressive country. Its block parties are the stuff of legend.

Metro 3730 N Clark St (Lake View), ⊛ metrochicago. com. Arguably the top venue in the city, this club, in an old cinema building, regularly hosts young British bands trying to break the States, plus DJ nights.

★ **Thalia Hall** 1807 S Allport St (Pilsen), ⊛ thaliahallchicago.com. Just three miles from the Loop, this historic venue was originally designed as an opera house in 1892. With adjacent bars and restaurants, come for dinner and a show played by a variety of rock, indie and pop music acts.

ENTERTAINMENT

Court Theatre 5535 S Ellis St (Hyde Park), ⊛ courttheatre. org. Based on the campus of the University of Chicago, the Court Theatre takes on a little bit of everything from Greek tragedies and Shakespeare to modern American plays.

Goodman Theatre 170 N Dearborn St, ⊛ goodmantheatre.org. Right in the Loop, the Goodman has been Chicago's traditional big-production house since 1925 and yearly staples include *A Christmas Carol* and a musical or two.

Second City 1616 N Wells St (Old Town), ⊛ secondcity. com. This band of comedic improvisers spreads its activities across three separate auditoriums. Greats including Stephen Colbert, John Belushi and Chris Farley have made merry here over the past fifty years.

Steppenwolf Theatre 1650 N Halsted St (Old Town), ⊛ steppenwolf.org. This prestigious ensemble, with alumni including John Malkovich and Gary Sinise, got its start in a church basement in 1974 and it continues to draw rave reviews. As part of an expanded campus, a new in-the-round theatre should be open next door in 2021.

The rest of Illinois

There is plenty more to **ILLINOIS** than the Windy City, though it's true that much of the cultural and social identity of this state revolves around Chicago. Primarily flat farmland that rolls into the Mississippi River and Great Plains beyond, the state

1

claims two giants of American history: **Abraham Lincoln**, who practised law from 1837 onward in **Springfield**, now the state capital and home to a wide range of Lincolniana; and **Ulysses S Grant**, whose home in **Galena** is a more modest tribute to the Civil War hero and eighteenth US president.

Springfield

Two hundred miles south of Chicago, the Illinois state capital of **SPRINGFIELD** spreads out from a neat, downtown grid. There is one primary reason people make a pilgrimage to this small, otherwise sleepy city: **Abraham Lincoln**. The sixteenth president of the United States honed his legal and political skills here, and his old homes, haunts and final resting place illuminate the life of one of America's greatest leaders.

Lincoln Home National Historic Site

426 S 7th St • Daily 9am–5pm (last tour 4.30pm) • Free, pay to park • ⓦ nps.gov/liho

The number-one Lincoln attraction is the only house he ever owned, and which he shared with his wife, Mary Todd, from 1844 to 1861, now preserved as the **Lincoln Home National Historic Site**. For a free narrated tour, pick up tickets at the on-site visitor centre. The excellent display "What a Pleasant Home Abe Lincoln Has" offers perspective on the neighbourhood as Lincoln knew it and films are shown regularly through the day – Abraham Lincoln: A Journey to Greatness (27min) and *At Home with Mr. Lincoln* and *Homage to Lincoln* (both 10min) – will help pass the time while you wait for the next available tour. The restored neighbourhood around the home contains twelve historic structures dating back to Lincoln's time. The **Dean House** (1850s) and **Arnold House** (1839) are open to the public (free, same hours), with more Lincoln and Springfield-related exhibits.

Abraham Lincoln Presidential Library and Museum

212 N 6th St • Daily 9am–5pm • Library free; museum charge • ⓦ alplm.org

Four blocks north of the Lincoln Home, the **Abraham Lincoln Presidential Library and Museum** is a state-of-the-art facility that charts Lincoln's career in exhaustive detail, with fascinating original documents and interactive displays. The core of the museum contains the Treasures Gallery, which holds dozens of original Lincoln family items.

Old State Capitol

1 Old State Capitol Plaza (Sixth and Adams sts) • Daily 9am–5pm • Free • ⓦ illinois.gov/dnrhistoric/Experience/sites/central/pages/old-capitol.aspx

In the reconstructed Greek Revival **Old State Capitol** (originally completed in 1840), Lincoln attended at least 240 Supreme Court hearings and proclaimed in 1858, "A house divided against itself cannot stand. I believe this government cannot endure permanently, half slave and half free". Objects, busts and papers relating to Lincoln and the Democrat Stephen A. Douglas, whom he debated (and subsequently lost to) in Illinois' 1858 US Senate election, and whom he defeated in the 1860 presidential race, can be found throughout the building. It's also where Barack Obama kicked off his presidential campaign in 2007.

Illinois State Capitol

401 S 2nd St • Mon–Fri 8am–4.30pm, Sat & Sun 9am–3.30pm • Free • ⓦ ilstatehouse.com

Built over a 20-year period in an elegant Renaissance Revival style, the current **Illinois State Capitol** held its first legislative session in 1877. Today, it still houses the offices of the Governor and the state's legislative branch. Visitors can take a self-guided tour to view the spectacular stained-glass dome interior and grand historical murals.

1

Lincoln Tomb State Historic Site

1500 Monument Ave (Oak Ridge Cemetery) • Daily 9am–5pm • Free • ⓦ lincolntomb.org

Marked by a 117ft-tall obelisk dedicated in 1874, the **Lincoln Tomb State Historic Site** lies in beautiful Oak Ridge Cemetery on the north side of town. Inside the vault are inscribed Edwin Stanton's oft-quoted words, "Now he belongs to the ages". Crypts in the burial chamber's south wall hold the remains of Lincoln's wife Mary (who died in 1882) and three of their sons.

ARRIVAL AND INFORMATION   SPRINGFIELD

By bus Greyhound buses drop off 5 miles northeast of downtown at Shaner's Towing (2815 N Dirksen Pkwy). Destinations Chicago (1 daily; 5hr 10min).
By train Amtrak trains roll in at 100 N 3rd St, downtown. Destinations Chicago (6 daily; 3hr 30min–4hr).

Visitor centre 1 S Old State Capitol Plaza, on the first floor of the old Lincoln-Herndon Law Office across from the Old State Capitol (Mon–Fri 9am–4:30pm; ☏ 217 789 2360, ⓦ visitspringfieldillinois.com).

ACCOMMODATION AND EATING

Cozy Dog Drive-In 2935 S 6th St, ⓦ cozydogdrivein.com. Route 66 diner that claims to be the birthplace of the Cozy Dog (aka the corn dog) in 1946, a deep-fried, batter-drenched hot dog on a stick, but also serves classic breakfast plates and cheap burgers. $̄

D'Arcy's Pint 661 W Stanford Ave, ⓦ darcyspintonline.com. This Irish-themed tavern serves up the ultimate

Horseshoe sandwich, a regional specialty comprised of thick-sliced bread topped with a choice of meats along with French fries and a "secret" cheese sauce. $̄$̄

The Inn at 835 835 S 2nd St, ⓦ connshg.com/inn-at-835. A charming ten-room B&B converted from a 1909 downtown apartment block. $̄$̄

Galena

The historic town of **GALENA**, in the far northwest corner of Illinois, has changed little since its nineteenth-century heyday when, thanks to its sheltered location just a few miles up the Galena River, it was a major port of call for Mississippi River steamboats. These days, the main foot traffic comes from weekend travellers who step back in time strolling along the gentle crescent of **Main Street**. Galena's most celebrated resident was **Ulysses S. Grant**, who moved to the town in 1860, working with his brothers as a clerk in a leather store owned by his father. When he returned after the Civil War in August 1865, it was as commander of the victorious Union army.

Grant Home State Historic Site

500 Bouthillier St • Wed–Sun 9am–4.45pm (Nov–Feb closes at 4pm) • Suggested donation • ⓦ granthome.com

The grateful citizens of Galena presented Ulysses S. Grant and his wife Julia with a house in 1865, known today as the **Grant Home State Historic Site**, a couple of blocks up Bouthillier Street on the far side of the Galena River. It was here, in the drawing room, that he received the news of his election as eighteenth US president in 1868. The family continued to own the house after Grant's death in 1885, and donated it to the city in 1904. Enthusiastic guides will give you a tour (continually throughout the day; 25–30min) of this handsome 1860 Italianate home, which has retained ninety percent of its original furnishings.

INFORMATION   GALENA

Galena Country Visitor Center 101 Bouthillier St (daily   9am–5pm; ☏ 877 464 2536, ⓦ visitgalena.org).

ACCOMMODATION AND EATING

DeSoto House Hotel 230 S Main St, ⓦ desotohouse.com. This 1855 landmark served as Grant's presidential campaign headquarters (rooms 209 and 211), and today sports beautifully renovated, Victorian-style rooms. $̄$̄$̄

Farmers' Guest House 334 Spring, ⓦ galenabedandbreakfast.com. A 5min walk from downtown, this B&B boasts top-notch full breakfasts and warm hospitality provided by owner Susan Steffan. The complimentary wine hour begins at 5pm, a good way to start the evening. $$$$

Fritz and Frites Bistro 317 Main St, ⓦfritzandfrites. com. A German and French bistro mash-up that serves schnitzel, steak frites and garlic-roasted chicken, plus a wild game sausage board. $$$

Log Cabin Steakhouse 201 N Main St, ⓦlogcabingalena. com. Classic supper club since 1937, serving expertly aged Allen Brothers' steaks, though the Greek owners ensure lots of Greek dishes also grace the menu. $$$

Indiana

Best known for college **sports** (especially the Fighting Irish of South Bend's University of Notre Dame) and the legendary **Indy 500** motor race, **INDIANA** nevertheless holds a few surprises. Since its foundation in 1816, the **Hoosier State** has nurtured plenty of non-sporty celebrities, from Michael Jackson to James Dean, Cole Porter, Steve McQueen and David Letterman, while the flourishing capital, **Indianapolis**, is a rich cultural hub. Fun **Bloomington** is the home of Indiana University (and its perennial standout college basketball team), and a smattering of historic sites in the rolling hills of the south includes the intriguing historic settlement of **Vincennes**, **New Harmony** and **Lincoln's Boyhood Home**.

Indiana Dunes National Park

1215 N State Rd 49, Porter, IN · Open daily 9am–4pm · charge · ⓦnps.gov/indu

Forty minutes east of Chicago along Lake Michigan's shore, past the steel town of Gary and the international Port of Indiana lies the Indiana Dunes. These 15 miles of secluded beaches on Lake Michigan's southern coast are the state's most visited destination year after year, offering unique wildlife not seen for miles around. The area is split into the national park and state park, each of which charge their own entry fees. But both share a visitor's centre in Porter that offers guided tours and a full itinerary of activities year-round, from swimming and kayaking to bird watching and snowshoeing.

Indianapolis

Founded on the White River in 1821 as the state capital, **INDIANAPOLIS** is best known for the **Indianapolis 500** each May, when half of America seems to focus

---

THE INDY 500

Seven miles northwest of downtown, the **Indianapolis Motor Speedway** stages two major events each year; the legendary **Indianapolis 500**, held on the last Sunday in May; and July's prestigious NASCAR Brickyard 400. The Indy 500 is preceded by two weeks of qualification runs that whittle the hopeful entrants down to a final field of 33 drivers, one of whom will scoop the $2.5 million first prize. The two-and-a-half-mile circuit was built as a test track for the city's motor manufacturers. The first five-hundred-mile race – held in 1911 and won in a time of 6hr 42min, at an average speed of 74.6mph – was a huge success, vindicating the organizers' belief that the distance was the optimum length for spectators' enjoyment. Cars now hit 235mph, though the official times of the winners are reduced by delays caused by accidents. The big race crowns one of the nation's largest festivals, attended by almost half a million spectators. Seats for the race usually sell out well in advance (ⓦindianapolismotorspeedway.com), but you may gain admittance to the infield, for a tailgate-style, rowdy atmosphere and limited viewing. Other times of year, visit the **Indianapolis Motor Speedway Museum** (daily: March–Oct 9am–5pm, Nov–Feb 10am–4pm; charge; ⓦindyracingmuseum.org) at the Speedway (4790 W 16th St), where you can also take track laps by bus or take a VIP tour of the grounds.

1

on the 24-hour car race. Indeed, sports tourism dominates here, with the Lucas Oil Stadium, home to the NFL's **Indianapolis Colts**, the latest in a bevy of major sports facilities downtown, and as home to the powerful **National Collegiate Athletic Association** (NCAA), the city frequently hosts major college basketball tournaments. Yet it's not all sports. The city is a vast suburban sprawl of almost two million, but its pristine, modern **downtown** harbours a handful of intriguing museums and monuments – **Indianapolis Museum of Art** is one of the region's best – a landscaped canal, a library dedicated to local son Kurt Vonnegut and the house of 23rd US president, Benjamin Harrison.

Downtown Indianapolis

The core of Indianapolis's spacious, relaxed **downtown** is the reasonably tasteful **Circle Centre** shopping and entertainment complex. One block north, streets radiate from **Monument Circle**, dominated by the 284ft **Soldiers and Sailors Monument** (temporarily closed), dedicated in 1902 and the closest the city has to a symbol. A few blocks north, overlooking University Park at 55 E Michigan St, the monumental **Indiana World War Memorial & Museum** (Wed–Sun 9am–5pm; free) was modelled after the Mausoleum of Halicarnassus and completed in 1924.

Indiana State House

200 W Washington St • Mon–Fri 8am–5pm, Sat 10am–2pm • Tours Mon–Fri 9am–3pm, on-demand; Sat 10.15am, 11am, noon & 1pm • Free • ⓦ in.gov/idoa

Completed in 1888, the **Indiana State House** is a grand Renaissance Revival edifice with an elegant, immaculately preserved interior of marble columns, giant staircases and a gorgeous stained-glass Rotunda – for the best view go up to the fourth floor. To enter the Senate and House of Representatives chambers you must take a tour.

Indiana State Museum

650 W Washington St • Wed–Mon 10am–5pm • charge • ⓦ indianamuseum.org

The Canal and White River State Park district, just west of downtown, is anchored by the illuminating **Indiana State Museum**, housed in a stylish contemporary building set on Central Canal itself. The lower level charts the development of Indiana through prehistory, with multimedia exhibits on everything from geology and an array of fossils to woolly mammoth skeletons and Native American culture in the state. Don't miss the Legacy Theater galleries on this floor, dedicated to African American history. Level 2 covers Indiana history from the era of Lincoln – his signed wooden mallet of 1829 is proudly displayed – to the modern day, with a room on Hoosier celebrities (the Jacksons, Axl Rose and James Dean among them). An artistic highlight is the soaring *Indiana Obelisk* in the centre of the museum, designed by famed Pop artist and local boy **Robert Indiana** (born Robert Clark).

Eiteljorg Museum of American Indians and Western Art

500 W Washington St • Mon–Sat 10am–5pm, Sun noon–5pm; tours at 1pm • charge • ⓦ eiteljorg.org

On display in the strikingly designed **Eiteljorg Museum of American Indians and Western Art** are works by Frederic Remington and Charles M. Russell, plus Georgia O'Keeffe's *Taos Pueblo*, but the real highlights are the Native American displays upstairs – the section on Indiana's Miami, Delaware and Potawatomi cultures is especially good. Harrison Eiteljorg was an Indianapolis industrialist who went West in the 1940s to speculate in minerals and fell so deeply in love with the art of the region that he brought tons of it back with him, especially from Taos, New Mexico, whose artists are well represented.

Kurt Vonnegut Museum and Library

543 Indiana Ave, at West St • Mon, Fri, & Sat 10am–7pm, Sun 10am–5pm • Charge, discount for ages 5-17 • ⓦ vonnegutlibrary.org

The **Kurt Vonnegut Museum and Library** reopened in 2019 and is dedicated to the writer, who was born in Indianapolis in 1922 – his great grandfather emigrated from Germany in 1851, becoming a successful local businessman. Kurt spent most of his later career in New York, where he died in 2007. At the Museum, you can sit at the same model typewriter Kurt would have used, view personal artefacts and memorabilia such as drawings, doodles and his typewriter and take in numerous ongoing exhibitions, too.

1

Eugene and Marilyn Glick Indiana History Center
450 W Ohio St • Tues–Sat 10am–5pm • charge • ⓦ indianahistory.org

State history is brought to life at the slick **Indiana History Center**, with video screens allowing access to information on every county, a special room dedicated to **Cole Porter** (with real live singer) and costumed actors role-playing scenes from key events.

Benjamin Harrison Presidential Site
1230 N Delaware St • Mon–Sat 10am–3.30pm, Sun noon–3.30pm • Tours (1hr 15min) on the hour and half-hour • charge • ⓦ bhpsite.org

Home to Indiana's only US president, the **Benjamin Harrison Presidential Site** north of downtown is an immaculately preserved Italianate mansion built in the 1870s, with all the rooms ornately furnished with period pieces and portraits, many of them family originals. Exhibits on the top floor and in the small Welcome Center add context to the 23rd president, who is largely forgotten today. **Benjamin Harrison** (1833–1901) was elected in 1888 as the Republican candidate, serving just one term – his chief achievements were the creation of the US National Forests and strengthening the US Navy.

Indianapolis Museum of Art at Newfields
4000 N Michigan Rd • Tues–Sun 11am–4pm • charge • ⓦ discovernewfields.org • Bus #34

Some five miles north of downtown, the lavish **Indianapolis Museum of Art** offers a beautifully presented (and easily digested) tour through world art history, with everything from medieval Spanish murals to Asian porcelain and African carvings on display. Highlights include the largest collection of **Turner paintings** outside Britain (galleries C301–303), the *Angel of the Resurrection*, a beautiful stained-glass window from the studio of Louis Comfort Tiffany (K207), paintings by Rembrandt, Rubens, El Greco and Caravaggio, and a small collection of Impressionist works by Monet, Renoir and Cézanne. Look out also for a special installation on Giovanni Bellini (C204) and the **Pont-Aven School** paintings (H208), with several from **Gauguin** – in a major art coup, the museum acquired a cache of seventeen of these paintings in 1998 for around $30 million.

The museum is set within a series of landscaped gardens adorned with massive sculptures and installations, dubbed **Newfields**, which includes the 100-acre **Virginia B. Fairbanks Art & Nature Park**. Your ticket also includes entry to **Oldfields** (aka **Lilly House**), a mansion on the grounds built in 1910s and purchased by pharmaceutical tycoon J.K. Lilly in 1932. The main floor has been refurnished in 1930s style, while upstairs hosts temporary exhibits.

ARRIVAL AND INFORMATION
INDIANAPOLIS

By plane Indianapolis International Airport (ⓦ indianapolisairport.com) is 10 miles southwest of downtown, on the #8 IndyGo bus route (45min; ⓦ indygo. net). The Go Green Shuttle (ⓦ goexpresstravel.com) provides shuttle bus rides to downtown (Lucas Oil Stadium, Convention Center and Marriott hotel) every 30min (daily 5am–11pm; 20–30min). Try Yellow Cabs for a ride into the city centre (☏ 317 487 7777).

By bus or train Both Greyhound buses and Amtrak trains (Chicago 3 days weekly; 5hr; Cincinnati 3 days weekly; 3hr 20min) arrive at 350 S Illinois St (☏ 317 267 3071), part of the fairly central Union Station complex. Megabus (Chicago, Cincinnati) drops off/picks up at N Delaware St between E Market St and E Wabash St.

Destinations (bus) Chicago (9 daily; 3hr 15min–4hr 10min); Cincinnati (2 daily; 2hr–3hr 5min); Columbus, OH (5 daily 3hr–3hr 50min).

Downtown Indy Visitor Center 111 Monument Cir #250; (8.30am-5pm Mon-Fri ⓦ downtownindy.org)

1

ACCOMMODATION AND EATING

Indianapolis has plenty of quality places to stay, with a cluster of budget options about five miles from downtown along the orbital I-495. Prices can double during the race months of May, August and September. The swish Circle Centre mall houses dozens of places to eat, but most are chains. You'd do better to stick to the more established restaurants downtown or head up to Broad Ripple Village (bus #17) at College Ave and 62nd St, which is packed with bars and cafés (along with galleries and shops).

★ **The Alexander** 333 S Delaware St, ⓦ thealexander. com. Every room in this hotel contains recently commissioned works of art, along with a mid-twentieth-century styling that's more SoCal than central Indiana. ⑤⑤⑤⑤
Crowne Plaza Indianapolis-Dwtn-Union Stn 123 W Louisiana St, ⓦ ihg.com. Stay in refurbished Pullman train cars, reborn as spacious, fully equipped hotel rooms (decorated after famous people such as Chaplin, Churchill and Cole Porter) in the old 1888 Union Station. ⑤⑤⑤
Bru Burger Bar 410 Massachusetts Ave, ⓦ bruburgerbar.com. Gourmet burger specialist with offerings such as the bourbon burger (peppercorn-bourbon glaze with horseradish cheese), and the 'melt your face' burger (with Habanero hot sauce and jalapeños). ⑤⑤
Indianapolis City Market 222 E Market St, ⓦ indycm. com. Opened in 1886, this landmark still offers snacks and craft beers at stalls such as Tomlinson Tap Room, Pat's Philly Pretzels and Gomez BBQ. ⑤

Indy Hostel 4903 Winthrop Ave, ⓦ indyhostel. us. Appealing small-scale hostel in a former family home, located in a friendly neighbourhood 6 miles from downtown. Female-only and mixed dorms, plus various private rooms. ⑤
Old Northside Bed and Breakfast 1340 N Alabama St, ⓦ oldnorthsideinn.com. Luxury B&B in an 1885 building, 1.5 miles north of downtown, with themed rooms, such as "Hollywood"; the Bridal Room has a huge canopy bed. ⑤⑤
Café Patachou on the Park 225 W Washington St, ☎ 317 632 0765, ⓦ cafepatachou.com. The most central branch of this "student union for adults" mini chain, with a focus on farm-to-table cuisine such as fluffy omelettes, tasty chicken salads, a special vegan Cuban breakfast, amazing stuffed cinnamon French toast and the signature turkey chili. ⑤⑤
★ **Shapiro's** 808 S Meridian St, ⓦ shapiros.com. Lauded deli since 1905, just a few blocks south of downtown, where you can fill up on lox, pastrami and other specialities in an old-style cafeteria atmosphere0. Leave room for the huge desserts. ⑤
St Elmo Steak House 127 S Illinois St, ⓦ stelmos.com. Venerable steakhouse opened in 1902, where all meals start with navy bean soup or Indiana brand Red Gold tomato juice, followed by juicy steaks or pork chops, with sides ordered à la carte. ⑤⑤⑤⑤

DRINKING AND NIGHTLIFE

The **nightlife** area in downtown is Massachusetts Avenue, where good bars and restaurants are easy to come by. Further afield is the chic Broad Ripple Village. Check the free weekly *NUVO* (ⓦ nuvo.net) "Indy's alternative voice", for full details of gigs and events.

★ **Chatterbox Jazz Club** 435 Massachusetts Ave, ⓦ chatterboxjazz.com. Ever-busy local bar, hosting live jazz nightly since the early 1980s (the bar's been here since 1896). ⑤
★ **The Rathskeller** 401 E Michigan St, ⓦ rathskeller.

com. German beer hall in the basement of the historic Athenaeum building (designed by Kurt Vonnegut's architect grandfather), offering food, live music and a *biergarten*. ⑤⑤
Slippery Noodle Inn 372 S Meridian St, ⓦ slipperynoodle. com. Indiana's oldest bar, established in 1850 next to Union Station, with cheap beer and live blues nightly. ⑤⑤
The Vogue Theater 6259 N College Ave, ⓦ thevogue. com. Popular Broad Ripple rock and indie venue in a former cinema, also featuring retro club nights. ⑤⑤

Bloomington

College town **BLOOMINGTON**, just 45 miles southwest of Indianapolis on Hwy-37, is by far the liveliest small city in Indiana and owes its vibrancy to the expansive, leafy campus of **Indiana University** (IU). The I.M. Pei-designed **Eskenazi Museum of Art** on campus at 1133 E 7th St (Mon–Fri 10am–5pm, Sat 10am–7pm, Sun noon–5pm; free) holds a small but carefully curated collection of painting and sculpture from medieval Italian pieces to Jackson Pollock's explosive drip painting, *No.11*. Other highlights include Picasso's enigmatic *The Studio* and several rare prints by Braque, Degas and Rembrandt, in addition to a vast collection of Mesoamerican, African, Asian and ancient Roman treasures. Don't miss the **Lilly Library** (Mon–Sat 9:30am–6pm free; ⓦ libraries.indiana.edu/lilly-library) nearby, a trove of rare books and manuscripts, from an original 1450s Gutenberg Bible, a 1480s *Canterbury Tales* and a giant original of Audubon's *Birds of America* (1840s), to Orson Welles' notes from *Citizen*

Kane. Downtown itself centres on **Courthouse Square** anchored by the stately 1907 Monroe County Courthouse, with restaurants and bars lining **Kirkwood Avenue** to the university's Sample Gates entrance.

ARRIVAL AND INFORMATION BLOOMINGTON

By bus Bloomington Shuttle (☎812 332 6004, ⓦgoexpresstravel.com) runs between here and Indianapolis airport (9 daily; 1hr 20min).

Visitor centre 2855 N Walnut St (Mon–Fri 8.30am–5pm, Sat 10am–3pm; ☎812 334 8900, ⓦvisitbloomington. com) and only useful if you have a car; there's a smaller

office downtown at 114 E Kirkwood Ave, inside the Buskirk-Chumley Theater (Tues Sun noon–5pm; ☎812 323 3020). You can also try the Indiana University Visitor Center, located more centrally at 900 E 7th St (Mon–Fri 9:30am-5:30pm, Sat 10am-2pm, Sun 12-3pm; ☎812 856 4648, ⓦvisitorcenter. indiana.edu)

ACCOMMODATION

Graduate Bloomington 210 E Kirkwood Ave, ⓦgraduatehotels.com/bloomington. **This** upscale chain of hotels designed specifically for university towns is located 1.4 miles from the university's campus, offers a modern feel and convenient location. $$$

Grant Street Inn 310 N Grant St, ⓦgrantstinn.com. This pleasant B&B, inside the 1883 Ziegler House, offers fine rooms decorated in a variety of styles from Victorian to upscale modern. $$

EATING AND DRINKING

Anyetsang's Little Tibet 415 E 4th St, ⓦanyetsangs. com. Take a trip to Lhasa at this cosy restaurant, with authentic Tibetan dumplings and dishes such as *kham amdo thugba* (stew) and lots for vegetarians. There are actually two Tibetan monasteries just outside town, founded by the Dalai Lama's brother (the Tibetan leader has also been here several times). $$

The Bluebird 216 N Walnut St, ⓦthebluebird.ws. Long-established nightclub and live music venue with a variety of acts from rock to folk. $$

B'Town Diner 211 N Walnut St, ⓦbtowndiner.com. Classic American breakfasts served all day, plus decent burgers and mac and cheese. $

★ **FARMbloomington** 108 E Kirkwood Ave, ⓦfarm-bloomington.com. Real food right from the farm, such as bone-in pork chops and *puttanesca* with locally grown

vegetables. $$

Lennie's Brewpub 514 E Kirkwood Ave, ⓦlenniesbloomington.com. The liveliest drinking spot around with different cream ales and IPA on tap – *Lennie's* (the restaurant section) is known for its pizza. $$

★ **Nick's English Hut** 423 E Kirkwood Ave, ⓦnicksenglishhut.com. IU institution since 1927, often full of celebrating students, serving pizzas and burgers with a range of draught beers. $$

Uptown Café 102 E Kirkwood Ave, ⓦthe-uptown.com. Go-to place for a more upscale brunch, with a full drink menu and a Creole take on American classics. $$$

★ The Village Deli 409 E Kirkwood Ave, ⓦvillagedeli. biz. Lively downtown diner offering a wide array of hearty American breakfast and lunch items. $

Vincennes

Founded as a fur trading post by French-Canadian adventurer François-Marie Bissot in 1732, **VINCENNES** thrived throughout the eighteenth century, and served as capital of Indiana Territory from 1800 to 1813. A sleepy place today on the banks of the Wabash River, just across from Illinois, the town's illustrious past is commemorated at the **Vincennes State Historic Sites** (1 W Harrison St; Wed-Mon 10am–5pm; charge; ⓦindianamuseum.org/historic-sites/vincennes). Enthusiastic guided tours take in the original Indiana Territory Capitol, a humble red-painted clapboard house, plus replicas of the territory's first school and print shop. Nearby is **Grouseland** (3 W Scott St; March–Dec Mon–Sat 9am–4pm, Sun 11am–4pm; Jan & Feb Tues–Sat 12am–3pm; charge; ⓦgrouselandfoundation.org), the stately 1804 mansion of first governor William Henry Harrison (later the ninth US president). Near Main Street is the much remodelled Old Cathedral and the **George Rogers Clark National Historical Park** (401 S 2nd St; daily 9am–5pm; free; ⓦnps.gov/gero), featuring a huge granite rotunda, its interior adorned with giant murals and a bronze statue of the US Independence hero. Learn about Clark's dramatic victory over the British at Fort Sackville (1779) at the visitor centre.

By car Vincennes is 75 miles southwest from Bloomington, but thanks to the new I-69 it's an easy day-trip; it's 120 miles from Indianapolis. You'll need a car to make the most of the area. Free parking is available all over the centre.

Visitor centre 702 Main St (Mon–Fri 8am–4pm; ☎ 812 886 0400, ⓦ visitvincennes.org).

New Harmony

The enchanting, perfectly preserved village of **NEW HARMONY**, 65 miles south of Vincennes, blends historic log cabins, clapboard and brick homes with contemporary monuments and a creative community specializing in arts, crafts and spiritual retreats. Founded in 1814 by the **Harmony Society**, a German Christian sect, the settlement was purchased by British social reformer **Robert Owen** in 1825 who briefly attempted to fashion his own utopian community here, albeit one based on science and reason instead of religion. Some sites such as Philip Johnson's thought-provoking **Roofless Church** at 420 North St are always open and free, but many of the older properties are part of the **Historic New Harmony** programme and can only be visited on a tour.

Visitor centre The Atheneum, 401 N Arthur St (temporarily closed), designed in 1979 by Richard Meier, of Getty Center fame. Tours of the older buildings start here (mid-March to Dec daily 1pm; charge), and they show a short movie and exhibits about New Harmony (charge).

ACCOMMODATION AND EATING

Ludwig Epple Guest House 520 Granary St, ⓦ newharmonyguesthouse.com. This circa 1820 clapboard home has been converted into a three-room guesthouse, with simple but comfortable furnishings. $\overline{\$\$}$

Red Geranium Restaurant 520 North St, ⓦ newharmonyinn.com/dining. Charming restaurant in the heart of the village, serving seasonal American and Midwestern cuisine such as crab dip, braised lamb and lemon pie. $\overline{\$\$\$}$

Lincoln Boyhood National Memorial

3027 E South St, Lincoln City (off Hwy-162) • Wed–Sun April–Nov 8am–5pm; Dec–March Wed–Sun 8am–3pm • Free • ⓦ nps.gov/libo

Tucked away within the rolling hills of southern Indiana, ninety miles south of Bloomington, the **Lincoln Boyhood National Memorial** commemorates the early life of America's favourite president. Lincoln's father moved the family here from Kentucky in 1816, when Abraham was seven, and he spent the next fourteen formative years in Little Pigeon Creek before moving to Illinois. The visitor centre contains a museum and videos, while the leafy grounds that Abraham once roamed contain his mother's grave, the site of the Lincoln log cabin and a Living Historical Farm with costumed role players.

Ohio

OHIO, the easternmost of the Great Lakes states, lies to the south of shallow Lake Erie. This is one of the nation's most industrialized regions, but the industry is largely concentrated in the east, near the Ohio River. To the south the landscape becomes less populated and more forested.

Enigmatic traces of Ohio's earliest inhabitants exist at the **Great Serpent Mound**, a grassy state park sixty miles east of Cincinnati, where a cleared hilltop high above a river was reshaped to look like a giant snake swallowing an egg, possibly by the Adena Indians around 800 BC. When the French claimed the area in 1699, it was inhabited by the **Iroquois**, in whose language Ohio means "something great". In the eighteenth century, the territory's prime position between Lake Erie and the Ohio River made it the subject of fierce contention between the French and British. Once the British acquired control of most land east of the Mississippi, settlers from New England began to establish communities along both the Ohio River and the Iroquois War Trail paths on the shores of the lake.

During the Civil War, Ohio was at the forefront of the struggle, producing two great Union generals, **Ulysses Grant** and **William Tecumseh Sherman**, and sending more than twice its quota of volunteers to fight for the North. Its progress thereafter has followed the classic "Rust Belt" pattern: rapid industrialization, aided by its natural resources and crucial location, followed by 1970s post-industrial gloom and a period of steady revitalization in the 21st century.

Although the state is dominated by its triumvirate of "C" towns (**Cleveland**, **Columbus** and **Cincinnati**), the **Lake Erie Islands** are its most visited holiday destination, attracting thousands of partying mainlanders. Cincinnati and Cleveland have both undergone major face-lifts and are surprisingly attractive, as is the comparatively unassuming state capital of Columbus.

Cleveland

It's a long time since the great industrial port of **CLEVELAND** – for decades the butt of jokes after the heavily polluted Cuyahoga River caught fire in 1969 – has been considered the "Mistake on the Lake". Although parts of the city are still recovering from the last recession, the most revitalized areas remain hubs of energy. Cleveland boasts a sensitive restoration of the Lake Erie and Cuyahoga River waterfront, a superb constellation of museums, a growing culinary scene and modern downtown super-stadiums. What with the now well-established **Rock & Roll Hall of Fame**, there's an unmistakable buzz about the place and in 2016 the Rock Box project saw clusters of speakers permanently installed in strategic downtown locations. There are regular live music events here and changing exhibitions featuring music's some of the world's greatest artists.

Founded in 1796, thirty years later Cleveland profited greatly from the opening of the **Ohio Canal** between the Ohio River and Lake Erie. During the city's heyday, which began with the Civil War and lasted until the 1920s, its vast iron and coal supplies made it one of the most important **steel** and **shipbuilding centres** in the world. **John D. Rockefeller** made his billions here, as did the many others whose restored old mansions like "Millionaires' Row".

Outside of the lively **downtown**, trendy **Ohio City**, just to the southwest, and the cultural institutions of **University Circle**, some distance east of the river, are the most rewarding areas to explore.

Downtown and around

Downtown Cleveland is a bustling place and its redevelopment has seen the emergence of several distinct subsections. Its main streets congregate on the stately nineteenth-century Beaux Arts **Public Square**, the subject of a $50 million investment/overhaul/face-lift in 2016. **Ontario Street**, which runs north–south through the Square, divides the city into east and west. Its dominant landmark is **Terminal Tower**, in the southwestern corner. Also on the square, the **Arcade** is a skylit shopping hall built in 1890, but the nearby **5th Street Arcades** contains an even more impressive selection of independent shops.

The Gateway District

At the southern end of downtown is the **Gateway District**, where new restaurants and bars surround **Progressive Field** stadium, home of the Indians baseball team (Ⓦindians. com), and the equally modern, multipurpose **Quicken Loans Arena** (Ⓦthearena.

1

com), aka "The Q", which hosts the Cavaliers basketball team, along with other major sporting and entertainment events.

The riverfront

West of The Q, at the **riverfront**, one of the nation's busiest waterways shares space with excellent bars, clubs and restaurants, all strung out along a boardwalk. At the lake end of the Cuyahoga River lies the **Flats**, where nineteenth century Irish immigrants settled, but today it is known for its nightlife, fourteen bridges and an atmospheric industrial setting.

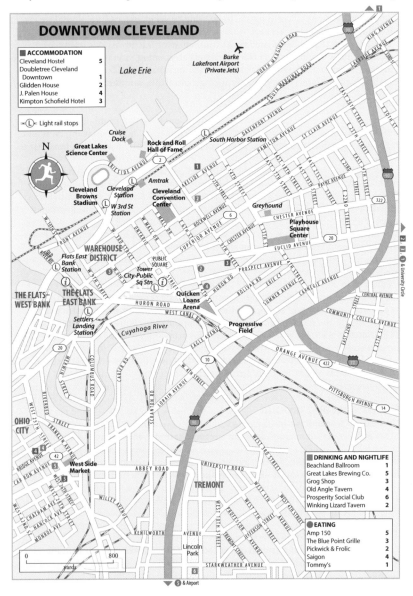

DOWNTOWN CLEVELAND

■ ACCOMMODATION

Cleveland Hostel	5
Doubletree Cleveland Downtown	1
Glidden House	2
J. Palen House	4
Kimpton Schofield Hotel	3

⊸Ⓛ⊸ Light rail stops

■ DRINKING AND NIGHTLIFE

Beachland Ballroom	1
Great Lakes Brewing Co.	5
Grog Shop	3
Old Angle Tavern	4
Prosperity Social Club	6
Winking Lizard Tavern	2

● EATING

Amp 150	5
The Blue Point Grille	3
Pickwick & Frolic	2
Saigon	4
Tommy's	1

The Warehouse District

A short but steady climb east from the river leads to the historic **Warehouse District**, a pleasant stretch of nineteenth-century commercial buildings between West Third and West Ninth streets, given over to shops, galleries, cafés and trendy restaurants.

North Coast Harbor

North of the busy Cleveland Memorial Shoreway (Hwy-2), the waters of Lake Erie lap gently into **North Coast Harbor**, a showpiece of Midwest regeneration, whose centrepiece is the iconic **Rock and Roll Hall of Fame**. Next door to the Rock Hall – as Clevelanders refer to it – is the giant **Great Lakes Science Center** 601 Erieside Ave (Wed–Sat 10am–5pm, Sun noon–5pm; charge, plus extra for OMNIMAX combo-ticket; ⓦgreatscience.com), one of America's largest interactive science museums, which cleverly outlines the interdependency of science, technology and the environment, with emphasis on the Lakes region. Across the road, the futuristic, 72,000-seat **Cleveland Browns Stadium** is the home of the Browns pro football team (ⓦclevelandbrowns.com).

Ohio City

To the west of the river, **Ohio City** is one of Cleveland's hipper neighbourhoods, with junk stores, exotic restaurants, Victorian clapboard houses and the bustling **West Side Market**, at Lorain Ave and W 25th St ⓦwestsidemarket.org), which sells all manner of

---

THE ROCK AND ROLL HALL OF FAME

Cleveland convincingly won a hotly contested bid to host the **Rock and Roll Hall of Fame** largely because **Alan Freed**, a local disc jockey, popularized the phrase "rock and roll" here back in 1951.

The museum's octogenarian architect – **I.M. Pei** – wanted the building "to echo the energy of rock and roll". A trademark Pei tinted-glass pyramid (he also designed the larger Louvre one), this white structure of concrete, steel and glass strikes a bold pose at North Coast Harbor on the shore of Lake Erie, especially when illuminated at night. The base of the pyramid extends into an impressive entrance plaza shaped like a turntable, complete with a stylus arm attachment.

The museum is much more than an array of **mementoes** and artefacts. Right from the start, the emphasis is on the contextualization of rock. The exhibits chart the art form's evolution and progress, acknowledging influences ranging from the blues singers of the Delta to the hillbilly wailers of the Appalachians. Elsewhere in the subterranean main exhibition hall, there's an in-depth look at seven crucial **rock genres** through the cities that spawned them: rockabilly (Memphis), R&B (New Orleans), Motown (Detroit), psychedelia (San Francisco), punk (London and New York), hip-hop (New York) and grunge (Seattle). Much space is taken up by exhibits on what the museum sees as the key rock artists of all time, including Elvis Presley, the Beatles, Jimi Hendrix, the Rolling Stones and U2. All inductees to the hall are selected annually by an international panel of rock "experts", but only performers who have released a record 25 years prior to their nomination are eligible.

Escalators lead to a level devoted to Freed, **studio techniques** and a great **archive** of rare live recordings, which you can listen to on headphones. The third floor houses the **Hall of Fame** itself, where an hourly video presentation of all inductees unfolds on three vast screens; the upper storeys contain the museum's **temporary exhibitions**. You can also cast your own vote for the upcoming year's inductees.

The best way to round off your visit is on Level 2, at **The Garage** – visitors can choose from guitars, bass guitars, keyboards and drumkits and either follow an on-screen tutorial, go solo or jam with other visitors (all levels welcome). Even if you don't want to take part, when others come together to jam, it's a great sight – and audio delight – to behold.

The museum is at 1100 E 9th St (daily 10am–5pm, charge, must make reservations in advance, ⓦrockhall.com). Weekends get very crowded and are best avoided.

1

ethnic foods – think Irish soda bread, German bratwurst and Russian delicacies. It's easily spotted by its red-brick clock tower. To the east, **Tremont** perfects small-town charm with hipster cafés and a pleasant park.

University Circle and around

Four miles east of downtown, **University Circle** is a cluster of more than seventy cultural and medical institutions and is also home to several major performing arts companies, as well as Frank Gehry's twisted-steel Weatherhead School of Management building at Case Western University. Adjacent to University Circle, **Murray Hill** is Cleveland's Little Italy; beyond this attractive area of brick streets, small delis and galleries is the trendy neighbourhood of **Coventry Village**.

University Circle museums and galleries

The eclectic Cleveland **Museum of Art**, fronted by a lagoon at 11150 East Blvd (Tues–Sun 10am–5pm; free; ⑩clevelandart.org), has a collection that ranges from Renaissance armour to African art, with a canteen-style café and snazzy restaurant on site. One of the area's newer attractions is **MOCA**, 11400 Euclid Ave (Thurs–Sun 11am–5pm, ⑩mocacleveland.org), an interactive modern art museum, featuring revolving exhibitions and housed in a stunning glass-and-steel polygonal structure. Also notable is the **Museum of Natural History**, 1 Wade Oval Dr (Tues–Sun 10am–5pm; charge, plus extra for planetarium; ⑩cmnh.org), with exhibits on dinosaurs and Native American culture.

University Circle gardens

The **Cleveland Botanical Garden**, 11030 East Blvd (Tues-Sat 10am–5pm, Sun noon–5pm; charge; ⑩cbgarden.org), has a glasshouse that features a cloudforest, a desert ecosystem, free-roaming chameleons and butterflies, a waterfall and a treetop walkway. Meanwhile, dotted along East and Martin Luther King Jr. boulevards in Rockefeller Park, 24 small landscaped cultural **gardens** are dedicated to and tended by Cleveland's diverse ethnic groups, including Croatians, Estonians and Finns.

Cleveland Metroparks Zoo

3900 Wildlife Way • Daily 10am–4pm • charge • ⑩ clemetzoo.com • By car, exit at W 25th or Fulton Rd; during summer, RTA runs special buses from downtown to the zoo

Five miles southwest of downtown via I-71, the **Cleveland Metroparks Zoo** features a "Wolf Wilderness", while the spectacular 164-acre **RainForest** building is populated by some seven thousand plants and 118 species of animals, including orangutans, American crocodiles and Madagascan hissing cockroaches.

Cuyahoga Valley National Park

Boston Mill Visitor Centre 6947 Riverview Road, Peninsula, OH • Open daily, some areas close at dusk • charge • ⑩ nps.gov/cuva

Less than 20 miles from downtown via I-77 S, Cuyahoga Valley National Park is not your average national park. Even more significant than its natural beauty and diversity in wildlife, this park is a testament to twentieth century conservation efforts. Back when nearby cities Akron and Cleveland where bustling industrial hubs, the Cuyahoga River was better known for catching on fire due to high levels of oil runoff. Coinciding with the creation of the Environmental Protection Agency, the area underwent intensive wetland cleanups and dam removal projects. These efforts have led to a resurgence of local wildlife such as beavers and bald eagles, and the fish in the river have recently been considered safe to eat for the first time in centuries, unsettling as this may sound, it is testament in itself to the epic conservation efforts that have taken place.

The park is made up of a patchwork of land parcels that include working farms, nature preserves, and private residences. It's proximity to the city ensures smooth cellular service, and the trails are some of the most accessible in the country, with bathrooms at every trailhead, wheelchair-friendly trails, and exhibits offered in Braille.

1

In the summer, be sure to visit the Countryside Farmer's Markets, which offer produce from the Cuyahoga Valley. The most well-known trail is the Brandywine Gorge Loop, which takes hikers around the 60-foot Brandywine Falls and its eponymous creek.

ARRIVAL AND DEPARTURE CLEVELAND

By plane Cleveland Hopkins International Airport is 10 miles southwest of downtown. The taxi ride takes 20 minutes, but the Regional Transit Authority (RTA; ☏216 621 9500, ⍟riderta.com) train is cheaper and takes just 10min longer.

By bus Greyhound arrives at 1465 Chester Ave, at the back of Playhouse Square.

Destinations Chicago (5 daily; 6hr 10min–10hr 55min); Cincinnati (4 daily; 4hr 40min–5hr 55min); Columbus (5 daily; 2hr 25min–2hr 55min); New York (9 daily; 9hr 10min–13hr 50min); Pittsburgh (6 daily; 2hr 25min–3hr 30min).

By train The Amtrak station is on the lakefront at 200 Cleveland Memorial Shoreway NE.

Destinations Chicago (2 daily; 6hr 46min–7hr); New York (1 daily; 12hr 33min); Pittsburgh (1 daily; 3hr 11min).

GETTING AROUND, INFORMATION AND TOURS

By bus The RTA runs an efficient bus service and a small train line, known locally as "the Rapid", until about 12.30am.

By light rail A light rail system – the Waterfront Line – connects Terminal Tower, the Flats, the Rock and Roll Hall of Fame and other downtown sights (every 15min, 6.15am–midnight).

By trolleybus Four free trolleys cover different parts of downtown (Mon–Fri 7am–7pm).

Visitor centre 334 Euclid Ave (Mon–Sat 9am–6pm; ☏800 321 1001, ⍟thisiscleveland.com); or try the booth on the baggage level of the airport (hours vary).

Tours *Goodtime III* (⍟goodtimeiii.com) runs 2hr boat cruises from the dock at 825 E 9th Street Pier.

ACCOMMODATION SEE MAP PAGE 78

Travellers without cars tend to stay at the downtown hotels, whose room-only prices are not cheap, but many of which offer packages that include admission to the Rock and Roll Hall of Fame or other attractions. B&Bs can be booked through ⍟positivelycleveland.com.

★ **Cleveland Hostel** 2090 W 25th St, ⍟thecleveland hostel.com. Excellent-value and spotless hostel in happening Ohio City, offering excellent shared facilities and well-priced dorm beds, as well as doubles, some with private bathrooms. $

Doubletree Cleveland Downtown 1111 Lakeside Ave, ⍟doubletree3.hilton.com. Good online deals, great lake views from the upper storeys and proximity to the Rock and Roll Hall of Fame make this reliable chain franchise a popular choice. $$$$

Glidden House 1901 Ford Drive, ⍟gliddenhouse.com. Sixty very comfortable and brightly coloured rooms and suites are housed in an imposing Gothic mansion. Large continental breakfast is included. $$$$

★ **J. Palen House** 2708 Bridge Ave, ⍟jpalenhouse. com. Extremely attractive and conveniently located Victorian house with a conical turret, oak beams, lavishly furnished rooms and a gourmet three-course breakfast. $$$$

Kimpton Schofield Hotel 2000 E 9th St, ⍟theschofield hotel.com. Set in an attractive historic landmark dating from 1902, this classily renovated hotel provides all the usual upscale comforts and services, including a free wine hour and light breakfast. $$$$

EATING SEE MAP PAGE 78

The city has a range of culinary delights, many of them ethnic. The excellent West Side Market (see page 79) in Ohio City abounds with cheap, unusual picnic food, while Little Italy and Coventry Village boast authentic Italian food and coffee bars, respectively.

★ **Amp 150** 4277 W 150th St, ⍟amp150.com. The airport Marriott hotel might seem an unlikely location, but it's worth the trip for top chef Dean Max's imaginative creations such as duck confit nuggets and beef delmonico. $$

The Blue Point Grille 700 W St Clair Ave, ⍟bluepointgrille.com. Warehouse District favourite, serving the best seafood in town, with specials such as Nag's Head grouper with lobster mashed potatoes. $$$

Pickwick & Frolic 2035 E 4th St, ⍟pickwickandfrolic. com. Cavernous restaurant with champagne lounge and martini bar. You can enjoy cabaret and stand-up comedy while dining on a range of pizza and starters or serious American meat and seafood dishes. $$

★ **Saigon Restaurant & Bar** 2061 E 4th St, ⍟saigoncleveland.com. Great-value place, with most of the exquisite Vietnamese items such as salt-baked squid and clay-pot catfish. $$

Tommy's 1824 Coventry Rd, ⍟tommyscoventry cleveland.com. Great-value food and much of it vegetarian Middle Eastern, dished up in a trendy, bright setting in lively Coventry Village. Try the famous shakes too. $$

The Warehouse District and East Fourth Street boast the greatest conglomeration of drinking, live music and dancing venues, although those in the know head across the river to more bohemian Ohio City and Tremont. Less than 5 miles east, both University Circle and youthful Coventry Village have good bars. The free weekly, the *Cleveland Scene* (ⓦclevescene.com), has listings of alternative music, cinema and other events.

Beachland Ballroom & Tavern 15711 Waterloo Rd, ⓦbeachlandballroom.com. It's more than 10 miles east of downtown, but this buzzing venue in a former Croatian social club draws great indie and rock bands. 5̄5̄

★ **Great Lakes Brewing Company** 2516 Market Ave, ⓦgreatlakesbrewing.com. At this venerable joint, Cleveland's best brewpub, famous for its IPAs, the huge

mahogany bar still bears the bullet holes made during a 1920s shoot-out involving lawman Elliot Ness. 5̄5̄

Grog Shop 2785 Euclid Heights Blvd, Cleveland Heights, ⓦgrogshop.gs. Near Coventry Village, the *Grog Shop* is a fun, sweaty, collegiate punk and alter-native venue, with bands on every night. 5̄

Old Angle Tavern 1848 W 25th St, ⓦoldangle.com. Friendly Irish pub with multiple screens for international sporting fixtures, decent pub grub, a selection of ales and lively music at night. 5̄5̄

Prosperity Social Club 1109 Starkweather Ave, ⓦprosperitysocialclub.com. Located in a 1938 ballroom in Tremont, this is a hip hangout, with a great jukebox, live music and a huge range of beers. 5̄

ENTERTAINMENT

Playhouse Square 1501 Euclid Ave, ⓦplayhousesquare. org. Within this impressive complex of four renovated old theatres the small Ohio Theater, with its gorgeous starlit-sky lobby ceiling, is home to the Cleveland Opera and Ballet, as well as comedy, musicals, concerts and the Great Lakes Theatre Festival. The Allen Theater is where the prestigious

Cleveland Play House company performs drama.

Severance Hall 11001 Euclid Ave, University Circle, ⓦclevelandorchestra.com. This grand Neoclassical venue is home to the well-respected Cleveland Orchestra, when they are not on tour.

The Lake Erie Islands

The **LAKE ERIE ISLANDS** – **Kelleys Island** and the three **Bass Islands** further north – were early stepping stones for the **Iroquois** on the route to what is now Ontario. French attempts to claim the islands in the 1640s met with considerable hostility, and they were left more or less in peace until 1813, when the Americans established their control over the Great Lakes by destroying the entire English fleet in the **Battle of Lake Erie**. A boom in **wine production** brought the islands prosperity in the 1860s, but last century they were hit successively by Prohibition, the emergence of the California wineries, an increase in motoring vacations and the lake's appalling pollution. Thankfully, the clean-up of recent decades has worked; today the islands are again a popular summer destination, with fishing, swimming and partying as the main attractions. **Sandusky** and nearby **Port Clinton** act as the main jump-off points to the islands.

The mainland

The large coal-shipping port of **SANDUSKY**, fifty miles west of Cleveland on US-2, is probably the most visited of the lakeshore towns, thanks to **Cedar Point Amusement Park**, five miles southeast of town (early May to Aug daily, hours vary; Sept & Oct weekends only; ⓦcedarpoint.com). The largest ride park in the nation – and considered by many to be the best in the world – Cedar Point boasts no fewer than seventeen roller coasters. The neighbouring **Soak City** water park (summer Mon–Thurs & Sun 10am–10pm, Fri–Sat 10am–midnight; ⓦsoakcitycp.com) is owned by Cedar Point and provides a good way to cool off, with eighteen acres of water slides and a wave pool. Aquatic fun continues through the winter a few miles further southeast at **Kalahari Waterpark** 7000 Kalahari Dr, Sandusky (daily 10am, closing times vary; ⓦkalahariresorts.com), America's largest indoor water park. The smaller resort town of **PORT CLINTON**, twelve miles west across the Sandusky Bay Bridge, is another departure point for the islands. Its pleasant lakefront is dotted with decent cafés and jet-ski rental outlets.

ARRIVAL AND INFORMATION

THE MAINLAND

By bus Greyhound buses stop way out at 6513 Milan Rd (US-250), Sandusky.

By train Amtrak trains pass through Sandusky once daily en route between Chicago and the East Coast. The unstaffed station at North Depot and Hayes A is in a dodgy area.

Visitor centre 125 E Water St, Sandusky (open daily 8:30am–4:30pm; ☎419 625 2984, ⒲shoresandislands. com).

ACCOMMODATION AND EATING

Kalahari 7000 Kalahari Drive, Sandusky, ⒲kalahariresorts. com. The luxury resort that includes the water park has huge rooms with jacuzzis and all mod cons, as well as a top tropical restaurant and a host of other facilities. $$$$

KOA East Shoreway Drive KOA, Sandusky, ⒲koa.com. Upscale campground with superb facilities such as a huge store, heated swimming pool and sports grounds. Cabins available as well as plenty of tent and RV spaces. $

★ **The Original Margaritaville** 212 Fremont Ave, Sandusky, ⒲themargaritavilleonline.com. Ribs and steaks supplement the wide Mexican menu in this fun spot with an on-site waterfall and live music at weekends. $$

Sunnyside Tower 3612 NW Catawba Rd, Port Clinton, ⒲sunnysidetower.com. Set on two lush acres, this Victorian-style B&B offers beautifully designed rooms and suites, plus a spacious lounge for socializing. $$$

Kelleys Island

About nine miles north of Sandusky, **KELLEYS ISLAND** lies in the western basin of Lake Erie. Seven miles across at its widest, it's the largest American island on the lake, but it's also one of the most peaceful and picturesque, home to fewer than two hundred permanent residents. With few buildings less than a century old, the whole island is a National Historic District. Its seventy-plus archeological sites include **Inscription Rock**, a limestone slab carved with 400-year-old pictographs; you can find it east of the dock on the southern shore. The **Glacial Grooves State Memorial**, on the west shore, is a 400ft trough of solid limestone, scoured with deep ridges by the glacier that carved out the Great Lakes.

Settled in the 1830s, Kelleys was initially a working island, its economy based on lumber, then wine, and later limestone quarrying. All but the last have collapsed, though a steady **tourist industry** has developed.

ARRIVAL AND INFORMATION

KELLEYS ISLAND

By plane Daily flights with Griffing Flying Service (3244 E State Rd, Port Clinton; ☎419 734 5400, ⒲flyinggriffing. com) leave daily from Sandusky and Port Clinton.

By ferry Kelleys Island Ferry Boat Line (⒲kelleysislandferry. com) operate from 510 W Main St in Lakeside Marblehead year-round, when weather permits, as frequently as every 30min at peak times.

By catamaran Jet Express (☎800 245 1538, ⒲jet-express.com) runs summer services from its docks at 101 W Shoreland Drive, Sandusky and 3 Monroe St, Port Clinton.

Chamber of Commerce 117 Addison Rd (daily 10am–3pm; ☎419 746 2360, ⒲kelleysislandchamber.com).

Website There is plenty of info at ⒲kelleysisland.com.

GETTING AROUND

By bike or golf cart Getting around the island is easy; cars are heavily discouraged and most people, when not strolling, use bikes or golf carts, available from Caddy Shack Square (⒲caddyshacksquare.com).

ACCOMMODATION AND EATING

Peeper's 109 W Lakeshore Drive, ⒲peepersbar.com. Locally owned bbq joint known for creative cocktails and shots, burnt ends, and hearty breakfast menu. $$

State Park Campground 920 Division St, ⒲kelleysislandchamber.com. The first-come, first-served state park on the north bay near the beach has more than 100 sites. Fairly basic but a lovely location. $

Sun And Surf 204 McGettigan Rd, ⒲stayonki.com. Modern, brightly decorated rooms, most with jacuzzis, are available in this attractive house with a lawn and jetty right onto the lake. $$$$

Village Pump 103 W Lakeshore Drive, ⒲villagepumpkioh. com. Lively place that serves good home-style food and drink; try its signature brandy Alexander. $$

South Bass Island

SOUTH BASS ISLAND is the largest and southernmost of the Bass Island chain, three miles from the mainland and northwest of Kelleys Island; the island's name derives

1

from the excellent bass fishing in the surrounding waters. Also referred to as **Put-in-Bay** after its one and only village, this is the most visited of the American Lake Erie Islands, its permanent population of 450 growing tenfold in the summer.

Just a year after its first white settlers arrived, British troops invaded the island during the War of 1812. The Battle of Lake Erie, which took place off the island's southeastern edge, is commemorated by **Perry's Victory and International Peace Memorial**, set in a 25-acre park. You can see the distant battle site from an observation deck near the top of the 352ft stone column (open seasonally). All this history is well documented at the **Lake Erie Islands Historical Museum**, 411 Catawba Ave (daily 11am–5pm; charge; ⓦleihs.org), which features dozens of model ships, memorabilia and exhibits on the shipping and fishing industries.

ARRIVAL AND INFORMATION

SOUTH BASS ISLAND

By plane Daily flights with Griffing Flying Service (see Kelleys Island) leave from Sandusky and Port Clinton.

By catamaran Jet Express (see Kelleys Island) runs summer services to Put-in-Bay from its dock at 101 W Shoreline Drive, Sandusky, and from 5 N Jefferson St, Port Clinton.

By ferry South Bass Island is served by Miller Ferry (5174 Water St, ⓦmillerferry.com) from late March to late Nov.

Visitor centre 440 Loraine Ave #267, Put-in-Bay (8am–8pm daily, ☎419 285 2832, ⓦvisitputinbay.com).

GETTING AROUND

By bike or golf cart You can rent bikes and golf carts from Boathouse Cart and Bike Rental at 216 Hartford Ave, Put-In-Bay (ⓦboathousecartrental.com).

By shuttle bus A service runs between the northern dock and the state park.

ACCOMMODATION

Arbor Inn B&B 511 Trenton Ave, ⓦarborinnpib.com. Set amid woods, this pleasantly chilled B&B has manicured gardens, which you can enjoy from the porch, and very comfortable rooms. $$$
Commodore Resort 272 Delaware Ave, ⓦcommodoreresort.com. With an attractive pool area

and decent bar-grill, this cheerful resort has wildly fluctuating rates for its nicely designed rooms. $$$
Fox's Den Campground 140 Conlan Rd, ⓦputinbay. com. This centrally located and well-equipped private campground is the only alternative to camping in the state park. $

EATING, DRINKING AND NIGHTLIFE

Beer Barrel Saloon 324 Delaware Ave, Put-In-Bay, ⓦbeerbarrelpib.com. Claims to have the longest uninterrupted bar in the world, complete with 160 bar stools, and provides booze, bar food and regular live music to partying holidaymakers. $$
The Boardwalk 341 Bayview Ave, ⓦthe-boardwalk. com. Actually a pair of similar restaurants sharing the

harbour boardwalk: the Main Deck and Upper Deck both do sandwiches, meat and seafood for $$$
Round House 228 Delaware Ave, Put-In-Bay, ⓦtheroundhousebar.com. Named after the rotund shape of its roof, this buzzing bar features daily live bands and DJs, plus a full range of drinks and snacks. $$

Columbus

Officially Ohio's largest city, although Cleveland's metropolitan area is greater, **COLUMBUS** is a likeable place to visit. State capital and home to the massive Ohio State University, the city's position in the rural heart of the state also makes it the only centre of culture for a good two-hour drive in any direction. Ohio became a state in 1803 and legislators designated this former patch of rolling farmland, on the high east bank of the Scioto River, its capital in 1812. The fledgling city was built from scratch, and its considered town planning is evident today in broad thoroughfares and green spaces.

Though Columbus has more people, it always seems to lag behind Cincinnati or Cleveland in terms of public recognition. As such, the place is best enjoyed for what it is – a lively college city with some good **museums**, gorgeous Germanic **architecture** and a particularly vibrant **nightlife**. Surprisingly, it also boasts one of the country's most active **LGBTQ scenes**.

Downtown Columbus

The spacious, orderly and easy-going **downtown** area holds several attractions. In the northwest corner of downtown, the area surrounding the impressive Nationwide Arena, home to NHL's Columbus Blue Jackets (Ⓦ bluejackets.com), dubbed the **Arena District**, has attracted a number of restaurants and nightspots. Just above it, left off High Street, is the restored Victorian warehouse of **North Market** (see page 86), while on the right side the strikingly deconstructivist **Greater Columbus Convention Center** is a massive pile of angled blocks designed by Peter Eisenman and completed in 1993.

Ohio Statehouse

1 Capitol Square • Mon–Fri 8am–5pm, Sat & Sun 11am–5pm • Free • Ⓦ ohiostatehouse.org

The **Ohio Statehouse** is a grand colonnaded edifice, pleasantly set in ten acres of park at the intersection of Broad and High streets, the two main downtown arteries. The highlights of this 1839 Greek Revival structure – one of the very few state capitols without a dome – are the ornate Senate and House chambers. A statue of Ohio native President William McKinley proudly stands outside the main entrance.

COSI

333 W Broad St • Wed–Sun 10am–5pm • charge, discount for kids • Ⓦ cosi.org

Housed in a streamlined structure across the river from the capitol, **COSI** (Center of Science and Industry) boasts more than 300,000 square feet of exhibit space. Most of it is geared toward familiarizing children with science, covering broad topics such as life, progress, space, the ocean and gadgets. It shows related movies (additional charge), as well as putting on live shows (prices vary).

Columbus Museum of Art

480 E Broad St • Tues–Sun 10am–5pm • charge, free Sun • Ⓦ columbusmuseum.org

About a mile east of High Street (US-23), a giant Henry Moore sculpture stands at the entrance to the inviting **Columbus Museum of Art**. Indoors, this airy space holds particularly good collections of Western and modernist art. There is also an admirable interactive element, allowing visitors to display their own creativity. The excellent new Margaret M. Walter wing opened in 2016, allowing the museum to display a much larger proportion of its collection.

The German Village

Just six blocks south of the Statehouse, I-70 separates downtown from the delightful **German Village** neighbourhood. During the mid-nineteenth century, thousands of German immigrants settled in this part of Columbus, building neat red-brick homes, the most lavish of which surround the 23-acre **Schiller Park**. Their descendants gradually dwindled in numbers by the 1950s and the area became increasingly run-down until it won a place on the National Register of Historic Places. The best way to explore its brick-paved streets, corner bars, old-style restaurants, Catholic churches and grand homes is to stop in at the **German Village Society Meeting Haus**, 588 S 3rd St (Mon–Fri 9am–4pm, Sat 10am–2pm, Sun 12-3pm April–Nov only; ☎614 221 8888, Ⓦ germanvillage.com), where popular walking tours run by the German Village Society start with a twelve-minute video presentation. The Society also oversees the immensely popular Haus und Garten Tour on the last Sunday in June and the Oktoberfest celebrations in late September. Book-lovers will adore the **Book Loft**, 631 S 3rd St (daily 10am–11pm; Ⓦ bookloft.com), whose books, many of them discounted, are crammed into 32 rooms of one grand building.

1

The Brewery District

Just west of High Street (US-23) are the warehouses of the **Brewery District**, where, until Prohibition, the German immigrants brewed beer by traditional methods. Many of the original buildings still stand, and in recent years the number of independent **microbreweries** has once again increased.

Short North Arts District

Across Nationwide Boulevard at the top end of downtown is the **Short North Arts District** (ⓦshortnorth.org), a former red-light district that's now Columbus's most vibrant enclave. Standing on either side of High Street – the main north–south thoroughfare – its entrance is marked by the iron gateways of the Cap at Union Station. Thereafter starts the trail of galleries, bars and restaurants that makes the area so popular with locals; it is also the heart of the gay community. The first Saturday of each month sees the **Gallery Hop**, when local art-dealers throw open their doors – complementing the artworks with wine, snacks and occasional performance pieces – and the socializing goes on well into the evening.

The university campus

Businesses beyond the Short North Arts District become a little more low-rent for a mile before High Street cuts through the **university campus** and suddenly sprouts cheap eating places and hip shopping. For bargain vinyl, head to Used Kids Records, 2500 Summit St (ⓦusedkidsrecords.com). The **Wexner Center for the Arts**, 1871 N High St (Tues–Thurs 9am–5pm, Sat 11am–7pm, Sun 11am–5pm; charge; ⓦwexarts.org), is another Eisenman construction, even more extreme than the Convention Center.

ARRIVAL, GETTING AROUND AND INFORMATION COLUMBUS

By plane Port Columbus International Airport is 7 miles northeast of downtown. Central Ohio Transit Authority's (COTA; ☏614 228 1776, ⓦcota.com) express route bus #52 runs from here through downtown, and taxis are also available.

By bus Greyhound stops at 111 E Town St.

Destinations Cincinnati (6 daily; 1hr 55min–2hr 55min); Cleveland (6 daily; 2hr 25min–2hr 50min).

Visitor centre 277 W Nationwide Blvd #125 (Thurs & Fri 10am-3pm, Sat 11am–3pm; ☏614 221 6623) and 188 Easton Town Center (Tues-Sun noon-6pm, ☏866 397 2657). Visit ⓦexperiencecolumbus.com.

ACCOMMODATION

Compared with other cities in the region, Columbus offers a good choice of convenient mid-range places to stay. Downtown rates are good, while even more savings can be had by staying in the German Village area.

50 Lincoln-Short North Bed & Breakfast 50 E Lincoln St, ⓦcolumbus-bed-breakfast.com. Enjoy a warm welcome and lavish furnishing in one of the seven rooms of this grand Short North house, now a delightful B&B. $$$

German Village Inn 920 S High St, ⓦgermanvillageinn. net. This family-run motel, on the south edge of the German Village/Brewery District, has simple but smart

rooms and is one of the best deals going. $$

Hilton Columbus Downtown 401 N High St, ⓦhilton. com. Luxurious new hotel between downtown and Short North, with gloriously appointed rooms featuring original artwork and a highly rated restaurant. Great online prepaid deals. $$$$

The Westin Great Southern 310 S High St, ⓦwestincolumbus.com. Columbus's grand red-brick Victorian hotel, with surprisingly moderate rates for some rooms, all of which are of high quality. $$$

EATING

The Short North and German Village neighbourhoods are crammed with places to eat, be they bottom-dollar snack bars or stylish and adventurous bistros. For a wide range of ethnic and organic snacks during the day, try the North Market, downtown at 59 Spruce St (Sun 10am–5pm, Tues–Sat 9am–7pm; ⓦnorthmarket.com), which also sells fresh produce.

Akai Hana 1173 Old Henderson Rd, ⓦakaihanaohio. com. Outstanding Japanese restaurant with a large selection of sushi, noodle and rice dishes. $$

Katzinger's Delicatessen 475 S 3rd St, German Village, ⓦkatzingers.com. A mesmerizing range of gut-busting sandwiches, plus Jewish delicacies and cheesecakes, are available at this slightly upmarket deli. $$

Marcella's 615 N High St, ⓦmarcellasrestaurant.com. Buzzing Italian restaurant with a lively bar. The food is a range of moderately upmarket pizzas, pasta, salads and main dishes such as veal saltimbocca. $\overline{\underline{\$\$\$}}$

★ **The Pearl** 641 N High St, ⓦthepearlcolumbus.com. Huge place with wood decor and a real buzz to it, serving nouveau cuisine such as braised short rib with horseradish mash. Oyster bar and lots of other seafood too. $\overline{\underline{\$\$\$}}$

Schmidt's 240 E Kossuth St, German Village, ⓦschmidthaus.com. This Columbus landmark (since 1886) serves a range of sausages, schnitzel and strudel in a former slaughterhouse, served by waitresses in German garb. $\overline{\underline{\$\$}}$

DRINKING AND NIGHTLIFE

This youthful university town is a rich source of local bands, from country revivalists to experimental alternative acts. The main nightlife areas are the bohemian Short North Arts District, also the LGBTQ hub, and the more mainstream Brewery District on the south side of the centre.

Axis Night Club 775 N High St, ⓦaxisonhigh.com. Very popular LGBTQ nightspot that gets steamier as the night wears on, as people gyrate to the latest disco and trance vibes. Cover on club nights varies. $\overline{\underline{\$\$}}$

Basement 391 Neil Ave, ⓦpromowestlive.com. One of the city's hottest music venues, where you are likely to hear up-and-coming bands of different genres. Good sound system. $\overline{\underline{\$\$}}$

Seventh Son Brewing Co. 1101 N 4th St, ⓦseventhsonbrewing.com. One of the best new microbreweries, which offers a panoply of fine brews such as Humulus Nimbus Super Pale Ale and Rookey Porter. There's a revolving food truck outside. $\overline{\underline{\$\$}}$

Short North Tavern 674 N High St, ⓦshortnorth. org. The oldest bar in the neighbourhood, with live bands playing at the weekend dressed in German garb. $\overline{\underline{\$}}$

★ **Skully's Music-Diner** 1151 N High St, ⓦskullys. org. Classic 1950s-style diner whose happy hour is often followed by cool indie-rock shows. $\overline{\underline{\$\$}}$

Village Idiot 1439 N High St ☏614 230 2544. Fun bar towards the university campus with games like darts and pool, plus a patio. Decent range of beers and a very cheap happy hour. $\overline{\underline{\$}}$

Cincinnati

CINCINNATI, just across the Ohio River from Kentucky, is a dynamic commercial metropolis with a definite European flavour and a sense of the South. Its tidy centre, rich in architecture and culture, lies within walking distance of the attractive **riverfront**, the lively **Over-the-Rhine** district to the north and arty **Mount Adams**.

The city was founded in 1788 at the point where a Native American trading route crossed the river. Its name comes from a group of Revolutionary War admirers of the Roman general Cincinnatus, who saved Rome in 458 BC and then returned to his small farm, refusing to accept any reward. Cincinnati quickly became an important supply point for pioneers heading west on flatboats and rafts, and its population skyrocketed with the establishment of a major steamboat **riverport** in 1811. Tens of thousands of **German** immigrants poured in during the 1830s.

Loyalties were split by the **Civil War**. Despite the loss of some important markets, the city decided that its future lay with the Union. In the prosperous postwar decade, Cincinnati acquired Fountain Square and the country's first professional baseball team, the **Reds** (ⓦreds.com); they, along with the **Bengals** football team (ⓦbengals.com), remain a great source of pride.

Downtown Cincinnati

Downtown Cincinnati rolls back from the Ohio River to fill a flat basin area ringed by steep hills. During the city's emergent industrial years, the filth, disease and crime drove the middle classes from downtown en masse. Nowadays, however, attractive stores, street vendors, restaurants, cafés, open spaces and gardens occupy the area. The city's rich blend of architecture is best appreciated **on foot**. Over, among and even right through the hotel plazas, office lobbies and retail areas, the **Skywalk** network of air-conditioned passages spans sixteen city blocks. A mile-long **riverside walk** begins at **Public Landing**, at the bottom of Broadway, and stretches east past painted showboats and the **Bicentennial Commons**, a 200th-birthday present from the city to itself in 1988.

1

Fountain Square

At the geographic centre of downtown, the **Genius of the Waters** in **Fountain Square** sprays a cascade of hundreds of jets, meant to symbolize the city's trading links. Surrounded by a tree-dotted plaza and all but enclosed by soaring facades of glass and steel, it's a popular lunch spot and venue for daytime concerts, as well as the second largest **Oktoberfest** in the world, after Munich's, in late September. Looming above Fifth and Vine streets, the 49 storey Art Deco Carew Tower (441 Vine St) marks the city's business district for miles around.

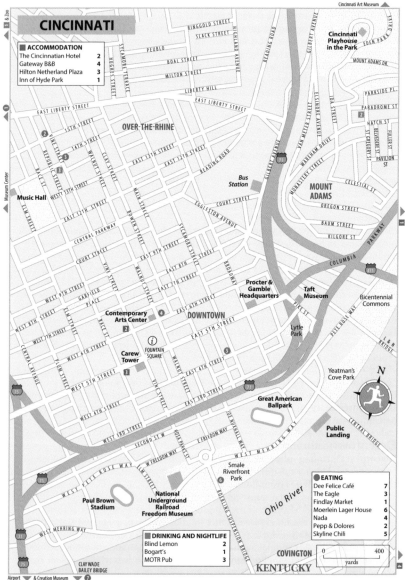

CINCINNATI

ACCOMMODATION
The Cincinnatian Hotel	2
Gateway B&B	4
Hilton Netherland Plaza	3
Inn of Hyde Park	1

EATING
Dee Felice Café	7
The Eagle	3
Findlay Market	1
Moerlein Lager House	6
Nada	4
Pepp & Dolores	2
Skyline Chili	5

DRINKING AND NIGHTLIFE
Blind Lemon	2
Bogart's	1
MOTR Pub	3

Procter & Gamble HQ

A few blocks east of Fountain Square are the Art Deco headquarters of the detergents and hygiene-product giant **Procter & Gamble**. The company was formed in 1837 by candle-maker William Procter and soap-maker James Gamble, to exploit the copious supply of animal fat from the slaughterhouses of "Porkopolis", as Cincinnati was then known. By sponsoring radio's The Puddle Family in 1932, the company created the world's first **soap opera**.

National Underground Railroad Freedom Museum

50 E Freedom Way • Wed–Sun 10am–5pm • charge • Ⓦ freedomcenter.org

South of I-71, Paul Brown Stadium, home of the Bengals, and the Reds' Great American Ballpark, are giant cement additions on the Cincinnati side of the Ohio River. In between the two sporting venues stands the engaging **National Underground Railroad Freedom Museum**, whose light and airy space chronicles the city's role in the emancipation of slaves as well as other worldwide struggles for freedom.

Contemporary Arts Center

44 E 6th St • Sat & Sun 10am–4pm, Wed–Fri 10am–7pm • Free • Ⓦ contemporaryartscenter.org

The left-field, multimedia art exhibitions at the superb **Contemporary Arts Center**, housed in a stunning building designed by the late Iraqi-born British architect Zaha Hadid, often lead to run-ins with the city's more conservative citizens. Exhibits occupy four floors and revolve every few months.

Taft Museum of Art

316 Pike St • Fri 11am–4pm, Sat & Sun 11am–5pm • charge, free on Sun • Ⓦ taftmuseum.org

Housed in an immaculate 1820 Federal-style mansion on the northeast fringe of downtown, the **Taft Museum of Art** contains priceless works by the likes of Rembrandt, Goya, Turner and Gainsborough in its permanent collection. It also hosts temporary exhibitions that change every two or three months.

North of downtown

Just over a mile northeast from downtown, the land rises suddenly and the streets start to conform to the contours of **Mount Adams**. Here, century-old townhouses coexist with avant-garde galleries, stylish boutiques, international restaurants and trendy bars. To explore these and enjoy unparalleled views of the river, take a taxi or the #49 bus from downtown.

Eden Park

Adjacent to the tightly packed streets of Mount Adams are the rolling lawns, verdant copses and scenic overlooks of **Eden Park**, where you will find the delightful **Krohn Conservatory** at 1501 Eden Park Drive (Tues–Sun 10am–8pm; charge; Ⓦ cincinnatiparks.com/krohn-conservatory). A loop road at the western end of the park leads to the **Cincinnati Art Museum**, on 953 Eden Park Drive (Tues–Sun 11am–5pm; charge; Ⓦ cincinnatiartmuseum.org). Its one hundred labyrinthine galleries span five thousand years, taking in an excellent Islamic collection as well as a solid selection of European and American paintings by the likes of Matisse, Monet, Picasso, Edward Hopper and Grant Wood.

Cincinnati Museum Center

1301 Western Ave • Thurs-Mon 10am–5pm • charge for each, discount for combination ticket, plus extra for OMNIMAX, discount with museum entry • Ⓦ cincymuseum.org

Northwest from downtown, Cincinnati's three-in-one **Museum Center** is housed in the magnificent Art Deco **Union Terminal**, approached via a stately driveway off Ezzard Charles Drive. Highlights of the **Museum of Natural History** are dioramas of Ice Age

1

Cincinnati and "the Cavern", which houses a living bat colony. The **Historical Society** holds a succession of well-presented, short-term exhibitions and the **Duke Energy Children's Museum** has a two-storey treehouse and eight other interactive exhibit areas.

Covington

Covington, directly across the Ohio River on the Kentucky side, is regarded as the southern side of Cincinnati. It can be reached from downtown Cincinnati by walking over the bright blue, 1057ft-long **John A. Roebling Suspension Bridge**, at the bottom of Walnut Street, which was built in 1867 and served as a prototype for the Brooklyn Bridge. A ten-minute walk southwest of the bridge brings you to the attractive, narrow, tree-lined streets and nineteenth-century houses of **MainStrasse Village**. It's a Germanic neighbourhood of antique shops, bars and restaurants that plays host to the lively **Maifest** on the third weekend of each May and is the centrepiece of the citywide **Oktoberfest** on the weekend after Labor Day. At Sixth and Philadelphia streets, 21 mechanical figures accompanied by glockenspiel music toll the hour on the German Gothic **Carroll Chimes Bell Tower**.

Creation Museum

2800 Bullitsburg Church Rd, Petersburg, KY • Wed–Sat 9am–6pm • charge, plus extra for Ark • ⓦ creationmuseum.org

South of MainStrasse Village, en route to the airport off I-275, one of the area's newest attractions is the multimillion-dollar **Creation Museum**. A truly "only in America" experience, the state-of-the-art dioramas, video show and planetarium (additional charge) argue an uncompromising creationist case and make Darwin out to be little short of Lucifer himself. There is also a full-scale **replica of the Ark** and a **petting zoo** (with more than two of some species).

Newport

Across the Licking River from Covington, the subdued town of **Newport** has become a lot livelier since the opening of a large shopping complex and the impressive **Newport Aquarium**, 1 Levee Way (Mon-Fri 10am–5pm, Sat & Sun 9am-8pm; charge; ⓦ newportaquarium.com). Clear underwater tunnels and see-through floors allow visitors to be literally surrounded by sharks and snapping gators.

ARRIVAL AND DEPARTURE   CINCINNATI

By plane Cincinnati-Northern Kentucky International Airport is 12 miles south of downtown, in Covington, Kentucky. Taxis to the city centre (☎ 859 586 5236) are also available.

By bus The Greyhound station is on the eastern fringe of the city centre, just off Broadway at 1005 Gilbert Ave. Destinations Cleveland (4 daily; 4hr 40min–5hr 15min); Columbus (5 daily; 1hr 55min–2hr 10min); Indianapolis

(5 daily; 2hr 5min–4hr 15min); Lexington (2 daily; 1hr 25min); Louisville (5 daily; 1hr 45min).

By train Amtrak trains arrive a mile northwest of downtown at the Union Terminal museum complex. Destinations Chicago (1 daily; 9hr 24min); Indianapolis (1 daily; 3hr 34min); New York (3 weekly; 18hr 31min); Washington DC (3 weekly; 14hr 52min).

GETTING AROUND AND INFORMATION

By bus The Metro bus network (☎ 513 621 4455, ⓦ go-metro.com) covers routes within the city and neighbouring Ohio counties. Buses on the Kentucky side are run by TANK (☎ 859 331 8265, ⓦ tankbus.org), including shuttle buses across to Cincinnati.

Visitor centre 5 Fountain Square Plaza (daily 11am–5pm; ☎ 513 534 5877); or contact the Cincinnati USA Regional Tourism Network (50 E Rivercenter Blvd; Mon-Fri 9am-5pm; ☎ 859 581 2260, ⓦ cincinnatiusa.com).

ACCOMMODATION   SEE MAP PAGE 88

Although Cincinnati's quality hotels are reasonable by big-city standards, budget travellers may have problems finding affordable downtown rooms. Uptown motels – over 2 miles north – are much cheaper, but you'll need a car or taxi to get around safely at night.

The Cincinnatian Hotel, Curio Collection by Hilton

601 Vine St, ⓦhilton.com. Exuding pure class with its marble lobby and wood-panelled rooms, this 1882 building houses the city's prime luxury hotel. $$$

Gateway B&B 326 E 6th St, Newport, Kentucky, ⓦgatewaybb.com. Comfortable, affordable Victorian place with cosy rooms decorated in period style, 5min from downtown Cincinnati and Covington, Kentucky. $$$

Hilton Netherland Plaza 35 W 5th St, ⓦhilton.com.

One of the classier *Hilton* franchises, located in a National Historic Landmark building, with a sumptuous Art Deco lobby, gym and well-furnished rooms. $$$-$$$$

Inn of Hyde Park 3539 Shaw Ave, ⓦinnofhydgepark. com. This small, welcoming inn has comfortable rooms and a common lounge. It's five miles east of downtown and is a good option if you have a car. The gourmet breakfast is a winner. $$$

EATING
SEE MAP PAGE 88

Cincinnati boasts excellent homegrown gourmet and continental restaurants. It's also famous for Cincinnati chilli, a combination of spaghetti noodles, meat, cheese, onions and kidney beans, served at chains such as *Skyline Chili* (see opposite).

Dee Felice Cafe 529 Main St, Covington, Kentucky, ⓦdeefelicecafe.com. This small and atmospheric spot specializes in Cajun cuisine with lots of fresh seafood dishes, and doubles as a jazz venue. $$

★The **Eagle** 1342 Vine St, ⓦeaglerestaurant.com. Billed as a food and beer hall featuring fried chicken, this Over-the-Rhine eatery offers southern classics and a blues soundtrack. $$

Findlay Market 1801 Race St, ⓦfindlaymarket.org. Ohio's oldest continuously operated market offers more than 50 full time food and artisan vendors. Open year round, Tuesday-Sunday. Prices vary.

★**Moerlein Lager House** 115 Joe Nuxhall Way, ⓦmoerleinlagerhouse.com. Large airy place with a deck overlooking the river, serving tempting seafood appetizers and main dishes such as hops-smoked pork belly, as well as a fine range of beers brewed on-site. $$

Nada 600 Walnut St, ⓦeatdrinknada.com. Very popular downtown Mexican, serving quite innovative dishes such as Durango BBQ pastor tacos and braised chicken enchiladas. $$

★**Pepp & Dolores** 1501 Vine St, ⓦpeppanddolores. com. A casual Italian restaurant inspired by the Sunday dinner traditions of Italian families. Menu features pasta made in house and a great date-night ambiance. $$$

Skyline Chili 254 E 4th St, ⓦskylinechili.com. The most central of the forty branches of this institution is the place to try Cincinnati chili (see opposite). Burritos also served. $

DRINKING AND NIGHTLIFE
SEE MAP PAGE 88

After dark, the hottest area with the widest appeal is the Over-the-Rhine district, which fans out from Main Street around 12th and 14th streets and buzzes every night. The next liveliest areas are ritzier Mount Adams and more collegiate Corryville, a 5min drive northwest from downtown.

Blind Lemon 936 Hatch St, ⓦtheblindlemon.com. Beyond the intimate, low-ceilinged bar, you'll find a relaxed

patio crowd. Live music (mostly acoustic) nightly. $$

Bogart's 2621 Vine St, ⓦbogarts.com. Established indie acts play this mid-sized venue a couple of miles north of downtown. It also hosts club nights and special events.

★**MOTR Pub** 1345 Main St, ⓦmotrpub.com. One of the hippest joints in this increasingly trendy area, with good food, a well-stocked bar and nightly free live music. $

ENTERTAINMENT

Entertainment listings for the whole city can be found in the free *Cincinnati CityBeat* (ⓦcitybeat.com).

Cincinnati Playhouse in the Park 962 Mt Adams Circle, ⓦcincyplay.com. This established company puts on drama, musicals and comedies, with performances throughout the year.

Cincinnati Music Hall 1241 Elm St, Over-the-Rhine, ⓦcincinnatiarts.org. This 1870s conglomeration of spires, arched windows and cornices is said to have near-perfect acoustics. Joint home to Cincinnati's Opera and Symphony Orchestra.

Michigan

Bill Bryson's verdict, in *The Lost Continent*, that **MICHIGAN** "is shaped like an oven mitt and is often about as exciting" is a little harsh (though it *is* shaped like an oven mitt), and the state that nurtured Michael Moore, Magic Johnson, Madonna and Stevie Wonder offers plenty of amusement. Though it's had its share of urban decay and mismanagement – the 2015 water contamination of **Flint**, and the well-documented,

1

seemingly endless decline of **Detroit** – the state has more in common with outdoorsy Oregon than the rest of the Midwest, with a rugged coastline along its two vividly contrasting peninsulas and untamed interiors of forests and plunging waterfalls. **Grand Rapids** and even Detroit itself are increasingly becoming America's most fascinating cities, but the further north you get, the more rewarding the scenery and local culture becomes, with quality microbreweries, decent wineries, endearingly friendly locals and their unique jargon and accent (don't ever compare it to Canadian); it's "pop", not soda, "roundabouts", not traffic circles, and kids go to "haahckey" practice after school.

Detroit

America's Motor City, **DETROIT** boasts a legacy that includes not only iconic automobiles such as the Cadillac, Chevrolet and Oldsmobile – thanks to the "Big Three" (Chrysler, Ford and GM) who set up shop here in the early twentieth century – but also Motown Records and the creation of techno music. Yet Detroit is perhaps best-known today for its almost surreal decline since the devastating **race riots of 1967**, from booming industrial hub to the largest municipal **bankruptcy** in US history in 2013; in 1950 the population was around 1.85 million, but by 2015 it had plummeted to just over 700,000. Vast swathes of the city lie abandoned; indeed, tourists are flocking once again to Detroit for what the locals angrily dismiss as "**ruin porn**". Thankfully there's much more to Detroit than this: a new city is emerging, from artists reclaiming abandoned factories and organic farming on empty lots, to the billion-dollar rejuvenation of **downtown**, vibrant neighbourhoods such as **Corktown** and community art initiatives such as the **Heidelberg Project**. Though it remains debatable how these changes will improve the lives of the city's poor – disproportionately African American – Detroit is undeniably one of America's most enigmatic cities.

Brief history

Detroit traces its foundation to Fort Pontchartrain du Détroit, established by the French officer **Antoine de Mothe Cadillac** in 1701 to strengthen France's control of the fur trade, particularly with the Ottawa and Huron. The British assumed control of the fort in 1760, but their poor treatment of the local tribes resulted in **Pontiac's Rebellion** in 1763, when the Ottawa and their allies unsuccessfully laid siege to Detroit. It wasn't until 1796 that the fort was surrendered to the Americans, and in 1805 a fire destroyed most of the still tiny settlement (and the fort). The town was gradually rebuilt in the nineteenth century, and by the Civil War (1861) it was a thriving port city of 45,000. Detroit's location at the heart of the Great Lakes made it a natural centre for industry, and manufacturing boomed in the 1870s and 1880s, fed by waves of Irish, German and Polish immigrants.

THE RUINS OF DETROIT

One of the most bizarre and controversial side effects of Detroit's economic collapse has been the rise of "ruin tourism" (aka "ruin porn") – tours of abandoned factories, churches and schools. The primary "attraction" (a giant building falling into atmospheric ruin) is the **Michigan Central Station** in Corktown, a grand edifice completed in 1914 and closed since 1988; Ford Motor Co purchased the station along with the Roosevelt Warehouse in 2018, and plans to turn it into a new corporate campus by 2022. Other targets include the 1911 **National Theatre** (currently being converted into the Monroe Blocks development), the **Packard Automotive Plant** (redevelopment into office space pending), and the 1910 **East Grand Boulevard Methodist Church** (development pending). Visiting these places can be dangerous (from unstable buildings and muggings) – go with a tour company such as City Tour Detroit (@citytourdetroit.com).

1

It was the existence of a flourishing machine tool and coach-building industry here that attracted **Henry Ford**, **Ransom Eli Olds**, the **Chevrolets** and the **Dodge** brothers to build their automobile empires in Detroit, beginning in the late 1890s. Thanks to the introduction of Ford's mass assembly line, Detroit boomed in the 1920s, and thousands of African Americans migrated from the South to work in the new factories. However, the auto barons sponsored the construction of segregated neighbourhoods and shed workers during times of low demand. Tensions between white and black workers led to the **Detroit race riot of 1943** – 25 blacks and nine whites were killed, the army called in to restore order. Though the good times returned after World War II, nothing was done to tackle inequality and racism, leading in **July 1967** to the bloodiest **race riot** in the USA in fifty years. More than forty people died and thirteen

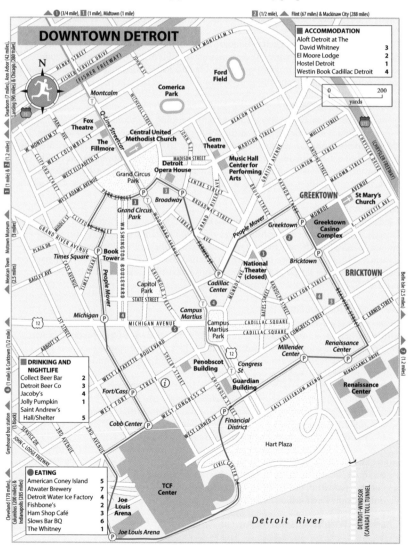

DOWNTOWN DETROIT

■ **ACCOMMODATION**
Aloft Detroit at The David Whitney	3
El Moore Lodge	2
Hostel Detroit	1
Westin Book Cadillac Detroit	4

0   200
yards

■ **DRINKING AND NIGHTLIFE**
Collect Beer Bar	2
Detroit Beer Co	3
Jacoby's	4
Jolly Pumpkin	1
Saint Andrew's Hall/Shelter	5

● **EATING**
American Coney Island	5
Atwater Brewery	7
Detroit Water Ice Factory	4
Fishbone's	2
Ham Shop Café	3
Slows Bar BQ	6
The Whitney	1

1

hundred buildings were destroyed. The **inner city** was left to fend for itself, while the all-important motor industry was rocked by the oil crises and Japanese competition in the 1970s. The city's long decline in subsequent years has been well documented, culminating in the bankruptcy of 2013, but today Detroit is not the mess some would have it, and suburban residents have started to return to the city's festivals, theatres, clubs and restaurants.

Downtown

Detroit's rapidly regenerating **downtown** is studded with monumental architecture, from Art Deco skyscrapers to giant stadiums and contemporary towers. Many offices are full again, or are being transformed into condos centred on **Campus Martius**, a new park/square opened in 2004. Downtown is safe during the day, but take care at night when many streets become deserted – though nightlife hub **Greektown** is fine (see page 98).

Don't miss the ornate **Guardian Building**, 500 Griswold St (open 24/7), an Art Deco gem completed in 1929 with a spectacular atrium. Hart Plaza and the **Riverfront**, overlooking Windsor (Canada), across the Detroit River, hosts free lunchtime concerts and lively weekend festivals all summer long.

The Renaissance Center

400 Renaissance Center (on Jefferson Ave) • ⓦ gmrencen.com

General Motors is headquartered in the seven gleaming towers of the **Renaissance Center (GMRenCen)**, completed in stages between 1977 and 1981 and rising 73 storeys (750ft) above the riverbank. Henry Ford II's grand design to revive Detroit (GM bought it in 1996), it's an attractive public space with a soaring glass atrium known as the GM Wintergarden, the huge GM World (car showroom) and a decent food court.

Midtown

Bus #465, FAST Woodward and Q-Line streetcar run up Woodward Ave

Three miles northwest of downtown, next to Wayne State University, the top-notch museums of the **Midtown** district are clustered within easy walking distance of one another. Tours however are currently postponed due to COVID-19. Be sure to observe the ornate **Fisher Building** (3011 W Grand Blvd; open 24 hours), Albert Kahn's 1928 masterpiece.

Detroit Institute of Arts

5200 Woodward Ave • Tues–Thurs 9am–4pm, Fri 9am–9pm, Sat & Sun 10am–5pm • charge, reservation required • ⓦ dia.org

One of America's most prestigious art museums, the colossal **Detroit Institute of Arts** traces the history of civilization from ancient Egypt to contemporary art. The building is part of the attraction, with a magnificently frescoed Great Hall and adjacent Rivera Court smothered in **Diego Rivera**'s enormous, show-stealing, 1933 *Detroit Industry* mural. Other highlights include a vast Italian collection with work from Donatello, Bellini, Botticelli, Tiepolo and Titian's *Judith*. Bruegel the Elder's *Wedding Dance* is a vibrant portrayal of bawdy Flemish peasant life, replete with codpieces, while John Singer Sargent's *Mosquito Nets* and Whistler's *Nocturne in Black & Gold* are two of many American masterpieces on show. There are special galleries dedicated to Rodin, Rubens and Rembrandt (including the last-named's haunting *Visitation*), plus several works by Picasso and Van Gogh (don't miss *The Diggers*). *The Nightmare*, by Henry Fuseli, is one of the most reproduced Romantic paintings. The British collection, one of the nation's largest, is also worth seeking out, with paintings by Constable, Gainsborough, Reynolds and Hogarth.

Charles H. Wright Museum of African American History

315 E Warren St • Tues–Sat 9am–4pm, Sun noon–5pm • charge • ⓦ thewright.org

THE MOTOWN SOUND

The legend that is Tamla Motown started in 1959 when Ford worker and part-time songwriter **Berry Gordy Jr** borrowed $800 to set up a studio. From his first hit onward – the prophetic *Money (That's What I Want)* – he set out to create a crossover style, targeting his records at white and black consumers alike.

Early Motown hits were pure formula. Gordy softened the blue notes of most contemporary black music in favour of a more danceable, poppy beat, with **gospel**-influenced singing and clapping. Prime examples of the early approach featured all-female groups such as the **Marvelettes** (*Needle in a Haystack*), the **Supremes** (*Baby Love*) and **Martha Reeves and the Vandellas** (*Nowhere to Run*), as well as the all-male **Miracles** (*Tracks of My Tears*), featuring the sophisticated love lyrics of lead singer **Smokey Robinson**. Gordy's "Quality Control Department" scrutinized every beat, playing all recordings through speakers modelled on cheap transistor radios before the final mix.

By the late 1960s Motown had acquired a harder sound, crowned by the acid soul productions of Norman Whitfield with the versatile **Temptations**. In 1968 the organization outgrew its premises on Grand Avenue; four years later it abandoned Detroit altogether for LA. Gordy signed **The Jackson 5** in 1969, leading to the "Jacksonmania" of the early 1970s, but by mid-decade the top sellers were the high-society soul of **Diana Ross** and the ballads of the **Commodores** – Gordy focused more on producing movies such as *The Wiz* (1978). Many artists left the label, including the crack songwriting team of Holland-Dozier-Holland, responsible for most of the **Four Tops**' hits; the team stayed in Detroit to produce the seminal **Chairmen of the Board** (*Gimme Just A Little More Time*). Today, Motown is owned by the giant **Universal Music Group**.

The impressive **Charles H. Wright Museum of African American History** is the largest African American museum in the world. Its core exhibit – **And Still We Rise** – begins with African history (with humanity's common ancestor "Mitochondrial Eve"), and includes harrowing replicas of a slave fort and slave boat, before moving through Abolition, Segregation and the modern Civil Rights movement, with special focus on Detroit. Exhibits cover the Nation of Islam, founded here by Wallace D. Fard in 1930, and popular ex-mayor Coleman Young.

Detroit Historical Museum

5401 Woodward Ave • Thurs–Sat 10am–5pm, Sun 1pm–5pm • Free • ⓦ detroithistorical.org

The history of the city, beginning with its establishment by the French in 1701, is showcased at the **Detroit Historical Museum** with multimedia exhibits and full-scale replicas of historic streets. Highlights include the **Kid Rock Music Lab**, which honours Detroit musical legends such as Stevie Wonder, Aretha Franklin, Eminem and Kid Rock himself, and allows folk young and old to experiment with musical innovation. **America's Motor City** chronicles Detroit's auto legacy (including the first car made here in 1896), while the city's role in the **Underground Railroad** gets its own illuminating section.

Ford Piquette Avenue Plant

461 Piquette Ave • Thurs–Sun 10am–4pm • charge • ⓦ fordpiquetteplant.org

Just north of Midtown, in what was once the heart of Detroit's car industry, the **Ford Piquette Avenue Plant** is a real gem, a relic of the city's golden age. Serving as Henry Ford's factory from 1904 to 1910, this is where he created the Model T in 1908, the car that brought motor transport to the masses for the first time. Tour guides illuminate the spacious floors of the old plant with tales of Ford's early career, adding context to the display of numerous vintage Ford cars and other long-defunct Detroit brands such as Hupp Motors and E-M-F Company.

1

DETROIT'S CONEY ISLANDS

Coney Island is a neighbourhood in Brooklyn, New York, but its famed hot dogs were adopted by Detroit in the early twentieth century, where they developed their own signature style – the hot dog sausage is grilled, placed into a steamed bun, then smothered by an all-meat, beanless chili, two strips of yellow mustard and chopped sweet onions. If you have wheels, check out *Duly's Place* (aka *Duly's Coney Island*, located at 5458 Vernor Hwy), which has been serving up hot dogs 24hr a day since it opened in 1921. Otherwise, there are plenty of spots downtown.

Heidelberg Project

3600 Heidelberg St · Daily 8am–7pm · Free · ⓦ heidelberg.org

Created in 1986 by artist Tyree Guyton, the **Heidelberg Project** spans a block on the city's east side, a series of art installations that has brought colour and life back to a virtually abandoned neighbourhood. Sadly, Guyton's work has been destroyed by order of city officials twice, and more recently by acts of arson – in 2016 he announced that he would gradually begin to dismantle parts of the project. Over the next few years the site will morph into what Guyton is calling Heidelberg 3.0, a larger community-activated arts village. Nevertheless, much of his artwork – multicoloured cars and recycled materials – will stay, and four decorated houses will remain (there are plans to transform the polka-dot-festooned Dotty Wotty House into a museum). The project area is generally safe, but don't stray beyond its borders – drive or take taxis to get here.

Dearborn

Though considered part of metropolitan Detroit, **DEARBORN** is a separately administered city, some eight miles west from downtown. It's best known for being the former home of **Henry Ford** and the vast museum he created (Ford Motor Co still has its world headquarters here), as well as having the largest **Arab American** population in the USA.

Arab American National Museum

13624 Michigan Ave, Dearborn · Thurs & Fri 11am–6pm, Sat noon–6pm · charge · ⓦ arabamericanmuseum.org · SMART bus #200

Arab immigrants (mostly Lebanese) started coming to Dearborn in the 1920s to work for Ford, and their legacy is sensitively portrayed in the **Arab American National Museum**. Exhibits focus on Arab culture and its achievements globally, before chronicling the experiences of Arab Americans, through hands-on and multimedia displays. Sections also honour notable Arab Americans such as Darrell Issa, Casey Kasem, Kathy Najimy and Rashida Tlaib, the local politician who in 2019 became the first Palestinian-American woman (and one of the first Muslim women) elected to Congress.

The Henry Ford Museum Complex

20900 Oakwood Blvd, Dearborn · ⓦ thehenryford.org

Founder of the company that still bears his name, Ford was also an inveterate collector of Americana, and today **The Henry Ford** complex of museums and historical re-creations in Dearborn is testimony to the immense wealth of its patron. Given the high cost involved (ask about combo passes), aim to spend most of the day here to make the most of it. While the separately managed **Fair Lane** (ⓦ henryfordfairlane.org), Henry and Clara Ford's Dearborn estate, is undergoing extensive rennovations, the grounds are open to visitors every day from 8am-5pm.

Henry Ford Museum of American Innovation

20900 Oakwood Blvd · Daily 9.30am–5pm · charge, additional for parking · ⓦ thehenryford.org · Bus #261 (FAST Michigan)

With an astounding 26 million artefacts to draw on, the fascinating **Henry Ford Museum of American Innovation** is a gargantuan curiosity shop, containing planes, numerous vintage cars, trains and row upon row of domestic inventions (as well as one of the earliest steam engines, a British **Newcomen Engine** from 1760). Presidential limousines, from FDR's "Sunshine Special" to the one JFK was shot in are here, as well as **George Washington's camp kit**, a rare copy of the **13th Amendment** (which abolished slavery) and the actual bus **Rosa Parks** was riding when she refused to give up her seat (see page 136), part of the excellent **With Liberty and Justice for All** section. Real oddities include the chair **Lincoln** was sitting in when he was assassinated, and even a test tube (allegedly) holding **Edison**'s last breath.

Greenfield Village

20900 Oakwood Blvd · Mid-April to Oct daily 9.30am–5pm; Nov Fri–Sun 9.30am–5pm · charge

Adjacent to the main museum, **Greenfield Village** was created by Ford in 1929 to replicate an early American town, sprinkled with a mix of replica cottages and actual properties he had moved here through the 1930s. It's essentially an historic theme park (Model-T and steam train rides cost extra), but there are some real gems here, from the actual **Wright Brothers' bicycle shop** and Ford's humble childhood home, to a replica of **Edison's Menlo Park complex** and the 1920s home of **Robert Frost** from Ann Arbor. Costumed interpreters demonstrate everything from weaving to puncture repair.

Ford Rouge Factory Tour

Tour buses depart every 20min Mon–Sat 9.30am–5pm (last bus back 5pm) · charge

Tour buses depart the Henry Ford Museum through the day for the **Ford Rouge Factory Tour**, at an actual Ford factory nearby in Dearborn, where you can view an assembly plant in action and vintage cars that were made here.

ARRIVAL AND DEPARTURE   DETROIT

By plane Detroit Airport (ⓦ metroairport.com) is 18 miles southwest of downtown. Metro Cabs (ⓣ 734 997 6500) and Metro Cars (ⓣ 800 456 1701) are both reasonable options cost-wise. SMART bus #125 (ⓣ 866 962 5515, ⓦ smartbus. org) goes downtown from both terminals, but only during peak periods (5–7am & 2–4pm). Better is the #261 FAST Michigan (daily 5am–11.25pm, every 15min–1hr), which runs downtown with limited stops. AirRide runs between the airport and Ann Arbor (roughly every hour; 45min–1hr;

ⓦ theride.org).

By bus Greyhound buses pull in at 1001 Howard St, downtown.

Destinations Ann Arbor (6 daily; 1hr–1hr 15min); Chicago (4 daily; 5hr 20min–6hr 25min); Cleveland (4 daily; 3hr 35min–4hr 10min); Grand Rapids (2 daily; 4hr 25min).

By train The Amtrak station is at 11 W Baltimore Ave (3 miles north of downtown), in an area best avoided late at night. Three trains a day head to Chicago (5hr–5hr 20min).

GETTING AROUND, INFORMATION AND TOURS

When it comes to orientation, it makes sense to think of Detroit as a region rather than a concentrated city (it covers some 140 square miles), and seeing everything will require wheels (local transport is patchy beyond downtown).

By elevated railway Downtown, the People Mover elevated railway loops around thirteen stations (Mon–Thurs 6.30am–midnight, Fri 6.30am–2am, Sat 9am–2am, Sun noon–midnight; ⓦ thepeoplemover.com).

By bus SMART (ⓦ smartbus.org) serves the entire metro region, while DDOT buses (ⓣ 313 933 1300, ⓦ detroitmi. gov/ddot) offer a patchier inner-city service. Bus #465 and FAST Woodward run between downtown and Midtown.

By light rail The Q-Line streetcar (ⓦ qlinedetroit.com) runs along central Woodward Ave from Congress St in

Downtown to Grand Blvd in New Center via Midtown (Mon–Thurs 6am–midnight, Fri 6am–2am, Sat 8am–2am, Sun 8am–11pm).

By taxi Try Checker Taxi (ⓣ 313 963 7000). If you have a smartphone, Uber and Lyft are useful in Detroit.

Visitor centre 211 W Fort St (Mon–Fri 9am–5pm; ⓣ 313 202 1800, ⓦ visitdetroit.com)

Tours Recommended are the fun themed tours provided by the Detroit Bus Co (ⓦ thedetroitbus.com/tours), and the bike tours by Wheelhouse (ⓦ wheelhousedetroit.com). The Detroit Experience Factory (ⓦ detroitexperiencefactory. org) run excellent tours with different themes and neighbourhoods – some are free.

ACCOMMODATION   SEE MAP PAGE 93

★ **Aloft Detroit at The David Whitney** 1 Park Ave, ⓦ marriott.com. Gorgeous boutique set inside the historic

1

Whitney building, a Neo-Renaissance palace from 1915. Rooms feature the slick, contemporary Aloft design, with fast free wi-fi. $$$$

★ **El Moore Lodge** 624 W Alexandrine St, ⓦ elmoore. com. One of the city's most lauded rehabilitations, a grand 1898 edifice with long-term residences, four stylish rooftop "urban cabins" dressed in reclaimed wood and cheaper bunk-bed rooms. $$$-$$$$

Hostel Detroit 2700 Vermont St, ⓦ hosteldetroit.com.

The city's only hostel is in lively Corktown, with cosy private rooms and dorms, plus owners who are keen to introduce Detroit to their guests. Advance reservations only, no walk-ins. Parking available for additional charge. $-$$

Westin Book Cadillac Hotel 1114 Washington Blvd, ⓦ bookcadillacwestin.com. Built in 1924, the magnificent *Book* was renovated and taken over by the *Westin* chain. It offers elegant rooms and a full range of amenities. $$$$

EATING

SEE MAP PAGE 93

Detroit's best restaurants are spread far and wide across the city, but there are plenty of downtown options; **Greektown**, basically one block of Monroe Avenue between Beaubien and St Antoine streets, is crammed with authentic Greek places. Less commercial, but offering just as high a standard, are the bakeries, bars and cantinas of **Corktown** and **Mexican Town**, west of downtown. The best restaurants tend to be in **Midtown**, while **East Dearborn** (especially Warren Ave, between Greenfield and Miller) is loaded with authentic Middle Eastern restaurants and bakeries.

American Coney Island 114 W Lafayette Blvd, ⓦ americanconeyisland.com. Detroit's own Coney Island hot dogs since 1917, using Dearborn Sausage and also serving local Atwater microbeers. Compare with fierce rival *Lafayette Coney Island* next door. $

★ **Atwater Brewery** 237 Jos Campau St, ⓦ atwaterbeer.com. This spacious Rivertown brewpub (1.5 miles east of RenCen) serves up excellent beer-battered fish, mussels, burgers and pizzas. $$

★ **Detroit Water Ice Factory** 1014 Woodward Av, ⓦ detroitwaterice.com. Dessert shop founded by *Detroit*

Free Press columnist and author Mitch Albom, knocking out delicious water ices in seventeen flavours including pumpkin, coconut and mango. Proceeds are donated to Albom's charity, S.A.Y. Detroit. $

Fishbone's 400 Monroe Ave (Greektown), ⓦ fishbonesusa.com. This noisy, fun and often packed chain restaurant is a Cajun joint serving whiskey ribs, crawfish, gumbo, sushi and lots more. $$

Ham Shop 330 Monroe Ave (Greektown), ☎ 313 965 0088. Basic greasy spoon knocking out bargain breakfast plates and lunch specials (Coney Island dogs and burgers). $

Slows Bar BQ 2138 Michigan Ave, ⓦ slowsbarbq. com. A lively, affordable mini-chain and bar that brings the Southern flavour north, with the best mac and cheese around, its famous yardbird sandwich, and craft beers on draught. $$

The Whitney 4421 Woodward Ave, ⓦ thewhitney.com. Located in a stately mansion built in 1894, this elegant restaurant serves upscale American cuisine, with specials such as beef Wellington, crab cakes, and a posh afternoon tea served daily at 2pm (advance reservations required). $$$$

DRINKING AND NIGHTLIFE

SEE MAP PAGE 93

Collect Beer Bar 1454 Gratiot Ave, ⓦ collect-beerbar. com. Rooftop beer bar in Eastern Market offering rotating draft beers. $

Detroit Beer Co 1529 Broadway, ⓦ detroitbeerco.com. Downtown microbrewery, with excellent beers made on the premises and happy hour daily. $$

Jacoby's 624 Brush St, ⓦ jacobysbar.com. The city's oldest tavern, open since 1904, serves German food and a vast selection of American and German beers. $$

Jolly Pumpkin 441 W Canfield St, ⓦ brewery. jollypumpkin.com. Pizzeria and microbrewery that's better known for its excellent French- and Belgian-style sour beers than for its food. $$

★ **Saint Andrew's Hall** 431 E Congress St, ⓦ saintandrewsdetroit.com. This cramped downtown club promotes top bands on the alternative circuit. It only holds 800 people, so get a ticket in advance. Downstairs is the *Shelter* club, with lesser-known touring bands followed by dance music.

Ann Arbor

The progressive heart of Michigan, **ANN ARBOR** lies just forty miles west of downtown Detroit along I-94, offering an exceptional variety of restaurants, microbreweries, live music venues and cultural activities. The **University of Michigan** has shaped the economy and character of the city ever since it was moved here from Detroit in 1837. Its central campus (east of State St) is a mishmash of architectural styles, from the Richardsonian Romanesque **Newberry Hall** (home of the Kelsey Museum of Archaeology) to the Art Deco **Burton Memorial Tower**. Though there's plenty to see, the main highlight is the

1

Museum of Art, 525 S State St (Tues–Wed 11am–5pm, Thurs & Fri 10am–8pm, Sat–Sun 11am–8pm; free; ⓦumma.umich.edu), with a carefully curated collection that includes Picasso's *Two Girls Reading*, Max Beckmann's *Begin the Beguine*, Monet's *Breakup of the Ice* and James McNeill Whistler's numbingly bleak *Sea and Rain*. Downtown itself is centred on **Main Street**, a short walk west of campus, twelve blocks of brightly painted shops, bookshops and street cafés.

ARRIVAL AND INFORMATION
ANN ARBOR

By bus Greyhound services stop at 325 Depot St (the Amtrak station). Megabus (Chicago 2 daily; 4hr 30min) stops three miles south of downtown at the Briarwood Mall, 900 Briarwood Circle (Parking Lot Pole 15).
Destinations Chicago (3 daily; 4hr 25min–5hr 20min); Detroit (7 daily; 45min–1hr 25min); Grand Rapids (2 daily; 3hr 15min); Lansing (2 daily; 1hr 45min).

By train Amtrak is on the north edge of downtown at 325 Depot St.
Destinations Chicago (3 daily; 4hr 12min–4hr 34min); Detroit (3 daily; 1hr).
Visitor centre 315 W Huron St (Mon–Fri 8.30am–5pm; ☎734 995 7281, ⓦannarbor.org).

ACCOMMODATION AND EATING

Bell Tower Hotel 300 S Thayer St, ⓦbelltowerhotel. com. The choice place to stay in Ann Arbor, in by far the most convenient location, and with elegant, comfy rooms. $$$$
Blue Tractor BBQ 207 E Washington St, ⓦbluetractor. net. Creative barbecue specialist (think chilli ginger spare ribs and *bulgogi* burgers), that also has its own microbrewery. $$
Burnt Toast Inn 415 W William St, ⓦburnttoastinn. com. This place is as warm and welcoming as a B&B should be; highlights include plush robes and yoga mats, and the

breakfasts are made with locally sourced ingredients. $$$
Frita Batidos 117 W Washington St, ⓦfritabatidos. com. Popular Latino joint knocking out Cuban-inspired fritas, coconut *batidos* (milkshakes), and churros. $$
★ **Zingerman's Delicatessen** 422 Detroit St, ⓦzingermansdeli.com. Ann Arbor institution since 1982, known for its smoky pastrami and black angus corned beef sandwiches, home-made chopped liver and chicken salad; they can also accommodate gluten-free diners, vegans and just about anyone else. $$

NIGHTLIFE

Ann Arbor's live music scene enjoys a nationwide reputation. Unlike many college towns, the place doesn't go to sleep during the summer, either. For news of gigs, grab a copy of the free, monthly *Current* (ⓦecurrent.com).
The Ark 316 S Main St, ⓦtheark.org. Lovers of folk, roots

and acoustic music will not be disappointed here.
Blind Pig 208 S 1st St, ⓦblindpigmusic.com. The best place in town to watch live rock, alternative and blues. Jimi Hendrix, Iggy Pop and MC5 have all graced the stage. $

Lansing

Thanks to its more central location (65 miles northwest of Ann Arbor), the small, sleepy city of **LANSING** replaced Detroit as the **capital of Michigan** in 1847. **Michigan State University** (MSU), with its Spartans sports teams, was founded soon after, and is now one of the largest universities in the nation. The **Michigan State Capitol**, at 100 N Capitol Ave (Mon–Fri 9am–5pm; free; ⓦcapitol.michigan.gov) was completed in 1879, its lavish interior featuring delicately painted murals, marble columns and a distinctive Renaissance Revival-style dome. A few blocks west, the vast **Michigan History Center**, 702 W Kalamazoo St (Fri & Sat 10am–4pm, Sun 1–5pm; charge, free Sun; ⓦmichigan.gov/ mhc), chronicles the history of the state from early native and French settlements to the 1960s, with excellent hands-on exhibits. Over in East Lansing, the **Eli & Edythe Broad Art Museum** (547 E Circle Drive; Thurs–Sun 10–6pm; free; ⓦbroadmuseum.msu.edu) is a cutting-edge contemporary art museum housed in a sensational, angular building, which was designed by Zaha Hadid.

ARRIVAL AND INFORMATION
LANSING

By bus Greyhound services stop at the CATA Transportation Center, 420 S Grand Ave.

Destinations Ann Arbor (1 daily; 1hr 40min); Chicago (3 daily; 5hr 25min–6hr 35min); Detroit (3 daily; 2hr–3hr);

Grand Rapids (4 daily; 1hr 10min); Mackinaw City (1 daily; 6hr 50min); Petoskey (1 daily 5hr 50min). | **Visitor centre** 500 E Michigan Ave (Mon–Fri 8.30am–5pm; ☎ 517 487 6800, ⓦ lansing.org).

Grand Rapids

Michigan's second-largest city and the former furniture capital of America, **GRAND RAPIDS** has garnered fame in the last few years for its high-quality **microbreweries**, some forty at the last count (and for being the setting for the *American Pie* movies). It was also the hometown of President **Gerald Ford**, who assumed the role after Nixon's resignation in 1974. Ford is buried with his wife Betty at the **Gerald R. Ford Presidential Museum**, 303 Pearl St (Mon–Sat 10am–5pm, Sun noon–5pm; charge; ⓦ fordlibrarymuseum.gov), an absorbing insight into the life of the 38th US president and his socially conscious wife (founder of the Betty Ford Center for substance abuse). Close to the modern downtown, **Heritage Hill** is loaded with historic homes, including the **Meyer May House**, 450 Madison Ave SE (tours Tues & Thurs 10am–1pm, Sun noon–3pm; free; ⓦ meyermayhouse.steelcase.com) designed by Frank Lloyd Wright in 1908. On the edge of town, the **Frederik Meijer Gardens & Sculpture Park** (1000 E Beltline Ave NE; Mon & Wed–Sat 9am–5pm, Tues 9am–9pm, Sun 11am–5pm; charge; ⓦ meijergardens.org) is worth half a day, with a fabulous Japanese Garden and over 50 major sculptures by Rodin, Henry Moore, Barbara Hepworth, Ai Weiwei and many others.

ARRIVAL AND INFORMATION GRAND RAPIDS

By bus Greyhound services stop at 250 Grandville Ave. Destinations Ann Arbor (2 daily; 3hr 15min); Chicago (2 daily; 5hr 10min); Detroit (2 daily; 3hr 30min–4hr 10min); Lansing (4 daily; 1hr 10min); Traverse City (1 daily; 3hr 40min).

Website See ⓦ experiencegr.com.

ACCOMMODATION AND EATING

Amway Grand Plaza Hotel 187 Monroe Ave NW, ⓦ amwaygrand.com. Stately, historic hotel dating from 1913 and now sporting a variety of refurbished rooms in period and contemporary styles. $̄$̄$̄$̄

CityFlatsHotel 83 Monroe Center St NW, ⓦ cityflatshotel.com. Centrally located boutique hotel with modern, eco-friendly rooms (cork flooring, reclaimed wood furnishings and the like). Parking in Monroe Center. $̄$̄$̄$̄

★ **Founders Brewing Co** 235 Grandville Ave SW, ⓦ foundersbrewing.com. Sample some of America's best craft beers at this German beerhall-inspired taproom, with excellent bar snacks. $̄

The Kitchen by Wolfgang Puck 187 Monroe Ave NW, ⓦ wolfgangpuck.com. Creative menus from the stable of celebrity chef Puck, dubbed "global comfort fare" and including noodles and meatloaf with smoked bacon. $̄$̄$̄

The Lake Michigan coast

In summer, ocean-starved Midwesterners make do with Michigan's **Gold Coast**, more than two hundred miles of sandy beaches and dunes studded with decent surf breaks at places such as **New Buffalo** (70 miles east of Chicago), and affluent resort towns such as **St Joseph**, another 26 miles north. This section of the Lake Michigan shore – from the Indiana border to the **Silver Lake Sand Dunes**, eighty miles northwest from Grand Rapids – buzzes with local tourist traffic all summer, but though the scene can be fun, the towns (and landscapes) further north are more worthwhile. The artsy village of **Saugatuck** (40 miles southwest of Grand Rapids), set around a charming harbour just off the lake, makes for a good pit stop, with plenty of galleries, posh boutiques and cafés along the boat-packed marina.

Traverse City

Some 140 miles north of Grand Rapids, **Traverse City** comes as a surprise in rustic northern Michigan, especially in summer. The favourite in-state **resort** for locals and for those escaping Chicago, the city buzzes with kiteboarding, kayaking, music and movie festivals, brewpubs and chic restaurants from May to September, making it a fun base at the "top of the mitt". Today, the area's claim to be the "**Cherry Capital of the World**" is no idle boast: thousands of acres of cherry orchards envelop the town, their wispy, white blossoms bringing a delicate beauty each May; be sure to visit **Cherry Republic**, 154 E Front St (Ⓦcherryrepublic.com) to sample the cherry ketchup, cherry-dusted tortillas and cherry butter or attend the **National Cherry Festival** (Ⓦcherryfestival.org), held during the first full week in July. Traverse City's neat **downtown** rests along the southern end of the west arm of **Grand Traverse Bay**, below the Old Mission Peninsula, with access to two sandy beaches.

ARRIVAL AND INFORMATION
TRAVERSE CITY

By bus the bus station (BATA) is at 115 Hall St; there's a daily service to Grand Rapids on Indian Trails (4hr 5min; Ⓦindiantrails.com) for Greyhound transfers to Chicago and Detroit. Buses also head north to Petoskey (1 daily; 1hr 45min) and Mackinaw City (1 daily; 2hr 45min).

Visitor centre 101 Grandview Pkwy, downtown (Tues–Sat noon–5pm; Ⓦtraversecity.com).

ACCOMMODATION, EATING AND DRINKING

Blue Tractor Barbeque 423 S Union St, Ⓦbluetractorcookshop.com. This downtown barbecue specialist is distinguished by its smoked baby back ribs and elaborate burgers. $$
North Peak Brewing Company 400 W Front St, Ⓦnorthpeak.net. This fine brewpub serves up excellent Atlantic salmon and burgers; its beers are made on the premises and range from oatmeal stouts to malty ambers. $$

Traverse City State Park Campground 1498 Munson Ave, Ⓦmidnrreservations.com. A solid choice for those who like the great outdoors, and the best budget option, this campground has electric hookups, access to a nearby beach and a small store. $
Wellington Inn 230 Wellington St, Ⓦwellingtoninn. com. Restored Neoclassical 1905 mansion downtown, with luxurious, period rooms and a sumptuous full breakfast. $$$$

Sleeping Bear Dunes National Lakeshore
Philip A. Hart Visitor Centre 9922 Front St (Hwy-72), Empire • Ⓦnps.gov/slbe • Daily 9am–4pm

The highlight of Michigan's northern coast is the untouched wilderness of **Sleeping Bear Dunes National Lakeshore**, a constantly resculptured area of towering dunes, beech-maple forests and precipitous 400ft drops. The area was named by the Ojibwe (Chippewa), who saw the mist-shrouded North and South Manitou islands as the graves of two drowned bear cubs, and the massive mainland dune as their grieving mother.

Check out the exhibits and video at the **visitor centre** in the village of Empire (24 miles west of Traverse City on Hwy-72), before heading for the stunning overlooks of the dunes and the lake along the hilly, seven-mile loop of the **Pierce Stocking Scenic Drive** off Hwy-109. You can also clamber up the strenuous but enjoyable **Dune Climb**, a 200ft-high sand pile two miles farther north on Hwy-109 for inspirational vistas. Drive another 1.7 miles to the **Glen Haven Historic Village**, restored to its 1920s heyday (Glen Haven General Store open from Memorial Day-June Fri–Sun noon–5pm, July-Labor Day daily noon–5pm; Cannery Boat Museum open daily 11am–5pm), while the nearby 1930s Life-Saving Station is now the **Sleeping Bear Point Coast Guard Station and Maritime Museum** (daily 11am–5pm).

The village of **Glen Arbor**, on Hwy-22 (8 miles north of the visitor centre), acts as the primary base for park activities and accommodation, though it's an easy day-trip from Traverse City.

Petoskey and around

In **PETOSKEY**, high above Little Traverse Bay, sixteen miles north of Traverse City along US-31, grand Victorian houses encircle the downtown's nicely restored **Gaslight District**. Ernest Hemingway spent most of his childhood summers here (his parents built a cottage on nearby Walloon Lake in 1898), and alludes to the town in his novel *The Torrents of Spring*.

1

Perched on the other side of Little Traverse Bay, ten miles from Petoskey, **Harbor Springs** is another affluent town, right on the water. Browse the boutique stores along charming Main Street, rent a boat or check out its two small beaches – Zorn Park and Zoll Street. Heading north, the "**Tunnel of Trees**" scenic drive follows a section of Hwy-119 for twenty miles to tiny **Cross Village** and the *Legs Inn*. Along this narrow winding road, occasional breaks in the overhanging trees afford sensational views of Lake Michigan and Beaver Island, with blossoms in spring and spectacular colours in the fall.

ACCOMMODATION AND EATING   **PETOSKEY AND AROUND**

★ **Legs Inn** 6425 N Lake Shore Drive, Cross Village, ⓦ legsinn.com. Built by Polish immigrant Stanley Smolak in the 1920s, this timber landmark full of driftwood carvings still knocks out authentic Polish cuisine such as pierogi (dumplings) as well as local smoked whitefish; you can also eat in the lovely garden overlooking the lake. Late May to late Oct.

North Perk Coffee 308 Howard St, Petoskey, ⓦ northperkcoffee.com. Excellent local coffee shop and small batch coffee roaster, with decent espresso, hot chocolate, doughnuts, iced lemonade and homemade ice cream. $̄

Stafford's Perry Hotel 100 Lewis St, Petoskey, ⓦ staffords.com. This centrally located hotel offers old-school glamour from another age, complete with a reading library. $̄$̄$̄

The Straits of Mackinac

The Upper and Lower peninsulas of Michigan are connected by the majestic **Mackinac Bridge**, soaring for five miles across the **Straits of Mackinac**, the busy waterway between lakes Michigan and Huron. Completed in 1957, "Mighty Mac" has a main span of 3800ft, making it America's third largest suspension bridge. **Mackinac Island** is the main attraction here, but the whole area is rich in history.

Mackinaw City

Some 35 miles northeast of Petoskey, **MACKINAW CITY** is a small tourist town that booms in the summer as the major embarkation point for Mackinac Island, though it does boast a few worthwhile attractions of its own. There's also plenty of cheap chain motel **accommodation** in Mackinaw City, though it pays to book ahead in mid-summer.

Michilimackinac State Park

106 W Straits Ave • May–October, hours and special events vary, ⓦ mackinacparks.com

Michilimackinac State Park, overlooking the Mackinac Bridge, contains **Colonial Michilimackinac**, an astounding re-creation of the fort and settlement founded here by the French in 1715. Occupied by the British in 1761, it was abandoned in 1781 when the whole post was evacuated to Mackinac Island. Today it's inhabited by costumed interpreters and packed with authentically constructed reproductions such as the Church of St Anne. Exhibits inside the buildings cover the French and British periods, and display some of the fascinating remains that have been dug up here, from Georgian coins to jaw harps. The **visitor centre** under the bridge shows a short video on the site.

Old Mackinac Point Lighthouse

526 N Huron Ave • Open daily May–October, 9am–4:30pm, June–September 9am–5:30pm, tours every half hour, last admittance half hour before closing • charge, discount for ages 5-12 • ⓦ mackinacparks.com

On the other side of the state park from Colonial Michilimackinac, the **Old Mackinac Point Lighthouse** preserves the lighthouse opened here in 1892 (it's been disused since 1958). Other than the tower itself (which you can climb), the site includes the Keepers' Quarters, restored to their 1910 appearance with exhibits on the history of the lighthouse, and the **Straits of Mackinac Shipwreck Museum**, which tells the story of the numerous shipwrecks that dot this treacherous coastline.

Mackinac Island

1

Viewed from an approaching boat, the tree-blanketed rocky limestone outcrop of **MACKINAC ISLAND** (pronounced "Mackinaw"), suddenly thrusting out from the swirling waters, is an unforgettable sight. As you near the harbour, large Victorian houses come into view, dappling the hillsides with white and pastel. On disembarking, you'll see rows of horses and buggies (all motorized transport is banned from the island) and inhale the omnipresent smell of fresh manure. Also ubiquitous on the island is **fudge**, relentlessly marketed as a Mackinac "delicacy" – **Murdick's**, 7363 Main St (ⓦoriginalmurdicksfudge.com), started the trend in 1887.

Mackinac's overcrowded **Main Street** can get irritating, but the island is worth visiting, not least for its ornate architecture, the chance to **cycle** the leisurely **eight-mile loop** (1–2hr) along the coast, and its rich history. French priests briefly established a mission to the Huron here during the winter of 1670–71 before moving to the mainland, and their legacy is preserved at the nineteenth-century **St Anne Catholic Church**, the island's most impressive shrine. In 1779 the British started moving back to the island from Michilimackinac, finally handing it over to the Americans in 1795. **John Jacob Astor** based his fur trade empire here until 1835 (you can visit his buildings on Market St), but the island was already attracting sightseers – since the opening of the **Grand Hotel** in 1887 it's depended almost entirely on the summer tourist trade. Since 1945, Michigan's governors have used the elegant **Governor's Summer Residence** (at the intersection of Huron Rd and Fort St; tours June–Aug Wed 9.30–11.30am; free; 15–20min) to host key events.

Fort Mackinac

7127 Huron Rd • Daily: May–June 9am–5pm, June–Sept 9.30am–7pm, Sept–Oct 9:30am–5pm, Oct 11am–4pm (last entry half hour before closing) • charge • ⓦ mackinacparks.com

To get a feel for the island's history, hike up to the whitewashed stone **Fort Mackinac**, a US Army outpost until 1895. Its ramparts afford a stupendous view of the village and lake below, and all its restored buildings – mostly nineteenth-century clapboard – contain absorbing exhibits on aspects of its past. The oldest is the **Officers' Stone Quarters**, begun by the British founders of the fort in 1780. Your ticket also includes access to several historic properties down in the village (June–Aug only, same hours), such as the **American Fur Co Store** and **Biddle House**, restored to its 1830s appearance.

ARRIVAL, INFORMATION AND GETTING AROUND
MACKINAC ISLAND

By catamaran Star Line (7271 Main St, May–Oct, schedule varies; ⓦmackinacferry.com) and Shepler's Ferry (7451 Lake Shore Dr, late April to Oct, schedule varies; ⓦsheplersferry. com); both companies offer high-speed crossings (15–20min) from the ferry terminal in Mackinaw City, at the end of Central Ave and do not require reservations.

Visitor Centre The state park visitor centre (7274 Main St; daily 9am–5pm; ⓦmackinacisland.org) sells tickets to the

Fort and other attractions.

By bike Numerous bike-rental outfits line Main St (see ⓦbikemackinac.com), offering similar prices, but if you intend to rent for more than half a day, shop around for the best deal.

Horse carriage Tours are running continually (daily 9am–5pm) through the summer (ⓦmict.com). Buy tickets at 7278 Main St, next to the docks.

ACCOMMODATION, EATING AND NIGHTLIFE

Grand Hotel 286 Grand Ave, ⓦgrandhotel.com. The island's majestic behemoth since 1887 and dripping with history, though the cheapest rooms are fairly standard. Sightseers be warned: you will be charged just to set foot in the lobby or stroll the famous 660ft-long porch and gardens. The restaurants are all good, but skip the overpriced lunch buffet, which is poor value and often mobbed by tour groups. Full-board rates only. $$$$

Murray Hotel 7260 Main St, ⓦmymurrayhotel.com. Decorated with plenty of chintz and carefully selected antiques, this hotel offers a large continental breakfast buffet. $$$$

Mustang Lounge 1485 Astor St, ⓦmustang-lounge. com. Popular local watering hole and restaurant built from a 1780s fur trader warehouse. Burgers and other pub favourites served. $$

1

Pink Pony 7221 Main St, ⓦpinkponymackinac.com. This bar and grill offers a fun atmosphere (raucous at times), great food (lake perch, whitefish, steaks), and a stellar view of the harbour. **$$$**

The Upper Peninsula

Michigan was forced to give up the valuable Toledo Strip to Ohio in order to become a state in 1837 – in exchange it received the **Upper Peninsula**, separated from the rest of the state by the **Straits of Mackinac** and considered virtually worthless at the time. Michigan had the last laugh, however – in the 1840s iron ore was discovered in the "UP" (pronounced "You-p"; locals are "Yoopers"), and the region subsequently boomed. Immigrants flooded in – Finns, Croatians and Cornish miners among them, the last introducing **Cornish pasties**, still sold all over northern Michigan. Today it's the great outdoors that provides the allure – the UP is smothered with forest and untamed wilderness, exemplified by the **Pictured Rocks National Lakeshore** and **Isle Royale National Park**, fifty miles offshore. The UP's only real city is **Marquette**, a college town with a quiet buzz that makes a good base for exploration.

Tahquamenon Falls State Park

41382 W Hwy M-123 • Daily 8am–10pm • charge per vehicle • ⓦdnr.state.mi.us

The centrepiece of the densely forested **Tahquamenon Falls State Park**, some seventy miles north of the Straits of Mackinac, is the Tahquamenon River and its waterfalls. The spectacular **Upper Falls** is a mini Niagara, some 200ft across with a 50ft drop. Four miles downstream are the **Lower Falls**, a series of five smaller but beautiful cascades – you can rent rowboats to reach the island in the centre of the falls (late May to mid-Oct; charge per person or per boat; cash only).

Pictured Rocks National Lakeshore

N8391 Sand Point Rd, Munising • Open 24hr year-round • Free entry • ⓦnps.gov/piro

Covering a 42-mile stretch of Lake Superior, the **Pictured Rocks National Lakeshore** offers a splendid array of multicoloured cliffs, rolling dunes and secluded sandy beaches. Over the millennia rain, wind, ice and sun have carved and gouged arches, columns and caves into the face of the lakeshore, all stained different hues. The best way to see the cliffs is by **boat** (see page 104). Hwy-58 runs along the edge of the park from the small village of **Grand Marais** to the summer boom town of **Munising**, but there are only a few sights on route, notably the **Log Slide** (a large dune) and **Miners Castle**, a jagged column of rock twelve miles east of Munising. With more time it's worth **hiking the trails** that run from Hwy-58 out to the shoreline, notably the loop to Chapel Falls and Chapel Beach and the trail to **Au Sable Light Station** (Burt Township, tours mid-June to Sept Wed–Sun 11am-5pm; charge). For an overview of the region's history, Native American culture and ecology, stop by the **Pictured Rocks Interpretive Center** in Munising (100 W Munising Ave; daily 10am–6pm; free; ⓦpuremichigan. org/property/picturedrocksinterpretivecenter).

INFORMATION AND TOURS

Visitor centres Munising Falls Visitor Center, 1505 Sand Point Rd (late May–Oct daily 9am–5pm, closed Nov–April; ☏906 387 3700) provides access to Munising Falls via a paved trail; Grand Sable Visitor Center, E21090 County Road H58, Seney (late May to Sept daily 9am–5pm; ⓦnps.org).

Tours Pictured Rocks Cruises offers a 2hr 30min narrated tour that leaves from the Munising City Dock, 100 City Park

PICTURED ROCKS NATIONAL LAKESHORE

Drive (late May to late Oct 1–7 trips daily; ⓦpicturedrocks. com). Glass Bottom Shipwreck Tours, farther along the lake at 1204 Commercial St, gives 2hr narrated cruises with surprisingly clear views of two shipwrecks – one intact (late May to early Oct 2–6 trips daily; ⓦshipwrecktours. com). Paddling Michigan arranges kayaking tours for 2hr (ⓦpaddlingmichigan.com)

ACCOMMODATION AND EATING

★**Falling Rocks Café & Bookstore** 104 E Munising Ave, Munising, ⓦfallingrockcafe.com. Cosy spot for quality coffee, pastries, light meals (smoked whitefish), local Jilbert Dairy ice cream, and books, with live music from local musicians Sat 7pm. Free wi-fi. Open daily from April-October. $$

Muldoon's Pasties & Gifts 1246 Hwy-28, Munising ☎ 906 387 5880, ⊛ muldoonspasties.com. Traditional (potato, ground beef, onion, rutabaga and carrot), chicken and vegetarian Cornish pasties made fresh every day. Open daily May-Oct. $

Terrace Motel 420 Prospect St, Munising, ⊛ exploringthenorth.com/terrace. Basic motel on the edge of downtown Munising, offering great value, with clean rooms, common room with a pool table and small sauna. Patchy but free wi-fi and cable TV. Open May-October. $$$

Marquette

Forty miles west of Munising is the unofficial capital of the UP, the low-key college town of **MARQUETTE**. Cafés and independent shops line the main drag, Washington Street, which runs down to Lake Superior, but there's not a lot in the way of traditional sights other than **St Peter Cathedral**, 311 W Baraga Ave, an incongruously grand Catholic edifice rebuilt after a fire in 1935. At 300 N Lakeshore Blvd, the **Marquette Maritime Museum & Lighthouse** (mid-May to mid-Oct, Tues–Sun 11am–4pm; charge, plus extra for lighthouse tour; ⊛ mqtmaritimemuseum.com) has exhibits on the fishing and freighting industries, as well as a video about the mysterious wrecking of the *Edmund Fitzgerald* in 1975. There are also tours of the adjacent Marquette Harbor Lighthouse, constructed in 1866.

ACCOMMODATION, EATING AND DRINKING   MARQUETTE

Donckers 137 W Washington St, ⊛ donckersonline. com. Chocolate shop and old-fashioned soda fountain downstairs, with diner upstairs, sporting a blend of retro 1950s and rustic UP style. Excellent breakfasts and pastries, plus free wi-fi. $$

Landmark Inn 230 N Front St, ⊛ thelandmarkinn.com. Rooms overlooking the lake are the real highlight here and the atmosphere is quite peaceful. Some of the rooms have modest historic importance, having played host to Amelia

Earhart and Abbott and Costello, among others. $$$

Ore Dock Brewing Co 114 W Spring St, ⊛ ore-dock. com. High-quality microbrewery, with live music Thurs–Sat, mostly local folk, jazz and rock bands. $$

Vierling Restaurant & Marquette Harbor Brewery 119 S Front St, ☎ 906 228 3533. Restaurant that specializes in Lake Superior whitefish and draught beers from Marquette Harbor Brewing (famed for its blueberry wheat beer). $$

Houghton and the Keweenaw Peninsula

The northernmost point in the UP offers remote, scenic drives, historic towns and innovative microbreweries. Originally founded as a copper mining town, the area still pays homage to its roots with dozens of designated historic sites where you can tour copper mines, lighthouses, and former mining towns dating as far back as 1846. Pass through hundreds of heritage sites and nature preserves, and catch a ferry to Isle Royale National Park from Houghton, the park headquarters for Isle Royale.

ACCOMODATION, EATING AND DRINKING

Brickside Brewery Copper Harbor, ⊛ bricksidebrewery. com. A small, local, family owned brewpub offering growlers to go and a small, rotating selection of beers brewed in house. $

Eagle Harbor Inn 460 W. North St, Eagle Harbor, ⊛ eagleharborinnmi.com. A short walk away from the beach, Eagle Harbor Lighthouse, and countless scenic hiking

trails, this inn offers quality dining and comfortable lodging for a reasonable price. $$

Keweenaw Brewing Company 408 Shelden Avenue, Houghton, ⊛ kbc.beer. Located in the centre of Downtown Houghton on the north side of US-41, their tap room features rotating beers on tap, home brewed birch, root or ginger beet, and several 'core' ales. $$

Isle Royale National Park

Open mid-April to Oct • Entry charge person per day

The 45-mile sliver of **Isle Royale National Park**, fifty miles out in Lake Superior, is geographically and culturally very, very far from Detroit. All cars are banned and, instead of freeways, 166 miles of hiking trails lead past windswept trees, swampy lakes, paddling loons and grazing moose. Aside from other outdoors types (fewer than 15,000 visitors come each year), the only traces of human life you're likely to see are ancient mineworks, possibly two millennia old, shacks left behind by commercial fishermen in the 1940s, and a few lighthouses and park buildings. Hiking, canoeing, fishing and scuba-diving among shipwrecks are the principal leisure activities.

Before you leave the mainland, visit the park headquarters in **Houghton** for advice on water purity, mosquitoes and temperatures that can drop well below freezing even in summer. Forget mobile phone or wi-fi service here.

ARRIVAL, INFORMATION AND ACCOMMODATION   ISLE ROYALE NATIONAL PARK

By ferry Ferries to Isle Royale leave from Copper Harbor (60 5th St; 3hr 45min; ⍵ isleroyale.com), the Houghton Visitor Center (6hr; ⍵ nps.gov/isro) and Grand Portage, Minnesota (402 Upper Road; 2hr; ⍵ grand-isle-royale.com).

By plane You can hop over by plane with Isle Royale Seaplanes from Hancock Portage Canal Seaplane Base, 21125 Royce Road, Hancock (30–45min; ⍵ isleroyaleseaplanes.com), or Cook County Airport, 123 Airport Road, Grand Marais, Minnesota.

Visitor centres Houghton Visitor Centre, 800 E Lakeshore Drive, Houghton (June to mid-Sept Mon–Fri 8am–6pm, Sat

10am–6pm; mid-Sept to May Mon–Fri 8am–4pm; ☏ 906 482 0984, ⍵ nps.gov/isro). Two small centres operate on the island itself, at Rock Harbor and at Windigo, usually open July & Aug only (daily 8am–6pm).

Rock Harbor Lodge ⍵ rockharborlodge.com. The only formal accommodation in the park features rooms with gorgeous views of the lake, along with Adirondack chairs that are perfect for relaxing in. The management also rents basic Windigo Camper Cabins some 45 miles from the lodge. Limited wi-fi in the lobby only. June to early Sept. Doubles & cottages $$$$, cabins $$

Wisconsin

America's self-proclaimed "Dairyland", **WISCONSIN** is perhaps one of the most intriguing destinations in the Midwest. While cheese is certainly a major product here – the Cheesehead Hat, designed by a Milwaukee Braves fan in 1987 and now a symbol of the state, is loved and loathed in equal measure – it's more than just one giant pasture. Beyond the rolling farmlands, red barns and silvery silos lie endless pine forests, some fifteen thousand sky-blue lakes, postcard-pretty valleys and dramatic bluffs. The state, whose Ojibwe name means "gathering of the waters", is bordered by Lake Michigan to the east, Lake Superior in the north and, to the west, the Mississippi and St Croix rivers, with the green **Wisconsin River Valley** beloved of Frank Lloyd Wright slicing through the middle. The state's human history is similarly diverse; Wisconsiners have invented the modern typewriter (1868), ice cream sundaes (1881) and the snowmobile (1924), and elected the nation's first Socialist mayor (1910). It's the home of Harley motorbikes, the Green Bay Packers and Les Paul guitars, and is the most German state in the union – almost every town once had a brewery. Today it remains a snowmobiling paradise, while Wisconsin's farm-to-table movement is one of the richest in the country, with wonderful farmers' markets and a dynamic culinary scene.

Milwaukee

Perched on Lake Michigan just ninety miles north of Chicago, **MILWAUKEE** is the largest city in Wisconsin, best known for its long history of **beer-making**, **Harley-Davidson** motorbikes and the stunning Calatrava-designed **Milwaukee Art Museum**. In recent years the city has been experiencing something of a renaissance, with revitalized downtown areas and a flourishing local food and drink scene – this despite some of its north side neighbourhoods still struggling with high crime and poverty.

Downtown Milwaukee is split north to south by the Milwaukee River and two-mile long **RiverWalk**, lined with restaurants and artwork (including the ever popular **Bronze Fonz**, based on the character from sitcom *Happy Days*, set in 1950s Milwaukee). **East Town**, the main business district, contains the ornate **Pabst Theatre** and **Milwaukee**

MILWAUKEE'S FESTIVALS

The eleven-day **Summerfest** (late June to early July; Ⓦ summerfest.com) is an extravaganza of live music and entertainment held in Henry Maier Festival Park. The 2019 line-up included Jason Aldean, Bon Iver, Lionel Richie, Jennifer Lopez, the Killers and Lil' Wayne. The **Wisconsin State Fair** (early Aug; Ⓦ wistatefair.com) takes place in West Allis, seven miles west of downtown Milwaukee, and it features everything from country music stars to a vast range of deep-fried culinary offerings.

City Hall, built in a lavish Flemish Renaissance Revival style in 1895 (check out the spectacular atrium). **West Town**, the old shopping district centred on Wisconsin Avenue, is also slowly being redeveloped, and merges into the **Marquette University** campus, noted for its **St Joan of Arc Chapel** (1421 W Wisconsic Ave; Mon–Sat 10am–4pm, Sun noon–4pm; free), originally built in France in the fifteenth century and reconstructed here in 1966. Just south of I-794 from downtown, the **Historic Third Ward** is an old warehouse district, now a gentrified zone of boutiques, loft apartments, bars and restaurants.

Milwaukee Art Museum

700 N Art Museum Drive • Fri–Sun 10am–5pm, Thurs till 8pm (open Mon in summer) • charge • Ⓦ mam.org

Overlooking Lake Michigan, the **Milwaukee Art Museum** is dominated by Santiago Calatrava's spectacular Quadracci Pavilion, its white, wing-like fins flapping up and down three times each day (noon & 5pm) to reduce heat gain and glare. Inside, the Windhover Hall is a futuristic, soaring space with a 90ft glass ceiling. Highlights of the permanent collection include one of the largest caches of work by **Georgia O'Keefe** (usually on Level 2) and an excellent array of modern and contemporary paintings, including Warhol, Rothko and Chuck Close. Other gems are scattered throughout the museum, such as Zurbarán's haunting *St Francis in His Tomb*, Picasso's hopeful *The Cock of the Liberation* and a handful of Impressionist works.

Discovery World

500 N Harbor Drive • Wed–Sun 9am–4pm • charge, discount for ages 3–17 • Ⓦ discoveryworld.org

Adjacent to the art museum, **Discovery World** is Milwaukee's family-friendly attraction, a hands-on science museum with interactive exhibits, aquarium (with a Lake Michigan tank), movie theatre and trips on a tall ship (late May to mid-Oct; additional charge; 2hr).

Milwaukee Public Museum

800 W Wells St • Wed–Mon 10am–5pm • charge • Ⓦ mpm.edu

The vast **Milwaukee Public Museum** chronicles the intertwined histories and mysteries of the earth, nature and humankind through dioramas such as "A Sense of Wonder" and a trip back in time (presented via old storefronts) to nineteenth-century Milwaukee. There's also a live butterfly habitat, a huge section on Native Americans (and the remaining tribes in Wisconsin) and some artefacts dug up from the ancient Mississippian culture settlement of Aztalan (fifty miles west). The **Dome Theater** (extra charge) with its giant, wraparound screen, shows films on the solar system's weather and the world of dinosaurs.

Pabst Mansion

2000 W Wisconsin Ave • Tours (1hr 15min) on the hour Mon–Sat 10am–3pm, Sun 11am–3pm • charge • Ⓦ pabstmansion.com • Bus #30

Patriarch of one of Milwaukee's "Big Four" breweries (the others being Schlitz, Miller and Blatz), Frederick Pabst had the lavish **Pabst Mansion** built in 1893. It's an exquisite example of ornate Flemish Renaissance architecture, heavily ornamented with oak, beech and cherry wood fixtures and plenty of Teutonic features – like all Milwaukee's

1

WISCONSIN: CHEESE, FISH FRIES AND CRAFT BREWS

Wisconsin has always been a rich farming region and today the artisan food movement is booming here. On the road you are likely to come across family-owned cheese producers, farmers' markets, microbreweries and wineries.

CHEESE

Cheddar is especially good in Wisconsin; look for Carr Valley Cheese (Ⓦcarrvalleycheese.com), which also produces the goat's cheese/chocolate blend Cocoa Cardona. Open since 1931, Baumgartner's Cheese Store & Tavern (1023 16th Ave; Ⓦbaumgartnercheese.com) in Monroe is known for its Limburger cheese and its mural-smothered bar, while Bleu Mont Dairy Farm (Ⓣ608 219 0366, can also be found at Dane County Farmer's Market in Madison) in Blue Mounds produces cave-aged cheddar with a cult-like following. One must-try snack sold everywhere in Wisconsin – fried cheese curds.

FISH FRIES AND SUPPER CLUBS

Wisconsin's great food traditions come together at supper clubs and fish fries. There are some three hundred supper clubs scattered across rural Wisconsin: think dim lighting, hand-muddled Old-Fashioned cocktails, Frank Sinatra tunes playing, huge steaks and relish trays. The Buckhorn Supper Club (11802 N Charley Bluff Rd; Ⓦthebuckhorn.net) on Lake Koshkonong in Milton is a classic example. Friday-night fish fries take place everywhere, typically comprising Lake Superior whitefish served with potato pancakes, brats, cheese curds and maybe a few Bloody Marys. A good place to try one is the Little Bohemia Lodge (142 US-51; Ⓦlittlebohemialodge.com) in Manitowish Waters, scene of an infamous Dillinger shoot-out in 1934.

BEER

Wisconsin brewers rarely export their best beers beyond the state. New Glarus Brewing (2400 WI-69; Ⓦnewglarusbrewing.com), in the Swiss-themed village of New Glarus, is locally celebrated for its Spotted Cow (a fruity ale) and Wisconsin Belgian Red, while Wisconsin Brewing (1079 American Way; Ⓦwisconsinbrewingcompany.com) in Verona is lauded for its IPAs. Milwaukee is another brewing hotspot (see page 111). Real connoisseurs opt for the local stouts (porters); Tyranena Brewing Company (1025 Owen St; Ⓦtyranena.com) in Lake Mills ages porters in old bourbon barrels, while Central Waters Brewing Co. (351 Allen St; Ⓦcentralwaters.com) in Amherst makes the robust and refreshing Mudpuppy Porter.

---

founding brewers, Pabst was born in Germany. Tours (the only way to visit) provide illuminating background on Pabst and his heirs, some of whom still live in Milwaukee (Pabst itself stopped brewing in 1996).

Best Place at the Historic Pabst Brewery

917 W Juneau Ave · **Tours** Mon noon, 2pm & 4pm; Thurs 2pm & 4pm; Fri 12pm, 1pm, 2pm, 3pm & 4pm; Sat 11am, 12pm, 1pm, 2pm 3pm &4pm; & Sun noon, 11am, 1pm & 3pm · charge · **Blue Ribbon Hall** open Mon 11am–4pm, Thurs 1pm–5pm, Fri 11am–6pm, Sat 10.30am–6pm, Sun 10:30am-4pm · Ⓦ bestplacemilwaukee.com

Remnants of the now shuttered Pabst Brewery have been preserved within the **Best Place at the Historic Pabst Brewery**, a clutch of historic structures that includes the ornate 1940s **Blue Ribbon Hall** (where beer is still served). The enthusiastic tours take in the office of "Captain" Pabst himself and his elegant 1880 corporate headquarters, and include a free beer.

Harley-Davidson Museum

400 W Canal St · Thurs-Mon 10am–5pm · charge · Ⓦ harley-davidson.com · Bus #80 or 15min walk south of Wisconsin Ave

Dedicated to the legendary motorbike company founded here by William S. Harley and Arthur Davidson in 1903, the **Harley-Davidson Museum** features over 450 vintage bikes, displayed in stylish modern premises just south of the river. Highlights include the oldest Harley ("Serial no. 1"), an ornate bike owned by Elvis and the monster-sized "King Kong". The Engine Room shows how the Harley engine works, while company history is chronicled with videos and memorabilia – there's even a small section on bike gangs such as the Hell's Angels, and famous bikes used in the movies. Hardcore fans should check out **Bike Nights** (Thurs in May-Aug) and the **Milwaukee Rally** in September.

ARRIVAL AND DEPARTURE　　　　　　　　　　　　MILWAUKEE

By plane Mitchell Airport (ⓦ mitchellairport.com), 8 miles south of downtown, is connected to the city centre by bus #80, and by shared-ride van service. Taxis, Uber and Lyft are also available.

By train Amtrak uses the Milwaukee Intermodal Station at 433 W St Paul Ave.
Destinations Chicago (7 daily; 1hr 40min).

By bus Greyhound (ⓦ greyhound.com), Badger Bus (ⓦ badgerbus.com), Lamers (ⓦ golamers.com), MegaBus (ⓦ megabus.com) and Coach USA (ⓦ coachusa.com) buses operate out of the Intermodal Station.
Destinations Chicago (9 daily; 1hr 45min–2hr); Green Bay (2 daily; 2hr 15min); Madison (11 daily with Badger and MegaBus; 1hr 35min); Minneapolis/St Paul (9 daily; 6hr–9hr).

GETTING AROUND AND INFORMATION

By bus Getting around Milwaukee is easy and inexpensive via the extensive bus system; use cash (exact fare) or stored-value cards (ⓦ ridemcts.com).

The Hop Streetcar The M-Line street tram runs downtown from the Intermodal Station to the Historic Third Ward, City Hall, Cathedral Square and Burns Common near the lake every 15–20min (ⓦ thehopmke.com).

By bike The Bublr Bikes (ⓦ bublrbikes.com) bike-share programme charges by 24hr time linit, or a thirty-day Bublr Pass allows unlimited 1hr rides.

Visitor centre 400 W Wisconsin Ave, in the Wisconsin Center (Mon–Fri 11am–2pm, summer also Sat & Sun 11am–2pm; ☎ 414 273 7222, ⓦ visitmilwaukee.org).

ACCOMMODATION

★ **The Brewhouse Inn & Suites** 1215 N 10th St, ⓦ brewhousesuites.com. For beer aficionados, this hotel is truly a dream come true. Located in the historic Pabst Brewery, it's all a bit steampunk – they've kept the six brew kettles on hand as decorative elements. The rooms are very comfortable, and there's an enormous stained-glass window etched with a picture of King Gambrinus, the patron saint of beer. $$$$

★ **Brumder Mansion Bed & Breakfast** 3046 W Wisconsin Ave, ⓦ milwaukeemansion.com. Fabulously decorated, enormous B&B with an in-house theatre, just minutes from downtown. Rooms include antiques, marble, rich draperies and stained glass. $$$

★ **Hotel Metro, Autograph Collection** 411 E Madison St, ⓦ hotelmetro.com. This retro Art Deco hotel has an historic feeling with a modern twist. Updated and eco-friendly, it's worth the extra cash for the fireplace and jacuzzi that sit in the centre of the room. $$$$

The Pfister Hotel 424 E Wisconsin Ave, ⓦ thepfisterhotel.com. This 1893 hotel sits nestled like a Victorian Grande Dame in the heart of downtown. Replenish yourself in the spa or visit the 23rd-floor martini lounge. There is even a world-class Victorian art collection. Rack rates are pricey, but often you can grab a special package for considerably less. $$$$

EATING AND DRINKING

One tradition not be missed in Milwaukee is the legendary Friday-night fish fries held all over the place, though the fish (typically cod and haddock) is often flown in these days (perch fishing is banned commercially in Lake Michigan). For picnics, visit Old World 3rd Street for Usinger's Famous Sausage (no.1030; ⓦ usinger.com) and the Wisconsin Cheese Mart (215 W Highland Ave; ⓦ wisconsincheesemart. com). The premier nightlife areas in downtown lie north of State Street on either side of the river (on Water St and Old World 3rd St), and in the Historic Third Ward. Walker's Point, on the southern edge of downtown, is also an up-and-coming area, with a burgeoning LGBTQ scene. As befits "Beer City", Milwaukee boasts a booming craft-beer culture, but it's also worth seeking its old-fashioned corner bars (often clapboard and shingle homes) and German-style beer gardens (open May–Oct).

Likewise Coffee 232 E Erie St, ⓦ likewise.com. Hipster-chic café serving high-quality, Fairtrade roasts, enhanced by high ceilings and free sparkling water. $$

Mader's 1041 N Old World 3rd St, ⓦ madersrestaurant. com. This German-themed restaurant is the ultimate in Teutonic kitsch, with a faux castle facade and Bavarian interior festooned with medieval suits of armour. Famed for its pork shank and amazing Sunday brunch buffet (11am–2pm). $$$

1

Milwaukee Ale House 233 N Water St, Ⓦ ale-house. com. Milwaukee's best old-style brewpub serves filling food and its own beer, such as the fine Sheepshead Stout. $\overline{\overline{55}}$

★ **Milwaukee Public Market** 400 N Water St, Ⓦ milwaukeepublicmarket.org. Modern food hall crammed with local vendors (of mostly prepared artisanal foods, not raw ingredients). Mon–Sat 10am–8pm, Sun 10am–6pm.

★ **Old German Beer Hall** 1009 N Doctor M.L.K. Jr Dr, Ⓦ oldgermanbeerhall.com. This Bavarian-style favourite is distinguished by its excellent hot pretzels, sausages and a charming game in the back room that involves pounding nails into a massive tree stump. $\overline{\overline{55}}$

★ **Sanford Restaurant** 1547 N Jackson St, Ⓦ sanford restaurant.com. This former grocery store is now a plush, gourmet dining experience with a seasonal, locally sourced menu that might include anything from chargrilled loin of elk to fried milkweed blossoms. $\overline{\overline{5555}}$

Von Trier 2235 N Farwell Ave, Ⓦ vontriers.com. A beer hall wuth Black Forest decor (it has the original elk chandelier from the Pabst Mansion) and lots of imported beers – the Weises is a house specialty. $\overline{\overline{55}}$

Madison

The capital of Wisconsin, **MADISON** is a bastion of progressive politics and culture, its splendid setting on an isthmus between two lakes and the **University of Wisconsin** (UW) attracts students from all over the world. Today this stimulating, youthful metropolis is home to a clutch of compelling museums, great restaurants and a student-fuelled nightlife scene. Forty miles west, and an easy day-trip from Madison, lie two architectural gems; Frank Lloyd Wright's masterful **Taliesin**, and the utterly weird **House on the Rock**.

Wisconsin State Capitol

2 E Main St • Mon–Fri 8am–6pm, Sat & Sun 8am–4pm, free tours hourly • Ⓦ tours.wisconsin.gov

Downtown is neatly laid out between lakes Mendota and Monona, with the towering **State Capitol** sitting on a hill at its centre, surrounded by the shady trees, lawns and park benches of **Capitol Square**. Completed in 1917 and lavishly decorated with marble and giant murals, the Capitol's huge granite dome rises 284ft, topped by a gilded bronze statue of "Wisconsin" by Daniel Chester French. An **observation deck** and small **museum** (summer only; Mon–Fri 9am–5pm; Sat 9am–3.45pm, Sun noon–3.45pm; free) provides panoramic views of the city.

Capitol Square museums

On the north side of Capitol Square, at 30 N Carroll St, the multi-storey **Wisconsin Historical Museum** (Thurs–Sat 11am–3pm; free, suggested donation; Ⓦ historicalmuseum. wisconsinhistory.org) chronicles state history with especially absorbing sections on local Native American cultures such as the Ojibwe and Ho-Chunks, and controversial political leaders such as "Fighting Bob" La Follette. Across the street, at 30 W Mifflin St, the **Wisconsin Veterans Museum** (Tues–Sat 10am–5pm; April–Sept also Sun noon–4pm; free; Ⓦ wisvetsmuseum.com) has detailed displays on every major US conflict since the Civil War, with special attention to the contribution of Wisconsin citizens.

Monona Terrace Community and Convention Center

1 John Nolen Drive • Open daily 8am-5pm; tours available on select dates and times • charge • Ⓦ mononaterrace.com

The lakeside **Monona Terrace Community and Convention Center**, a few blocks south of the Capitol, is a wonderful example of **Frank Lloyd Wright**'s grand vision. Surprisingly intimate and full of architectural detail, the Center, with its curves, arches and domes, was only completed in 1997. Enjoy the views from the *Lake Vista Café* on the roof.

University of Wisconsin-Madison

A welcoming eight-block-long pedestrian mall lined with restaurants, cafés, bars and stores, **State Street** links the Capitol with the attractive central campus of the **University of Wisconsin-Madison** (Ⓦ wisc.edu). The university's **Chazen Museum of Art**, 800 University Ave, is worth a look (Mon-Fri 10am–7pm, Sat & Sun 11am–5pm; free;

BEST OF THE BREWERY TOURS

The only major brewer still operating in Milwaukee is Miller (which combined with Molson to form MillerCoors in 2007), but the city's microbreweries have been growing rapidly since the 1980s.

Lakefront Brewery 1872 N Commerce St, ⓦ lakefrontbrewery.com. Founded in 1987; tours (45min) include two 16oz pours of beer (and souvenir pint glass). Also holds a popular fish fry on Fridays (4–9pm), accompanied by live polka (get here early). Tours Mon–Thurs noon–8pm, Fri noon-4pm, Sat 11am–8pm, Sun noon–4pm.

MillerCoors 4251 W State St, ⓦ millercoors.com. One-hour tours of the legendary brewery, including the underground caves where Frederick Miller originally cooled his beers, and a few samples in the Bavarian-style *Miller Inn*. Temporarily closed due to COVID-19.

Sprecher Brewing 701 W Glendale Ave, Glendale, ⓦ sprecherbrewery.com. Famed for its root beer and sodas as much as its beers. Tours include the brewhouse, lager cellar and Bavarian murals on the bottling room wall; four beer samples and unlimited soda included. Tours every on the hour, Wed–Fri 2pm-5pm, Sat noon-5pm, Sun noon, noon-2pm.

ⓦ chazen.wisc.edu), especially strong in Russian Social Realist art, Japanese prints and ceramics, the drawings and sculptures of Alexander Calder, John Steuart Curry and Wisconsin painters John Wilde and Sylvia Fein. Look out also for Vasari's *Adoration of the Shepherds* and *Critical Success*, a sardonic Jean Cocteau drawing of a bull beheading a matador.

The **Memorial Union**, 800 Langdon St, contains a pub, *Der Rathskeller*, with tables strewn beneath huge, vaulted ceilings and live music most nights. Outside, the spacious **UW Terrace** offers beautiful sunset views over Lake Mendota and an intimate bar and music venue in the warmer months, when students sunbathe on the piers jutting into the lake. The **Badger Bash**, a huge celebration involving the acclaimed UW Marching Band, is held here before every football home game (the **Wisconsin Badgers** play at nearby Camp Randall Stadium).

First Unitarian Society

900 University Bay Drive • Mon-Fri 10am-2pm; Tours: May & Sept Mon–Fri 10am; June–Aug Mon–Fri 10am & 2.30pm; Sun 10.10am year-round • charge; book online; free on Sun • ⓦ fusmadison.org/welcome/meeting-house/tours

Completed in 1951, the innovative copper-and-glass **Unitarian Meeting House**, three miles west of the Capitol, was designed by Frank Lloyd Wright (Wright's parents were founding members of the church, which is still an active Unitarian congregation). Its sweeping, dramatically curved ceiling and triangle motif are definitely worth the drive or bike ride out here.

ARRIVAL AND INFORMATION   MADISON

By bus Greyhound buses drop off/pick up in front of the Phillips 66 gas station, 4 Collins Ct (just off I-90), an inconvenient seven miles from downtown. Buses run to/ from Milwaukee (2 daily; 1hr 30min), Chicago (1 daily; 3hr 50min) and Minneapolis (2 daily; 5hr 15min–5hr 50min).

Badger Coaches makes frequent trips daily to Milwaukee from various locations in downtown (ⓦ badgerbus.com).
Visitor centre 452 State St (Wed-Sun 11am–5pm; ☏ 608 262 4636, ⓦ visitmadison.com).

ACCOMMODATION

Madison Concourse Hotel 1 W Dayton St, ⓦ concoursehotel.com. The city's premier luxury hotel offers spacious, well-appointed rooms just steps from State Street. Parking additional cost. $$$$

Mansion Hill Inn 424 Pinckney St, ⓦ mansionhillinn. com. The hosts here provide a relaxed setting within a restored 1857 Romanesque Revival mansion located close to the campus. $$$$

EATING AND DRINKING

Madison has one of the strongest farm-to-table dining and craft beer scenes in the country. Its Dane County Farmers'

Market (ⓦ dcfm.org) is the largest in the nation (mid-April to mid-Nov: Capitol Square Sat 8am–noon; Jan-April:

Garver Feed Mill 3241 Garver Green Sat 8am-12pm; and at 200 Block Martin Luther King, Jr Blvd Wed 8.30am–1.45pm).

Babcock Hall Dairy Store 1605 Linden Drive, ⓦ babcockhalldairystore.wisc.edu. The best ice cream in town served on the UW campus. $

★ **Graze Restaurant** 1 S Pinckney St Floor 2, ⓦ grazemadison.com. The locally sourced dishes here include whitefish cakes, designer mac and cheese and a beet and walnut burger. $$

★ **Marigold Kitchen** 118 S Pinckney St, ⓦ marigoldkitchen.com. Charming, sunny spot serving delicious, creative breakfast and lunch dishes – such as challah French toast and chilli poached eggs – focusing on local, organic ingredients. $$

★ **The Old Fashioned** 23 N Pinckney St, ⓦ theoldfashioned.com. Named for the state's signature brandy cocktail, this gastropub (with a massive range of Wisconsin craft beers) serves locally-sourced Wisconsin food, such as fried cheese curds, walleye and perch, brats and a killer version of its eponymous cocktail. $$$

Old Sugar Distillery 931 E Main St #8, ⓦ oldsugardistillery.com. Fashionable warehouse pub and distillery of small-batch whiskey, rum, ouzo, brandy and honey liquor, served neat or in a number of creative cocktails. $$

Taliesin

5481 County Rd C (off Hwy-23), Spring Green • CURRENTLY CLOSED TO THE PUBLIC, plans to reopen June 2022; **Visitor centre** May–Oct daily 9am–5.30pm; Nov–April Fri–Sun 10am–4.30pm • **Highlights tour** May–Oct daily 10.15am, 1.45pm & 3.15pm • (discount for Hillside Studio only) • **House tour** May–Oct daily 11am, noon & 3pm; April & Nov Fri–Sun 11am & 2pm • ⓦ taliesinpreservation.org

Frank Lloyd Wright's final home and one of his masterpieces, **Taliesin** is a pricey but essential highlight for fans of architecture or American history. The 600-acre estate comprises five Lloyd Wright structures, the most important of which is Taliesin itself, completed in 1911 and a stunning example of the **Prairie School**. Many of Wright's most famous buildings were designed in the studio here (including the Guggenheim Museum). Nearby, the **Hillside Home School** was completed by Wright in 1902, also in the Prairie School style, and today remains a prestigious postgraduate college for architects. Illuminating **tours** (the only way to visit the site) leave from the **Frank Lloyd Wright Visitor Center**, which was designed by Wright in 1953 as a restaurant; it now features a café and a bookstore.

Tours add context to the architecture but also the traumatic events that took place here. Lloyd Wright left Chicago (see page 59) in 1909, abandoning his family for his mistress Mamah Cheney (the wife of a client). They eventually moved to the Wisconsin River valley three miles south of **Spring Green**, the home of his mother's Welsh family, the Lloyd-Joneses. Lloyd Wright was born in nearby Richland Center, and named his new home Taliesin in homage to his Welsh roots. Tragically, Mamah was murdered at the house by a deranged servant in 1914 (along with her two children by her former husband, and four others), and the house was burned down. A heartbroken Wright (who was in Chicago during the attack) rebuilt, but the house burned again in 1925 (this time by accident). He again rebuilt, "Taliesin III" remaining his primary residence (with third wife Olgivanna) until he died in 1959.

House on the Rock

5754 WI-23 • Mid-March to mid-May & mid-Oct to Dec Thurs–Mon 9am–5pm; mid-May to mid-Oct daily 9am–5pm; last entry at 4pm • chares per section or for all three; see website for open days mid-Nov to mid-March • ⓦ thehouseontherock.com

From 1945 onward, Alex Jordan built the whimsical **House on the Rock**, six miles south of Taliesin on Hwy-23, on and out of a natural, 60ft, chimney-like rock – for no discernible reason. He certainly never lived in it, nor did he intend it to become Wisconsin's number-one tourist attraction. The first section of this multilevel series of furnished nooks and chambers includes the Asian Garden, the Infinity Room (which juts out across the valley for 218ft) and the Original House, whose interior design is Frank Lloyd Wright meets *The Flintstones*. The second section plays host to a chaotic tribute to aviation (with hundreds of model planes), "Music of Yesterday" (with antique music machines) and one of the world's largest fireplaces. The third section has a massive circus display, Japanese Garden and the world's **largest carousel**. Taken as one riotous and bizarre experience, the net effect is overwhelming and disorienting, but kitsch fun.

Apostle Islands National Lakeshore

Bayfield Visitor Center and Headquarters, 415 Washington Avenue, Bayfield, WI • Open daily, with some seasonal closures due to unsafe ice conditions • free park entry, charges apply for boats, cruises, rentals, etc. • ⓦ nps.gov/apis

Considered the jewels of Lake Superior, the northernmost mainland point in the state of Wisconsin features 12 miles of coastline and an archipelago of 21 small islands spread over 700 square miles of water. From Meyers Beach on the mainland, you can kayak or walk across the frozen Lake Superior (depending on the season). Most of the park is only accessible by boat, so check out the cruise schedules offered through the visitor centre if planning an excursion. Each island offers its own contributions to the region's history and indigenous culture, as well as access to sea caves, breathtaking cliffs, and more historic lighthouses than any other national park.

Minnesota

Welcome to **MINNESOTA**, America's "Land o' Lakes" (there are actually 11,842, to be precise), kayaking and cycling paradise, and the source of the Mississippi. It's a state characterized by massive wilderness reserves such as the Superior and Chippewa national forests, and 95 percent of the population lives within ten minutes of one of those lakes – the very name Minnesota is a Sioux word meaning "land of sky-tinted water" and even water skiing was invented here (on Lake Pepin) in 1922. Freshwater walleye fish and wild rice (a traditional Ojibwe food) are sold everywhere.

Today more than half of all Minnesotans live around the Twin Cities of **Minneapolis** and **St Paul**, the Midwest's great civic double act for their combined cultural, recreational and business opportunities. Smaller cities include the northern shipping port of **Duluth**, the gateway to **Lake Superior** and the remote waterfalls and forests of the **North Shore Scenic Drive**.

Minneapolis

With a centre of gleaming skyscrapers towering over the Mississippi, **MINNEAPOLIS** is the Midwest's most liveable city, a bike-friendly, modern metropolis blessed with a huge network of parks, rivers and the "Chain of Lakes", an excellent light-rail network and

---

PRINCE OF PAISLEY PARK

One of the most influential musicians of all time, **Prince** Rogers Nelson was born in 1958 in Minneapolis, a city he adored and remained close to his whole life. He released his debut album *For You* in 1978, beginning a career that was honoured by an Oscar (for *Purple Rain* in 1985), two Brit Awards, a Golden Globe and seven Grammies. **Paisley Park Studios** was completed in 1988, ostensibly as a base for the singer's label, Paisley Park Records, but it came to be Prince's permanent home, an elaborately furnished retreat where he continued to make music and where he often held parties for his neighbours. Prince died here suddenly in 2016 (of an accidental drug overdose), sending much of Minneapolis into a period of mourning; at **First Avenue**, the club where Prince filmed *Purple Rain*, fans began leaving floral tributes, and a makeshift memorial grew outside Paisley Park in the suburb of Chanhassen. Tours (daily 9am–9pm, book well in advance) of Paisley Park, 7801 Audubon Rd, Chanhassen, began in October 2016 (buy tickets at ⓦ officialpaisleypark.com).

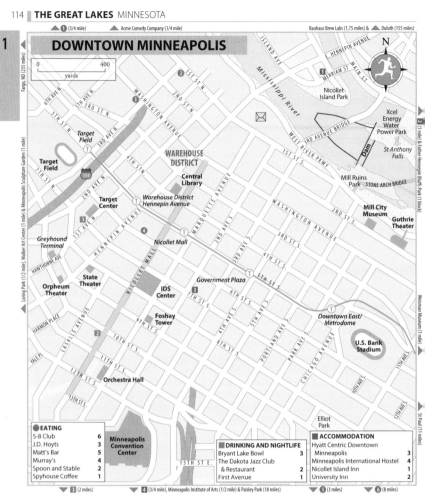

DOWNTOWN MINNEAPOLIS

EATING		
5-8 Club		6
J.D. Hoyts		3
Matt's Bar		5
Murray's		4
Spoon and Stable		2
Spyhouse Coffee		1

DRINKING AND NIGHTLIFE	
Bryant Lake Bowl	3
The Dakota Jazz Club & Restaurant	2
First Avenue	1

ACCOMMODATION	
Hyatt Centric Downtown Minneapolis	3
Minneapolis International Hostel	4
Nicollet Island Inn	1
University Inn	2

some of America's best restaurants and theatres. Though it's often viewed as a better place to live than to visit, lacking major showstoppers – outside of the US the city is most famous for its association with the late musician **Prince** – it also boasts an impressive roster of **art museums** and the **Mall of America**, the western world's **largest shopping mall**, guaranteed to blow the mind of even the most jaded shopaholic.

With neighbouring St Paul (see page 117), Minneapolis forms the **Twin Cities**, a major metropolitan area of 3.5 million, though the two centres are quite distinct, their downtowns some twelve miles apart.

Downtown Minneapolis is anchored by pedestrianized **Nicollet Mall**, most lively between 10th Street S and 5th Street S (the famous **Mary Tyler Moore statue** stands at Nicollet and 7th St; the hit 1970s *Mary Tyler Moore Show* was set in the city). **Hennepin Avenue**, the other main drag, is a block west. The best place to access the riverfront, just north of downtown, is **Mill Ruins Park**, where the historic **Stone Arch Bridge** makes an ideal vantage point for viewing what remains of **St Anthony Falls**, transformed into a concrete spillway in the 1870s.

In 2020, the eyes of the world landed on Minneapolis, after unarmed **George Floyd**, an African-American, was unlawfully killed by a white police officer while being arrested, with his actions filmed and the footage shared worldwide. The ensuing civil unrest in the city – three nights of rioting and looting – precipitated national and global protests against police brutality towards people of colour, and lack of accountability for their actions. In April 2021, the police officer responsible was convicted of second and third-degree murder and manslaughter, a result greeted with a celebratory march in the Minneapolis streets, although the sense of justice was tempered by news of the shooting of another unarmed black man, Daunte Wright, elsewhere in the city.

Foshay Tower

821 Marquette Ave • Thurs–Mon 11am–5pm • charge, discount ages 4-14 • ⓦ exploreminnesota.com

The best panorama of downtown's skyscrapers can be had from the observation deck of **Foshay Tower**, a 447ft Art Deco beauty completed in 1929 and now a hotel. Buy tickets in the hotel lobby.

Mill City Museum

704 2nd St S • Thurs & Fri 10am–4pm, Sat & Sun 10am–5pm • charge • ⓦ mnhs.org/millcity

From around 1860 to 1930 Minneapolis was the flour-milling capital of the world, a potentially underwhelming accolade commemorated at the surprisingly fun and illuminating **Mill City Museum**. A series of hands-on exhibits are complemented by the Flour Tower multimedia show (an eight-storey elevator ride through the mill's history) and the "Minneapolis in 19 Minutes Flat" movie. The museum is cleverly built into the ruins of the Washburn A Mill, completed in 1880 on the riverfront.

Minneapolis Institute of Art

2400 3rd Ave S • Tues-Sun 10am–5pm • Free • ⓦ new.artsmia.org

Art lovers should aim to spend half a day at the vast **Minneapolis Institute of Art (Mia)**, one mile south of downtown, covering cultural artefacts from 2000 BC to the present, from Buddhist statues and Yoruba carvings to Innu caribou coats and samurai armour. The paintings collection is superb, with examples from all the European old masters and almost every period. Highlights include El Greco's wonderfully expressive *Christ Driving the Money Changers from the Temple* (gallery 341), Goya's haunting *Self-Portrait with Dr. Arrieta* (321), Rembrandt's *Lucretia* (311) and Poussin's landmark *Death of Germanicus* (313). Matisse is well represented (with *Three Bathers* and *Boy with a Butterfly Net* in gallery 371) while Max Beckmann's *Blind Man's Buff* triptych (377) is a stunning work of symbolism. The American collection features exceptional work by John Singer Sargent and Georgia O'Keeffe, while Picasso (*After the Lance*), Miró (*Spanish Playing Cards*) and Manet (*The Smoker*) all feature.

Walker Art Center

725 Vineland Pl • Sun 11am–5pm, Thurs 11am–9pm, Fri & Sat 11am–6pm • charge, free on Thurs 5–9pm and first Sat of month • ⓦ walkerart.org

In the Loring Park district just west of downtown, the **Walker Art Center** is a contemporary art and performance space that focuses primarily on temporary exhibitions, though its permanent collection of sculpture and paintings contains some real gems. Look out for German Expressionist Franz Marc's *Large Blue Horses*, Edward Hopper's *Office at Night* and Chuck Close's *Big Self-Portrait*. Opened in 1971, the centre's most striking feature is an aluminium mesh and glass expansion by Swiss architects Herzog & de Meuron in 2005.

The attached eleven-acre outdoor **Sculpture Garden** (daily 6am–midnight; free) features pieces by Calder, Louise Bourgeois and Frank Gehry, plus the gigantic, whimsical *Spoonbridge and Cherry* by Claes Oldenburg and Coosje van Bruggen.

Weisman Art Museum

333 E River Pkwy • Thurs & Fri 10am–5pm, Wed 10am-8pm, Sat & Sun 11am–5pm • Free • ⓦ wam.umn.edu • Green Line to East Bank Station

1

Designed by Frank Gehry for the University of Minnesota (two miles east of downtown) in his trademark glimmering stainless-steel style (reminiscent of Bilbao's Guggenheim), the **Weisman Art Museum** is a fabulous showcase for modern and contemporary art. Exhibitions revolve, but the permanent collection is especially rich in American Modernism (with Chuck Close, Alfred Maurer and Georgia O'Keefe well represented), ceramics, Mimbres pottery (from the American Southwest), and, oddly, traditional Korean furniture. Gehry's stunning *Standing Glass Fish* installation is on display in the lobby.

ARRIVAL AND DEPARTURE   MINNEAPOLIS

By plane Minneapolis-St Paul International Airport (Ⓦmspairport.com) lies about 12 miles south of downtown. Super Shuttle Minneapolis (Ⓣ612 827 7777, Ⓦsupershuttle.com) takes travellers between the airport and major hotels for around $16 per person. Taxis to Minneapolis cost slightly more than taxis to St Paul. You can also take the METRO Blue Line (Ⓣ612 373 3333, Ⓦmetrotransit.org) into Minneapolis or bus #54 to St Paul

(both daily 4am–1am).
By bus The Greyhound bus station is at 950 Hawthorne Ave (Ⓣ612 371 3325, Ⓦgreyhound.com) on the edge of downtown.
Destinations Chicago (4 daily; 8hr 10min–9hr 45min); Duluth (3 daily; 3hr–3hr 35min); Madison (1 daily; 5hr 50min).

GETTING AROUND AND INFORMATION

By light rail The METRO Green Line links Minneapolis with St Paul, while the Blue Line runs to the airport, Minnehaha Falls and Mall of America. Stored-value Go-To Cards are available, or as an unlimited 7 day pass.
By bus Metro Transit buses (Ⓣ612 373 3333; Ⓦmetrotransit.org) run all over the city.

By bike Nice Ride bike share system (Ⓦniceridemn.com) charges for single rides per 30min, or unlimited 30min rides per day.
Visitor centre 505 Nicollet Mall Suite 100 (Wed-Sat 10am–3pm; Ⓣ612 397 9278, Ⓦminneapolis.org).

ACCOMMODATION   SEE MAP PAGE 114

★ **Hyatt Centric Downtown Minneapolis** 615 2nd Ave S, Ⓦhyatt.com. The city's top hotel is well worth a splurge, with luxurious rooms, sensational views, free bikes and a free wine hour every evening. $$$
Minneapolis Hostel 2400 Stevens Ave, Ⓦminneapolishostel.com. This conveniently situated independent hostel has private rooms, spacious dorms, fast free wi-fi and decent shared kitchen. Dorms $, doubles $$

Nicollet Island Inn 95 Merriam St, Ⓦnicolletislandinn.com. Attractive hotel set uniquely on an island in the middle of the Mississippi, worth considering because of its romantic location and excellent restaurant. $$$
University Inn 925 SE 4th St, Ⓦuniversityinnmn.com. A few blocks from University of Minnesota's campus, this simple, modern hotel is good value and convenient for those with university business. $$$

EATING   SEE MAP PAGE 114

5-8 Club 5800 Cedar Ave, Ⓦ5-8club.com. One of two local tavern that claims to be the home of the original Juicy Lucy. Four locations in the Twin Cities. $
J.D. Hoyt's Supper Club 301 Washington Ave N, Ⓦjdhoyts.com. A traditional supper club serving down-home food at good prices. The grilled catfish is quite good and the grilled bananas are worth a try. $$$
Matt's Bar & Grill 3500 Cedar Ave S, Ⓦmattsbar.com. Hole-in-the-wall that has a cult following due to its "Jucy Lucy", the locally celebrated hamburger with molten cheese inside the patty. Cash only. $
★ **Murray's** 26 S 6th St, Ⓦmurraysrestaurant.com.

Steakhouse institution since 1946, with specials such as the silver butter knife steak, hickory-smoked shrimp, and its famed raspberry pie. $$$$
★ **Spoon and Stable** 211 1st St N, Ⓦspoonandstable.com. Gavin Kaysen's fashionable restaurant, housed in a former horse stable, is justly lauded for its Midwest-inspired dishes such as sourdough bigoli and bison tartare. $$$$
Spyhouse Coffee 907 N Washington Ave, Ⓦspyhousecoffee.com. Chain of local coffee roasters, with coffeeshops across the city offering a rustic yet modern vibe that is quintessentially Minneapolis. $$

DRINKING AND NIGHTLIFE   SEE MAP PAGE 114

Acme Comedy Company 708 N 1st St, Ⓦacmecomedycompany.com. Iconic stop for stand-up

comedy, check out their dinner-show packages. $$
Bauhaus Brew Labs 1315 Tyler St NE,

bauhausbrewlabs.com. Family owned craft brewery with a large open air patio, taproom, and live shows. $$

Bryant Lake Bowl & Theater 810 W Lake St, bryantlakebowl.com. Vintage bowling alley, bar, restaurant and cabaret theater in Uptown offering a one-of-a-kind night out. $$

★ **The Dakota Jazz Club & Restaurant** 1010 Nicollet Mall, dakotacooks.com. Gourmet Midwestern food and great local and national jazz acts downtown. $$

First Avenue 701 First Ave, first-avenue.com. The landmark rock venue where Prince's *Purple Rain* was shot still packs them in with top bands and dance music. $$

St Paul

Minnesota's capital city, **ST PAUL** has traditionally been the staid, slightly older sibling of Minneapolis, careful to preserve its buildings and traditions, though the **Lowertown** neighbourhood has developed into something of a hipster hub in recent years (think craft cocktails, farmers' markets, craft brews and food trucks). Downtown itself is built, like Rome, on seven hills: the 1905 **Minnesota State Capitol**, a Cass Gilbert masterpiece (75 Rev Dr Martin Luther King Jr Blvd; Mon 8:30am-5, Tues–Fri 8am–5pm; mnhs.org/capitol), and the **Cathedral of St Paul**, 239 Selby Ave (7:30am–6pm daily), occupy one each, the latter a gorgeous Beaux Arts edifice completed in 1915.

In the heart of downtown, the castle-like **Landmark Center** (75 W 5th St; Mon & Wed-Fri 8am–5pm, Thurs 8am-8pm, Sat 10am–5pm, Sun noon–5pm; landmarkcenter.org), a former post office and courthouse completed in 1902, now

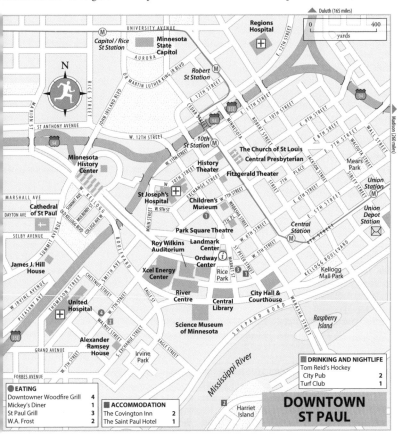

DOWNTOWN ST PAUL

● **EATING**
Downtowner Woodfire Grill	4
Mickey's Diner	1
St Paul Grill	3
W.A. Frost	2

■ **ACCOMMODATION**
The Covington Inn	2
The Saint Paul Hotel	1

■ **DRINKING AND NIGHTLIFE**
Tom Reid's Hockey City Pub	2
Turf Club	1

contains five art galleries and the visitor centre. The Landmark Center overlooks **Rice Park**, the prettiest little square in the city. A sculpture garden with characters from Charles Schulz's *Peanuts* comic strip, the artist himself a St Paul native, has been added to the adjacent **Landmark Plaza**. Just to the south at 120 W Kellogg Blvd, an immense steel iguana is the doorkeeper at the hands-on **Science Museum of Minnesota** (Wed, Thurs & Sun 9am–5pm, Fri & Sat 9am–8pm; charge, discount for ages 4–12, Ⓦsmm. org), which also has a domed Omnitheater (additional cost, discount for kids) for giant-screen films.

Minnesota History Center
345 Kellogg Blvd • Thurs-Sat 10am–4pm, Sun 11am–4pm • charge • Ⓦ mnhs.org

Interactive exhibits and thematic galleries bring the past to life at the **Minnesota History Center**, an inventive museum that includes a replica iron mine, a simulation of a tornado, tackles the state's obsession with Vikings and provides an illuminating take on Minnesota's long history of immigration, beginning with Germans in the 1800s and ending with recent waves of Somali and Hmong refugees.

Summit Avenue

A well-preserved five-mile Victorian boulevard, **Summit Avenue** runs southwest from the Cathedral of St Paul. **F. Scott Fitzgerald** (who was born nearby in 1896), finished his first success, *This Side of Paradise*, in 1919 while living in a modest rowhouse at 599 Summit Ave. He disparaged the avenue as a "museum of American architectural failures". The only mansion you can visit along here is the **James J. Hill House** at no. 240, a railroad baron's sumptuous Richardsonian Romanesque mansion from 1891 (1hr 15min tours every 30min Thurs–Sat 10am–3.30pm, Sun 11am–4pm; charge, reservations recommended; Ⓦmnhs.org/ hillhouse). **Walking tours** of the street also run from Hill House (May–Sept Sat 11am & 2pm, Sun 2pm; charge, discount ages 5-17, reservations recommended). The lavish **Minnesota Governor's Residence** is at no. 1006 (daily 8am-9pm, tours June–Aug, see Ⓦmn.gov/admin/governors-residence).

ARRIVAL AND INFORMATION
ST PAUL

By plane See page 116.

By bus The Greyhound bus station is at the Union Depot, 240 Kellogg Blvd.
Destinations Chicago (3 daily; 7hr 35min–9hr 15min); Milwaukee (5 daily; 5hr 30min–8hr).

By train Amtrak uses the Union Depot at 240 Kellogg Blvd. To/from Minneapolis, take the METRO Green Line (see page

116) from here.
Destinations Chicago (2 daily; 7hr 55min); Milwaukee (2 daily; 6hr 7min).

Visitor centre Landmark Center, 175 W Kellogg Blvd #502 (Mon–Fri 8am–5pm; ☎651 292 3225, Ⓦvisitsaintpaul. com).

ACCOMMODATION
SEE MAP PAGE 117

The Covington Inn 100 Harriet Island Rd, Ⓦcovingtoninn.com. A one-of-a-kind B&B in a converted towboat on the Mississippi, facing downtown, with just four cosy rooms. $$$

★**The Saint Paul Hotel** 350 Market St, Ⓦsaintpaulhotel.com. This grand, 1910 establishment is

Minnesota's top hotel. Rooms tend to be smaller than those of other luxury hotels, but the staff and atmosphere make up for it. The *St Paul Grill* provides some of the city's finest dining, while the classy bar has tons of great scotches and cognacs. $$$

EATING
SEE MAP PAGE 117

Downtowner Woodfire Grill 253 7th St W, Ⓦdowntownerwoodfire.com. This Persian bistro is ideal if you plan to catch a local football game or just enjoy dinner. Weekends feature live jazz music starting at 8pm. $$

★**Mickey's Diner by willy** 1950 7th St W,

Ⓦmickeysdinerbywilly.com. Opened as a satellite location to the original Mickey's in 1960, this location offers the same no-nonsense, wise-cracking staff, gut-busting breakfast plates, burgers and home-made baked beans. $

★**St Paul Grill** 350 Market St (Saint Paul Hotel),

ⓦstpaulgrill.com. Best place for a splurge, with traditional American dishes in this classic downtown hotel. $$$
★ **W.A. Frost and Company** 374 Selby Ave #1825, ⓦwafrost.com. This former pharmacy and F. Scott Fitzgerald hangout has been converted into a plush restaurant with a garden patio. The fusion menu features dishes such as mushroom Wellington and squash ravioli; the wine cellar stocks some 3000 bottles. $$$

DRINKING AND NIGHTLIFE SEE MAP PAGE 117

Tom Reid's Hockey City Pub 258 W 7th St, ⓦtomreids.com. This pre- and post-game hangout is where locals gather to honour the state's favourite sport. $$
Turf Club 1601 University Ave W, ⓦturfclub.net. Retro live music venue open since the 1940s, now hosting indie bands, plus DJ and jazz at the weekends. Hours depend on shows scheduled. $

ENTERTAINMENT

Fitzgerald Theater 10 E Exchange St, ⓦthefitzgeraldtheater.com. Built in 1910 and known as the former venue for Garrison Keillor's weekly *A Prairie Home Companion* radio recording. It hosts a wide programme of concerts and lectures.
History Theatre 30 E 10th St, ⓦhistorytheatre.com. Original plays deal with events and personalities from the region's past, such as productions based on Vietnam War oral histories and swing music showcases.
Penumbra Theatre 270 N Kent St, ⓦpenumbratheatre.org. African American theatre company focusing, not surprisingly, on works by African American playwrights.

Duluth

Thanks to the Great Lakes and their interconnecting canals, the city of **DULUTH** is considered an "Atlantic" seaport, even though it's an astounding 2342 miles from the ocean. Perched at the western extremity of Lake Superior, it remains an important shipping hub for iron ore and coal, the city cascading down from granite bluffs to a busy **harbour**, shared with Superior, Wisconsin. Duluth's compact **downtown** is a blend of modern towers and older Victorian buildings, though the heated **Skywalk** (an enclosed pedestrian walkway) keeps folks off the streets – it's often cold here, even in summer. Most of the action takes place along the **downtown Waterfront** area (aka Canal Park), which pokes out into the harbour along Lake Avenue and Canal Park Drive, lined with restaurants, hotels and shops. If the weather is good, drive **Skyline Parkway**, an exhilarating twenty-mile road that follows the ridge above the city, with stellar views and sights such as 80ft-tall **Enger Tower**.

Lake Superior Maritime Visitor Center

600 Canal Park Dr • Late March to early Oct daily 10am–9pm; early Oct to late March Fri-Sun 10am-4:30pm • Free • ⓦlsmma.com

At the southern tip of Canal Park, the **Lake Superior Maritime Visitor Center** is the best place to gain an understanding of Duluth port and its history, with absorbing displays on locks, shipwrecks and lighthouses. Outside, watch big ships from around the world pass under the delightfully archaic **Aerial Lift Bridge** and through the Duluth Ship Canal.

Great Lakes Aquarium

353 Harbor Drive #100 • Daily 10am–6pm • charge, discount for ages 3–17 • ⓦglaquarium.org

The **Great Lakes Aquarium** has the distinction of being America's only all-freshwater aquarium, with giant tanks of local species such as lake trout, sturgeon, burbot and walleye, plus otter shows and sturgeon touch pools sure to enthrall little ones.

1

The St. Louis County Depot

506 W Michigan St • Daily 10am-5pm • Museums, railroad, and combo ticket available • Ⓦ duluthdepot.org

Completed in 1892, Duluth's grand old train station is now **The Depot** complex housing the **Lake Superior Railroad Museum**, displaying vintage trains, the **Duluth Art Institute** (with changing exhibits of mostly regional artists) and the **St Louis County Historical Society**, with displays charting the history of the area. The Depot is also the starting point for excursions on the **North Shore Scenic Railroad** to Two Harbors (mid-April to mid-Oct daily; see Ⓦ northshorescenicrailroad.org).

Glensheen Mansion

3300 London Rd • Open daily, 9am-4:30pm • charge for tours • Ⓦ glensheen.org

The stately lakeside Jacobean Revival mansion of **Glensheen**, three miles from downtown Duluth, was completed in 1908 for Chester Congdon, a lawyer who struck it rich investing in iron and copper mining. Today tours take in the vast interior of finely crafted original furnishings, and the immaculate grounds.

ARRIVAL, INFORMATION AND TOURS   DULUTH

By bus Greyhound/Jefferson Lines buses pull in at 228 W Michigan St, downtown, with services to/from Minneapolis (3 daily; 3hr–3hr 25min).

Visitor centre 225 W Superior St, Suite 110 inside the Holiday Center (Mon–Fri 8.30am–5pm; ☎ 218 722 4011, Ⓦ visitduluth.com).

Boat tours VistaFleet, 323 Harbor Drive, operates a variety of harbour cruises (May–Oct; ☎ 218 722 6218, Ⓦ vistafleet.com).

ACCOMMODATION AND EATING

Fitger's Brewhouse Brewery & Grille 600 E Superior St, Ⓦ fitgersbrewhouse.com. A brewpub where the pale ale is quite fine and the Lake Superior smoked fish wrap makes an uncommonly good accompaniment. $$

Northern Waters Smokehaus 394 S Lake Ave #106 (DeWitt-Seitz Marketplace). Smoked fish is popular in Duluth and this place has the best offerings in town, housed in a landmark 1909 warehouse. They also do non-fish sandwiches such as the Silence of the Lambwich and the Pastrami Mommy. $$

South Pier Inn 701 S Lake Ave, Ⓦ southpierinn.com. Excellent location on the waterfront in Canal Park (by the Aerial Bridge), with modern, comfy rooms and lake views. $$$

The North Shore Scenic Drive

The **North Shore Scenic Drive** (aka Hwy-61) follows the thickly forested Lake Superior shoreline for 150 miles northeast from Duluth to the US/Canadian border, its precipitous cliffs interspersed with pretty little ports, numerous waterfalls and picture-postcard picnic sites.

At **Gooseberry Falls State Park** (daily 8am–10pm; Joseph N. Alexander visitor centre 3206 MN-61; open daily 8am–10pm; free; Ⓦ dnr.state.mn.us), forty miles from Duluth, the Gooseberry River plunges over a series of 30ft cascades to its outlet in Lake Superior. Like all the other state parks along Hwy-61, it provides **campsites**, plus access to the rugged 310-mile **Superior Hiking Trail** (Ⓦ superiorhiking.org), divided into easily manageable segments for day-trekkers. Eight miles further on, **Split Rock Lighthouse** (3713 Split Rock Lighthouse Rd; April to Oct daily 10am–6pm, Nov to mid-May Friday-Mon 10am–4pm; charge; Ⓦ mnhs.org/splitrock) occupies a stunning location on the cliffs, its restored tower and keeper's home an enlightening museum.

Just beyond **Cascade River State Park** the road dips into the little port of **GRAND MARAIS** (110 miles from Duluth), the best base for exploring the region, with plenty of accommodation and a pleasant harbourfront lined with shops and restaurants. The town's visitor centre has lists of **outfitters** for those heading west into the **Boundary Waters Canoe Area Wilderness**, a paradise for canoeing, backpacking and fishing. It's one of the most heavily used wilderness areas in the country; overland trails, or "portages", link more than a thousand lakes and in winter you can ski and dogsled cross-country.

Grand Portage National Monument

1

170 Mile Creek Rd, Grand Portage • Heritage Center late May to mid-Oct daily 8.30am–5pm; mid-Oct to late May Mon–Sat 8.30am–4.30pm; Historic Depot summer daily 9am–5pm • Free • ⓦ nps.gov/grpo

Some 145 miles from Duluth, the **Grand Portage National Monument** marks the location of one the most important fur-trading posts in America. In 1731, Native Americans introduced the French to an 8.5-mile portage route that linked Lake Superior to the Pigeon River and the vast Canadian wilderness beyond. From 1784 to 1802, the North West Company made its main summer base at this "Grand Portage", and a clutch of authentically reconstructed buildings (aka **Historic Depot**) now stand on the excavated site, manned by costumed interpreters. The adjacent **Heritage Center** contains exhibits and movies about the site and the culture of the local **Ojibwe** people that were crucial to the fur trade – today the site lies on the Grand Portage Indian Reservation. In summer, ferries run daily from here to remote **Isle Royale National Park** (see page 105). Five miles on, literally at the Canadian border, **Grand Portage State Park** (9393 E MN-61; daily 8am-10pm; free; ⓦ dnr.state.mn.us) contains the tumbling 120ft **High Falls** of the Pigeon River, the main reason a portage was needed all those years ago.

Voyageurs National Park

Open 24hr • Free

Set along the border lakes between Minnesota and Canada, **VOYAGEURS NATIONAL PARK** is like no other in the US national park system. To see it properly, or indeed to grasp its immense beauty at all, you need to leave your car behind and venture into the wild by boat. Once out on the lakes, you're in a great, silent world. Kingfishers, osprey and eagles swoop down for their share of the abundant walleye; moose and bear stalk the banks.

You can't do Voyageurs justice on a day-trip, though daily cruises from the Kabetogama and Rainy Lake visitor centres do at least allow a peek at the lake country. If you're here for a few days, rent a **motorboat** or canoe and camp out. It's easy to get lost in this maze of islands and rocky outcrops, and unseen sandbanks lurk beneath the surface, so it's important to plan your trip with park rangers. During **freeze-up** – usually from December until March – the park takes on a whole new aura as a prime destination for skiers and snowmobilers.

ARRIVAL AND INFORMATION

VOYAGEURS NATIONAL PARK

By car Most travellers access Voyageurs from Hwy-53, which runs northwest from Duluth. After just over 100 miles, at Orr, it intersects with Rte-23, which runs northeast toward Crane Lake, at the eastern end of the park.

Visitor centres About 28 and 31 miles beyond Hwy-53's junction with Rte-23, highways 129 and 122 lead, respectively, to the visitor centres at Ash River (late May to late Sept Thurs–Sun 10am–4pm; ☎ 218 374 3221) and Kabetogama Lake (late May to late Sept daily 9am–5pm; ☎ 218 875 2111). Another prime visitor centre is at Rainy Lake, at the westernmost entrance, 36 miles farther on via International Falls (daily late May to late Sept 9am–5pm; late Sept to late May Thurs–Sun 10am–4.30pm; ☎ 218 286 5258, ⓦ nps.gov/voya).

ACCOMMODATION

Camping You can camp on one of the many scattered islands, most plentiful around Crane Lake. There are also first-come, first-served state-owned campgrounds on the mainland at Ash River and Woodenfrog, near Kabetogama. ̄§

Kettle Falls Hotel 12977 Chippewa Trail, Kabetogama, ⓦ kettlefallshotel.com. A perfectly rustic way to experience Voyageurs (only accessible by shuttle bus and ferry from Ash River visitor centre), with a wide range of lodging options, day-trips and boat rentals. Shared bathrooms. ̄§§

ILLUSTRATION OF LINCOLN RETURNING HOME AS PRESIDENT IN 186

Contexts

History

The history of the Great Lakes region is indelibly linked to the history of North America and the development of the United States. These few pages survey the peopling and political development of the disparate regions that now form the USA.

First peoples

The true pioneers of North America, nomadic hunter-gatherers from Siberia, are thought to have reached what's now **Alaska** around seventeen thousand years ago. Thanks to the last ice age, when sea levels were 300ft lower, a "**land-bridge**" – actually a vast plain, measuring six hundred miles north to south – connected Eurasia to America.

Alaska was at that time separated by glacier fields from what is now Canada, and thus effectively part of Asia rather than North America. Like an air lock, the region has "opened" in different directions at different times; migrants reaching it from the west, unaware that they were leaving Asia, would at first have found their way blocked to the east. Several generations might pass, and the connection back towards Asia be severed, before an eastward passage appeared. When thawing ice did clear a route into North America, it was not along the Pacific coast but via a corridor that led east of the Rockies and out onto the Great Plains.

This migration may well have been spurred by the pursuit of large mammal species, and especially **mammoth**, which had already been harried to extinction throughout almost all of Eurasia. A huge bonanza awaited the hunters when they finally encountered America's own indigenous "**megafauna**", such as mammoths, mastodons, giant ground sloths and enormous long-horned bison, all of which had evolved with no protection against human predation.

Filling the New World

Within a thousand years, ten million people were living throughout both North and South America. Although that sounds like a phenomenally rapid spread, it would only have required a band of just one hundred individuals to enter the continent, and advance a mere eight miles per year, with an annual population growth of 1.1 percent, to achieve that impact. The mass **extinction** of the American megafauna was so precisely simultaneous that humans must surely have been responsible, eliminating the giant beasts in each locality in one fell swoop, before pressing on in search of the next kill.

At least three distinct waves of **migrants** arrived via Alaska, each of whom settled in, and adapted to, a more marginal environment than its predecessors. The second, five thousand years on from the first, were the "**Nadene**" or Athapascans – the ancestors of the Haida of the Northwest, and the Navajo and Apache of the Southwest – while the third, another two thousand years later, found their niche in the frozen Arctic and became the **Aleuts** and the **Inuits**.

c.60 million BC	15,000 BC	11,000 BC
Two mighty islands collide, creating North America as a single landmass, and throwing up the Rocky Mountains	First nomadic peoples from Asia reach Alaska	Almost all North America's large mammals become extinct, possibly due to over-hunting

Early settlements

The earliest known settlement site in the modern United States, dating back 12,000 years, has been uncovered at Meadowcroft in southwest Pennsylvania. Five centuries later, the Southwest was dominated by the so-called **Clovis** culture, while subsequent subgroups ranged from the Algonquin farmers of what's now New England to peoples such as the Chumash and Macah, who lived by catching fish, otters and even whales along the coasts of the Pacific Northwest.

The **Moundbuilders** of the **Ohio** and **Mississippi** valleys developed sites such as the Great Serpent Mound in modern Ohio. The most prominent of these early societies, now known as the **Hopewell** culture, flourished during the first four centuries AD.

Estimates of the total indigenous population before the arrival of the Europeans vary widely, but an acceptable median figure suggests around fifty million people in the Americas as a whole. Perhaps five million of those were in North America, speaking around four hundred different languages.

Christopher Columbus

Five more centuries passed before the crucial moment of contact with the rest of the world came on October 12, 1492, when **Christopher Columbus**, sailing on behalf of the Spanish, reached the Bahamas. A mere four years later the English navigator John Cabot officially "discovered" Newfoundland, and soon British fishermen were setting up makeshift encampments in what became **New England**, to spend the winter curing their catch.

Over the next few years various expeditions mapped the eastern seaboard. In 1524, the Italian **Giovanni da Verrazano** sailed past Maine, which he characterized as the "Land of Bad People" thanks to the inhospitable and contemptuous behaviour of its natives, and reached the mouth of the Hudson River. The great hope was to find a sea route in the Northeast that would lead to China – the fabled **Northwest Passage**. To the French **Jacques Cartier**, the St Lawrence Seaway seemed a promising avenue, and unsuccessful attempts were made to settle the northern areas of the Great Lakes from the 1530s onwards. Intrepid trappers and traders ventured ever further west.

The growth of the colonies

The sixteenth-century rivalry between the English and the Spanish extended right around the world. Freebooting English adventurers-cum-pirates contested Spanish hegemony along both coasts of North America. Sir Francis Drake staked a claim to California in 1579, five years before **Sir Walter Raleigh** claimed **Virginia** in the east, in the name of his Virgin Queen, Elizabeth I. The party of colonists he sent out in 1585 established the short-lived settlement of **Roanoke**, now remembered as the mysterious "Lost Colony".

The Native Americans were seldom hostile at first encounter. To some extent the European newcomers were obliged to make friends with the locals; most had crossed the Atlantic to find religious freedom or to make their fortunes, and lacked the skills to make a success of subsistence farming.

Between 1620 and 1642, sixty thousand migrants – 1.5 percent of the population – left England for America. Those in pursuit of economic opportunities often joined the

c.2500 BC	900 AD	1050
Agriculture reaches North America from Mexico	Mississippian settlements – city-like conglomerations of earthen mounds – appear throughout the Southeast	Ancestral Puebloan culture reaches its peak at Chaco Canyon in the Southwest

longer-established colonies, thereby serving to dilute the religious zeal of the Puritans. Groups hoping to find spiritual freedom were more inclined to start afresh.

From their foothold in the Great Lakes region, meanwhile, the **French** sent the explorers Joliet and Marquette to map the Mississippi and its connecting waterways in 1673. Upon establishing that the river did indeed flow into the Gulf of Mexico, they turned back, having cleared the way for the foundation of the huge and ill-defined colony of **Louisiana** in 1699.

The American Revolution

The American colonies prospered during the **eighteenth century**. Boston, New York and Philadelphia in particular became home to a wealthy, well-educated and highly articulate middle class. Frustration mounted at the inequities of the colonies' relationship with Britain, however. The Americans could only sell their produce to the British, and all transatlantic commerce had to be undertaken in British ships.

Full-scale independence was not an explicit goal until late in the century, but the main factor that made it possible was the economic impact of the pan-European **Seven Years War**. Officially, war in Europe lasted from 1756 to 1763, but fighting in North America broke out a little earlier. Beginning in 1755 with the mass expulsion of French settlers from Acadia in eastern Canada (triggering their epic migration to Louisiana, where the **Cajuns** remain to this day), the British went on to conquer all of Canada. In forcing the **surrender of Québec** in 1759, General Wolfe brought the war to a close; the French ceded Louisiana to the Spanish rather than let it fall to the British, while Florida passed briefly into British control before reverting to the Spanish. All the European monarchs were left hamstrung by debts, and the British realized that colonialism in America was not as profitable as in those parts of the world where the native populations could be coerced into working for their overseas masters.

There was also another major player – the **Iroquois Confederacy**. Iroquois culture in the Great Lakes region, characterized by military expansionism and even human sacrifice, dates back around a thousand years. Forever in competition with the Algonquin and the Huron, the southern Iroquois had by the eighteenth century formed a League of Five Nations – the Seneca, Cayuga, Onondaga, Oneida and Mohawk, all in what's now upstate New York. Wooed by both the French and British, the Iroquois charted an independent course. Impressed by witnessing negotiations between the Iroquois and the squabbling representatives of Pennsylvania, Virginia and Maryland, Benjamin Franklin wrote in 1751 that "It would be a very strange thing if…ignorant savages should be capable of forming a scheme for such a union…that has subsisted ages and appears indissoluble; and yet that a like union should be impracticable for ten or a dozen English colonies".

An unsuccessful insurrection by the Ottawa in 1763, led by their chief **Pontiac**, led the cash-strapped British to conclude that, while America needed its own standing army, it was reasonable to expect the colonists to pay for it. In 1765, they introduced the **Stamp Act**, requiring duty on all legal transactions and printed matter

1492	1607	1610	1619
Christopher Columbus makes landfall in the Bahamas	English colonists establish Jamestown in Virginia	Santa Fe is founded as capital of New Mexico; horses begin to spread across the Southwest	Twenty African slaves arrive in Virginia on a Dutch ship

in the colonies to be paid to the British Crown. Arguing for "no taxation without representation", delegates from nine colonies met in the Stamp Act Congress that October. By then, however, the British prime minister responsible had already been dismissed by King George III, and the Act was repealed in 1766.

However, in 1767, Chancellor Townshend made political capital at home by proclaiming "I dare tax America", as he introduced legislation including the broadly similar Revenue Act. That led Massachusetts merchants, inspired by **Samuel Adams**, to vote to boycott English goods; they were joined by all the other colonies except New Hampshire. Townshend's Acts were repealed in turn by a new prime minister, Lord North, on March 5, 1770. By chance, on that same day a stone-throwing mob surrounded the Customs House in Boston; five people were shot in what became known as the **Boston Massacre**. Even so, most of the colonies resumed trading with Britain, and the crisis was postponed for a few more years.

In May 1773, Lord North's **Tea Act** relieved the debt-ridden East India Company of the need to pay duties on exports to America, while still requiring the Americans to pay duty on tea. Massachusetts called the colonies to action, and its citizens took the lead on December 16 in the **Boston Tea Party**, when three tea ships were boarded and 342 chests thrown into the sea.

The infuriated British Parliament thereupon began to pass legislation collectively known as both the "Coercive" and the "Intolerable" Acts, which included closing the port of Boston and disbanding the government of Massachusetts. Thomas Jefferson argued that the acts amounted to "a deliberate and systematical plan of reducing us to slavery". To discuss a response, the first **Continental Congress** was held in Philadelphia on May 5, 1774, and attended by representatives of all the colonies except Georgia.

The Revolutionary War

War finally broke out on April 18, 1775, when General Gage, the governor of Massachusetts, dispatched four hundred British soldiers to destroy the arms depot at **Concord**, and prevent weapons from falling into rebel hands. Silversmith **Paul Revere** was dispatched on his legendary ride to warn the rebels, and the British were confronted en route at Lexington by 77 American "Minutemen". The resulting skirmish led to the "shot heard 'round the world".

Congress set about forming an army at Boston, and decided for the sake of unity to appoint a Southern commander, **George Washington**. One by one, as the war raged, the colonies set up their own governments and declared themselves to be states, and the politicians set about defining the society they wished to create. The writings of pamphleteer Thomas Paine – especially *Common Sense* – were, together with the Confederacy of the Iroquois, a great influence on the **Declaration of Independence**. Drafted by Thomas Jefferson, this was adopted by the Continental Congress in Philadelphia on July 4, 1776. Anti-slavery clauses originally included by Jefferson – himself a slave-owner – were omitted to spare the feelings of the Southern states, though the section that denounced the King's dealings with "merciless Indian Savages" was left in.

At first, the Revolutionary War went well for the British. General Howe crossed the Atlantic with twenty thousand men, took New York and New Jersey, and ensconced himself in Philadelphia for the winter of 1777–78. Washington's army was encamped

1620	**1664**	**1682**
Puritan colonists reach New England aboard the Mayflower, and settle at Plymouth	The Dutch settlement of New Amsterdam, captured by the English, becomes NYC	Quaker settlers found Philadelphia. The Sieur de la Salle claims the Mississippi valley for France as Louisiana

THE US CONSTITUTION

As signed in 1787 and ratified in 1788, the **Constitution of the United States** stipulated the following form of government:

All **legislative** powers were granted to the **Congress of the United States**. The lower of its two distinct houses, the **House of Representatives**, was to be elected every two years, with its members in proportion to the number of each state's "free Persons" plus "three fifths of all other persons" (meaning slaves). The upper house, the **Senate**, would hold two Senators from each state, chosen by state legislatures rather than by direct elections. Each Senator was to serve for six years, with a third of them to be elected every two years.

Executive power was vested in the **President**, who was also Commander in Chief of the Army and Navy. He would be chosen every four years, by as many "**Electors**" from each individual state as it had Senators and Representatives. Each state could decide how to appoint those Electors; almost all chose to have direct popular elections. Nonetheless, the distinction has remained ever since between the number of popular votes, across the whole country, received by a presidential candidate, and the number of state-by-state "electoral votes", which determines the actual result. Originally, whoever came second in the voting automatically became **vice president**.

The President could **veto** acts of Congress, but that veto could be overruled by a two-thirds vote in both houses. The House of Representatives could **impeach** the President for treason, bribery or "other high crimes and misdemeanors", in which instance the Senate could remove him from office with a two-thirds majority.

Judicial power was invested in a **Supreme Court**, and as many "inferior Courts" as Congress should decide.

The Constitution has so far been altered by 27 **Amendments**. Numbers **14** and **15** extended the vote to black males in 1868 and 1870; **17** made Senators subject to election by direct popular vote in 1913; **19** introduced women's suffrage in 1920; **22** restricted the President to two terms in 1951; **24** stopped states using poll taxes to disenfranchise black voters in 1964; and **26** reduced the minimum voting age to 18 in 1971.

not far away at Valley Forge, freezing cold and all but starving to death. It soon became clear, however, that the longer the Americans could avoid losing an all-out battle, the more likely the British were to over-extend their lines as they advanced through the vast and unfamiliar continent. Thus, General Burgoyne's expedition, which set out from Canada to march on New England, was so harried by rebel guerrillas that he had to surrender at Saratoga in October 1777. Other European powers took delight in coming to the aid of the Americans. Benjamin Franklin led a wildly successful delegation to France to request support, and soon the nascent American fleet was being assisted in its bid to cut British naval communications by both the French and the Spanish. The end came when Cornwallis, who had replaced Howe, was instructed to dig in at Yorktown and wait for the Royal Navy to come to his aid, only for the French to seal off Chesapeake Bay and prevent reinforcement. Cornwallis surrendered to Washington on October 17, 1781.

The ensuing **Treaty of Paris** granted the Americans their independence on generous terms – the British abandoned their Native American allies, including the Iroquois, to

1759	1765	1770
British General James Wolfe forces the surrender of Québec, ending the French and Indian War	New England responds to British legislation with the cry "no taxation without representation"	In the Boston Massacre, British sentries fire on a mob and kill five colonists

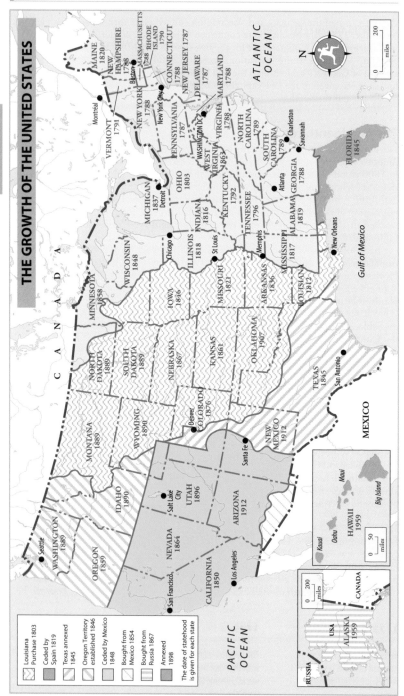

THE GROWTH OF THE UNITED STATES

Legend:
- Louisiana Purchase 1803
- Ceded by Spain 1819
- Texas annexed 1845
- Oregon Territory established 1846
- Ceded by Mexico 1848
- Bought from Mexico 1854
- Bought from Russia 1867
- Annexed 1898
- The date of statehood is given for each state

the vengeance of the victors – and Washington entered New York as the British left in November 1783. The Spanish were confirmed in possession of Florida.

The victorious US Congress met for the first time in 1789, and the tradition of awarding political power to the nation's most successful generals was instigated by the election of George Washington as the first **president**. He was further honoured when his name was given to the new capital city of **Washington DC**, deliberately sited between the North and the South.

The nineteenth century

During its first century, the territories and population of the new **United States of America** expanded at a phenomenal rate. The white population of North America in 1800 stood at around five million, and there were another one million African slaves (of whom thirty thousand were in the North). Of that total, 86 percent lived within fifty miles of the Atlantic, but no US city could rival Mexico City, whose population approached 100,000 inhabitants (both New York and Philadelphia reached that figure within twenty years, however, and New York had passed a million fifty years later).

It had suited the British to discourage settlers from venturing west of the Appalachians, where they would be far beyond the reach of British power. However, adventurers such as **Daniel Boone** started to cross the mountains into Tennessee and Kentucky during the 1770s. Soon makeshift rafts, made from the planks that were later assembled to make log cabins, were careering west along the Ohio River (the only westward-flowing river on the continent). Jean Baptiste Point du Sable, an African American trader, became the first to establish a settlement on the Chicago River.

The Louisiana Purchase

In 1801, the Spanish handed Louisiana back to the French, on condition that the French would keep it forever. However, Napoleon swiftly realized that attempting to hang on to his American possessions would spread his armies too thinly, and chose instead to sell them to the United States for $15 million, in the **Louisiana Purchase** of 1803. President Thomas Jefferson swiftly sent the explorers **Lewis and Clark** to map out the new territories, which extended far beyond the boundaries of present-day Louisiana. With the help of Sacagawea, their female Shoshone guide, they followed the Missouri and Columbia rivers all the way to the Pacific; in their wake, trappers and "mountain men" came to hunt in the wilderness of the Rockies. The **Russians** had already reached the Pacific Northwest, and established fortified outposts to trade in beaver and otter pelts.

The War of 1812 and Andrew Jackson

British attempts to blockade the Atlantic, primarily targeted against Napoleon, gave the new nation a chance to flex its military muscles. British raiders succeeded in capturing Washington DC, and burned the White House, but the **War of 1812** provided the USA with a cover for aggression against the Native American allies of the British. **Tecumseh** of the Shawnee was defeated near Detroit, and **Andrew**

1773	1775	1776
In the Boston Tea Party, two hundred colonists respond to British duties by tipping tea into the sea	The Revolutionary War begins with the "shot heard 'round the world"; George Washington leads the Continental Army	The Declaration of Independence is signed on July 4

Jackson moved against the Creek of the southern Mississippi. Jackson's campaign against the Seminole won the USA possession of Florida from the Spanish; he was rewarded first with the governorship of the new state, and later by his election to the presidency. While in office, in the 1830s, Jackson went even further, and set about clearing all states east of the Mississippi of their native populations. The barren region that later became Oklahoma was designated as "Indian Territory", home to the "Five Civilized Tribes". The Creek and the Seminole, and the Choctaw and Chickasaw of Mississippi were eventually joined by the Cherokee of the lower Appalachians there, after four appalling months on the forced march known as the "**Trail of Tears**".

Manifest Destiny and the Mexican War
It took only a small step for the citizens of the young republic to move from realizing that their country might spread across the whole continent to supposing that it had a quasi-religious duty – a "**Manifest Destiny**" – to do so. At its most basic, that doctrine amounted to little more than a belief that might must be right, but the idea that they were fulfilling the will of God inspired countless pioneers to set off across the plains in search of a new life.

The Civil War
From its inception, the unity of the United States had been based on shaky foundations. Great care had gone into devising a **Constitution** that balanced the need for a strong federal government with the aspirations for autonomy of its component states. That was achieved by giving Congress two separate chambers – the **House of Representatives**, in which each state was represented in proportion to its population, and the **Senate**, in which each state, regardless of size, had two members. Thus, although in theory the Constitution remained silent on the issue of **slavery**, it allayed the fears of the less populated Southern states that Northern voters might destroy their economy by forcing them to abandon their "peculiar institution".

However, the system only worked so long as there were equal numbers of "Free" and slave-owning states. The only practicable way to keep the balance was to ensure that each time a new state was admitted to the Union, a matching state taking the opposite stance on slavery was also admitted. Thus, the admission of every new state became subject to endless intrigue. The 1820 **Missouri Compromise**, under which Missouri joined as a slave-owning state and Maine as a Free one, was straightforward in comparison to the prevarication and chest-beating that surrounded the admission of Texas, while the Mexican War was widely seen in the North as a naked land grab for new slave states.

The Great Lakes role in abolition and Union
Abolitionist sentiment in the North was not all that great before the middle of the nineteenth century. At best, after the importation of slaves from Africa ended in 1808, Northerners vaguely hoped slavery was an anachronism that might simply wither away. As it turned out, Southern plantations were rendered much more profitable by the development of the cotton gin, and the increased demand for manufactured cotton goods triggered by the **Industrial Revolution**. However, the

1779	1787	1789	1858
First written records documented Jean Baptiste Pointe DuSable as the first settler of Chicago	The Constitution is signed in Philadelphia	George Washington is inaugurated as the first president of the United States	Abraham Lincoln declares "A house divided against itself cannot stand"

rapid growth of the nation as a whole made it ever more difficult to maintain a political balance between North and South.

Matters came to a head in 1854, when the **Kansas-Nebraska Act** sparked guerrilla raids and mini-wars between rival settlers by allowing both prospective states self-determination on the issue. That same year, the **Republican Party** was founded to resist the further expansion of slavery. Escaped former slaves such as Frederick Douglass were by now spurring Northern audiences to moral outrage, and Harriet Beecher Stowe's *Uncle Tom's Cabin* found unprecedented readership. Abolitionists and freed former slaves in the North began to help fugitive slaves escape from the South on the Underground Railroad, a series of well-traveled paths that led from the border states of Kentucky and Tennessee through the northern states. Thousands of African Americans escaped slavery this way, settling in northern cities along the Great Lakes. Many others, distrustful of receiving fair treatment by the American government, crossed the Great Lakes and resettled in Canada.

In October 1859, **John Brown** – a white-bearded, wild-eyed veteran of Kansas's bloodiest infighting – led a dramatic raid on the US Armory at Harpers Ferry, West Virginia, intending to secure arms for a slave insurrection. Swiftly captured by forces under Robert E. Lee, he was hanged within a few weeks, proclaiming that "I am now quite certain that the crimes of this guilty land will never be purged away but with blood".

The Republican presidential candidate in 1860, the little-known state senator **Abraham Lincoln** from Illinois, won no Southern states, but with the Democrats split into Northern and Southern factions he was elected with 39 percent of the popular vote. Within weeks, on December 20, South Carolina became the first state to secede from the Union; the **Confederacy** was declared on February 4, 1861, when it was joined by Mississippi, Florida, Alabama, Georgia, Louisiana and Texas. Its first (and only) president was **Jefferson Davis**, also from Kentucky; his new vice president remarked at their joint inauguration that their government was "the first in the history of the world based upon the great physical and moral truth that the negro is not equal to the white man". Lincoln was inaugurated in turn in March 1861, proclaiming that "I have no purpose, directly or indirectly, to interfere with the institution of slavery in the States where it exists. I believe I have no lawful right to do so, and I have no inclination to do so". He was completely inflexible, however, on one paramount issue: the survival of the Union.

The coming of war

The **Civil War** began in April 1861. Over four years, the **Union** of 23 Northern states, holding more than 22 million people and including all of what is now New England, wore down the **Confederacy** of eleven Southern states, with nine million. As for potential combatants, the North initially drew upon 3.5 million white males aged between 18 and 45 – and later recruited blacks as well – whereas the South had more like one million. In the end, around 2.1 million men fought for the Union, and 900,000 for the Confederacy. Of the 620,000 soldiers who died, a disproportionate 258,000 came from the South – one quarter of its white men of military age. Meanwhile, not only did the North continue trading with the rest of the world while maintaining its industrial and agricultural output, it also stifled the Confederacy with a devastating **naval blockade**.

1860	**1861**	**1862**
Lincoln's election prompts South Carolina and other Southern states to secede and form the Confederacy	The artillery attack on Fort Sumter in South Carolina marks the start of the Civil War	President Lincoln's Emancipation Proclamation declares that all slaves in states or areas of states still in rebellion to be free

After years of bitter war and bloodshed, Lincoln took the political decision to match his moral conviction by issuing his **Emancipation Proclamation** in 1862, though the **Thirteenth Amendment** outlawing slavery only took effect in 1865.

The aftermath of the Civil War can almost be said to have lasted for a hundred years. While the South condemned itself to a century as a backwater, the rest of the re-United States embarked on a period of expansionism and prosperity.

Industry and immigration

The late nineteenth century saw massive **immigration** to North America, with influxes from Europe to the East Coast paralleled by those from Asia to the West. As in colonial times, national groups tended to form enclaves in specific areas – from the Scandinavian farmers of Minnesota and the northern Plains to the Basque shepherds of Idaho..

The fastest growth of all was in the nation's greatest **cities**, especially New York, Chicago and Boston. Their industrial and commercial strength enabled them to attract and absorb migrants not only from throughout Europe but also from the Old South – particularly former slaves, who could now at least vote with their feet.

The various presidents of the day, from the victorious General Grant onwards, now seem anonymous figures compared to the industrialists and financiers who manipulated the national economy. These "**robber barons**" included such men as John D. Rockefeller, who controlled seventy percent of the world's oil almost before anyone else had realized it was worth controlling; Andrew Carnegie, who made his fortune introducing the Bessemer process of steel manufacture; and J.P. Morgan, who went for the most basic commodity of all – money. Their success was predicated on the willingness of the government to cooperate in resisting the development of a strong labour movement. Strikes on the railroads in 1877, in the mines of Tennessee in 1891 and in the steel mills of Pittsburgh in 1892 were forcibly crushed. But while these early fights were often deadly and not victorious for workers, they laid an important foundation for a growing movement of unionization.

Two significant strikes begun in Chicago in the 1880s met similar fates. In Pullman, In 1894, 4,000 Pullman workers went on strike, after George Pullman cut wages without decreasing the cost of the workers' rent. This strike was endorsed nationally by the American Railway Union, leading to 100,000 railroad workers refusing to operate Pullman railcars. After police killed two striking workers, a rally held in the following days turned deadly when someone threw a stick of dynamite, causing police to fire into the crowd. The Haymarket Massacre is commemorated globally as International Workers' Day every May 1.

The nineteenth century had also seen the development of a distinctive American voice in **literature**, which rendered increasingly superfluous the efforts of passing English visitors to "explain" the United States. From the 1830s onwards, writers explored new ways to describe their new world, with results as varied as the introspective essays of Henry Thoreau, the morbid visions of Edgar Allan Poe, the all-embracing novels of Herman Melville and the irrepressible poetry of Walt Whitman, whose endlessly revised *Leaves of Grass* was an exultant hymn to the young republic. Virtually every leading participant in the Civil War wrote at least one highly readable volume of memoirs, while public figures as disparate as Buffalo

1865	1870	1876
General Robert E. Lee of the Confederacy surrenders to Union General Ulysses Grant on April 9; five days later, Lincoln is assassinated	Senator Hiram R. Revels of Mississippi becomes the first black man to sit in Congress	Sioux warriors defeat the Seventh Cavalry, and kill General George Custer, at Little Bighorn

Bill Cody and the showman P. T. Barnum produced lively autobiographies. The boundless national self-confidence found its greatest expression in the vigorous vernacular style of **Mark Twain**, whose depictions of frontier life, fictionalized for example in *Huckleberry Finn*, gave the rest of the world an abiding impression of the American character.

A decade into the twentieth century, the United States had advanced to the point that it knew, even if the rest of the world wasn't yet altogether sure, that it was the strongest, wealthiest country on earth.

The twentieth century

The first years of the twentieth century witnessed the emergence of many features that came to characterize modern America. In 1903 alone, Wilbur and Orville Wright achieved the first successful powered **flight** and Henry Ford established his Ford Motor Company. Ford's enthusiastic adoption of the latest technology in mass production – the assembly line – gave Detroit a head start in the new **automobile** industry, which swiftly became the most important business in America. Both **jazz** and **blues** music first reached a national audience during that same period, while Hollywood acquired its first **movie** studio in 1911, and its first major hit in 1915 with D.W. Griffith's unabashed glorification of the Ku Klux Klan in *Birth of a Nation*. This film also led to a rebirth of the Ku Klux Klan, and the violence, discrimination, and lynching of hundreds of African Americans led those who remained to flee for safety and opportunity in the cities of the North. In what was called the "Red Summer" of 1919, racial riots broke out in major cities across the United States, killing hundreds.

In response to the changes and increasing adversity faced by many groups, this was also a time of growing **radicalism**. Both the NAACP (National Association for the Advancement of Colored People) and the socialist International Workers of the World ("the Wobblies") were founded in the early 1900s, while the campaign for women's suffrage also came to the forefront. Writers such as Jack London and Upton Sinclair, who exposed conditions in Chicago's stockyards in *The Jungle*, proselytized to the masses.

Though President Wilson kept the USA out of the **First World War** for several years, American intervention was, when it came, decisive. With the Russian Revolution illustrating the dangers of anarchy, the USA also took charge of supervising the peace. However, even as Wilson presided over the negotiations that produced the Treaty of Versailles in 1919, isolationist sentiment at home prevented the USA from joining his pet scheme to preserve future world peace, the League of Nations.

Prohibition and the Roaring Twenties

Back home, the 18th Amendment forbade the sale and distribution of alcohol, while the 19th finally gave all American women the vote. Quite how **Prohibition** ever became the law of the land remains a mystery; certainly, in the buzzing metropolises of the Roaring Twenties, it enjoyed little conspicuous support. There was no noticeable elevation in the moral tone of the country, and Chicago in particular became renowned for the street wars between bootlegging gangsters such as Al Capone and his rivals.

1876	1892	1894
Mark Twain's The Adventures of Tom Sawyer is the first book to be written on a typewriter	New York's Ellis Island opens; twelve million immigrants pass through before it closes in 1954	4,000 Pullman workers go on strike. By the end of the year their numbers will rise to 100,000 workers

The two Republican presidents who followed Wilson did little more than sit back and watch the Roaring Twenties unfold. Until his premature death, **Warren Harding** enjoyed considerable public affection, but he's now remembered as probably the worst US president of all, thanks to the cronyism and corruption of his associates. It's hard to say quite whether **Calvin Coolidge** did anything at all; his laissez-faire attitude extended to working a typical four-hour day, and announcing shortly after his inauguration that "four-fifths of our troubles would disappear if we would sit down and keep still".

The Depression and the New Deal

By the middle of the 1920s, the USA was an industrial powerhouse, responsible for more than half the world's output of manufactured goods. Having led the way into a new era of prosperity, however, it suddenly dragged the rest of the world down into economic collapse. The consequences of the **Great Depression** were out of all proportion to any one specific cause. Possible factors include American over-investment in the floundering economy of postwar Europe, combined with high tariffs on imports that effectively precluded European recovery. Conservative commentators at the time chose to interpret the calamitous **Wall Street Crash** of October 1929 as a symptom of impending depression rather than a contributory cause, but the quasi-superstitious faith in the stock market that preceded it showed all the characteristics of classic speculative booms. On "Black Tuesday" alone, enough stocks were sold to produce a total loss of ten thousand million dollars – more than twice the total amount of money in circulation in the USA. Within the next three years, industrial production was cut by half, the national income dropped by 38 percent, and, above all, unemployment rose from 1.5 million to 13 million.

National self-confidence, however shaky its foundations, has always played a crucial role in US history, and President Hoover was not the man to restore it. Matters only began to improve in 1932, when the patrician **Franklin Delano Roosevelt** accepted the Democratic nomination for president with the words "I pledge myself to a new deal for America", and went on to win a landslide victory. At the time of his inauguration, early in 1933, the banking system had all but closed down; it took Roosevelt the now-proverbial "Hundred Days" of vigorous legislation to turn around the mood of the country.

Taking advantage of the new medium of radio, Roosevelt used "Fireside Chats" to cajole America out of crisis; among his earliest observations was that it was a good time for a beer, and that the experiment of Prohibition was therefore over. The **New Deal** took many forms, but was marked throughout by a massive growth in the power of the federal government. Among its accomplishments were the National Recovery Administration, which created two million jobs; the Social Security Act, of which Roosevelt declared "no damn politician can ever scrap my social security program"; the Public Works Administration, which built dams and highways the length and breadth of the country; the Tennessee Valley Authority, which by generating electricity under public ownership for the common good was probably the closest the USA has ever come to institutionalized socialism; and measures to legitimize the role of the unions and revitalize the "Dust Bowl" farmers out on the plains.

1896	1896	1901
The Haymarket Massacre results in the deaths of 7 policeman and 2 strikers	Ruling in Plessy v Ferguson, the Supreme Court creates the doctrine of "separate but equal" provision for whites and blacks	Following the assassination of President McKinley, 42-year-old Theodore Roosevelt becomes the youngest-ever president

After the work-creation programmes of the New Deal had put America back on its feet, the deadly pressure to achieve victory in **World War II** spurred industrial production and know-how to new heights. The USA stayed out of the war at first, until it was finally forced in when the Japanese launched a pre-emptive strike on Hawaii's Pearl Harbor in 1941. In both the Pacific and in Europe, American manpower and economic muscle eventually carried all before it. By dying early in 1945, having laid the foundations for the postwar carve-up with Stalin and Churchill at Yalta, Roosevelt was spared the fateful decision, made by his successor Harry Truman, to use the newly developed atomic bomb on Hiroshima and Nagasaki.

The coming of the Cold War

With the war won, Americans were in no mood to revert back to the isolationism of the 1930s. Amid much hopeful rhetoric, Truman enthusiastically participated in the creation of the **United Nations**, and set up the **Marshall Plan** to speed the recovery of Europe. However, as Winston Churchill announced in Missouri in 1946, an "**Iron Curtain**" had descended upon Europe, and Joseph Stalin was transformed from ally to enemy almost overnight.

The ensuing **Cold War** lasted for more than four decades, at times fought in ferocious combat (albeit often by proxy) in scattered corners of the globe, and during the intervals diverting colossal resources towards the stockpiling of ever more destructive arsenals. Some of its ugliest moments came in its earliest years; Truman was still in office in 1950 when war broke out in **Korea**. A dispute over the arbitrary division of the Korean peninsula into two separate nations, North and South, soon turned into a standoff between the USA and China (with Russia lurking in the shadows). Two years of bloody stalemate ended with little to show for it, except that Truman had by now been replaced by the genial **Dwight D. Eisenhower**, the latest war hero to become president.

The Eisenhower years are often seen as characterized by bland complacency. Once Senator **Joseph McCarthy**, the "witch-hunting" anti-Communist scourge of the State Department and Hollywood, had finally discredited himself by attacking the army as well, middle-class America seemed to lapse into a willful stupor. Great social changes were taking shape, however. World War II had introduced vast numbers of women and members of ethnic minorities to the rewards of factory work, and shown many Americans from less prosperous regions the lifestyle attainable elsewhere in their own country. The development of a **national highway system**, and a huge increase in automobile ownership, encouraged people to pursue the American Dream wherever they chose. As cities grew more diverse and suburbs more accessible, working class and middle-class white Americans began to move out of the city into surrounding suburbs, a trend known as White Flight.

Also during the 1950s, **television** reached almost every home in the country. Together with the LP record, it created an entertainment industry that addressed the needs of consumers who had previously been barely identified. **Youth culture** burst into prominence from 1954 onwards, with Elvis Presley's recording of *That's All Right Mama* appearing within a few months of Marlon Brando's moody starring role in *On the Waterfront* and James Dean's in *Rebel Without a Cause*.

1919	1920	1925
The "Red Summer" of white supremacist terrorism and racial riots sweep across the country	The 18th Amendment heralds the introduction of Prohibition; the 19th Amendment gives women the vote	F. Scott Fitzgerald, who dubs this era the Jazz Age, publishes The Great Gatsby

The civil rights years

Racial segregation of public facilities, which had remained the norm in the South ever since Reconstruction, was finally declared illegal in 1954 by the Supreme Court ruling on *Brown v. Topeka Board of Education*. Just as a century before, however, the Southern states saw the issue more in terms of states' rights than of human rights, and attempting to implement the law, or even to challenge the failure to implement it, required immense courage. When fifteen-year-old Chicagoan Emmet Till was lynched in Mississippi for allegedly winking at a white woman, his mother's choice to have an open casket funeral launched the civil rights movement to the American consciousness. The action of Rosa Parks in refusing to give up her seat on a bus in Montgomery, Alabama, in 1955, triggered a successful mass boycott, and pushed the 27-year-old **Rev Dr Martin Luther King, Jr.** to the forefront of the civil rights campaign.

The election of **John F. Kennedy** to the presidency in 1960, by the narrowest of margins, marked a sea-change in American politics, even if in retrospect his policies do not seem exactly radical. At 43 the youngest man ever to be elected president, and the first Catholic, he was prepared literally to reach for the moon, urging the USA to victory in the Space Race in which it had thus far lagged humiliatingly behind the Soviet Union. The two decades that lay ahead, however, were to be characterized by disillusion, defeat and despair. If the Eisenhower years had been dull, the 1960s in particular were far too interesting for almost everybody's liking.

Kennedy's sheer glamour made him a popular president during his lifetime, while his assassination suffused his administration with the romantic glow of "Camelot". His one undisputed triumph, however, came with the **Cuban missile crisis** of 1962, when the US military fortunately spotted Russian bases in Cuba before any actual missiles were ready for use, and Kennedy faced down premier Khrushchev to insist they be withdrawn. On the other hand, he'd had rather less success the previous year in launching the abortive **Bay of Pigs** invasion of Cuba, and he also managed to embroil America deeper in the ongoing war against Communism in Vietnam by sending more "advisers" to Saigon.

Although a much-publicized call to the wife of Rev Martin Luther King, Jr. during one of King's many sojourns in Southern jails was a factor in his election success, Kennedy was rarely identified himself with the **civil rights** movement. The campaign nonetheless made headway, lent momentum by television coverage of such horrific confrontations as the onslaught by Birmingham police on peaceful demonstrators in 1963. The movement's defining moment came when Dr. King delivered his electrifying "I Have a Dream" speech later that summer. King was subsequently awarded the Nobel Peace Prize for his unwavering espousal of Gandhian principles of nonviolence. Perhaps an equally powerful factor in middle America's recognition that the time had come to address racial inequalities, however, was the not-so-implicit threat in the rhetoric of **Malcolm X**, who argued that black people had the right to defend themselves against aggression.

After Kennedy's assassination in November 1963, his successor, **Lyndon B. Johnson**, pushed through legislation that enacted most of the civil rights campaigners' key demands. Even then, violent white resistance in the South

1929	1932	1941
The Wall Street Crash plunges the USA into economic turmoil	Franklin D. Roosevelt pledges "a new deal for the American people"	A surprise Japanese attack on Pearl Harbor precipitates US entry into World War II

continued, and only the long, painstaking and dangerous work of registering Southern black voters en masse eventually forced Southern politicians to mend their ways.

Johnson won election by a landslide in 1964, but his vision of a "**Great Society**" soon foundered. He was brought low by the war in **Vietnam**, where US involvement escalated beyond all reason or apparent control. Broad-based popular opposition to the conflict grew in proportion to the American death toll, and the threat of the draft heightened youthful rebellion. San Francisco in particular responded to psychedelic prophet Timothy Leary's call to "turn on, tune in, drop out"; 1967's "Summer of Love" saw the lone beatniks of the 1950s transmogrify into an entire generation of hippies.

Dr King's long-standing message that social justice could only be achieved through economic equality was given a new urgency by riots in the ghettoes of Los Angeles in 1965 and Detroit in 1967, and the emergence of the Black Panthers, a Black Power political organization that valued community driven social programs and armed self defence. King also began to denounce the Vietnam War; meanwhile, after refusing the draft with the words "No Vietcong ever called me nigger", **Muhammad Ali** was stripped of his title as world heavyweight boxing champion.

In 1968, the social fabric of the USA reached the brink of collapse. Shortly after Johnson was forced by his plummeting popularity to withdraw from the year-end elections, Martin Luther King was gunned down in a Memphis motel. Next, JFK's brother **Robert Kennedy**, now redefined as spokesman for the dispossessed, was fatally shot just as he emerged as Democratic front-runner for president. This was the backlash to the Summer of Love, and it didn't take a conspiracy theorist to see that the spate of deaths reflected a malaise in the soul of America. The culminating event was the Chicago Democratic Convention in August, where police brutally suppressed riots and protests outside of the convention centre, with Mayor Daley imfamously ordering them, "shoot to kill".

Richard Nixon to Jimmy Carter

Somehow the misery of 1968 resulted in the election of Republican **Richard Nixon** as president. Nixon's conservative credentials enabled him to bring the USA to a rapport with China, but the war in Vietnam dragged on to claim a total of 57,000 American lives. Attempts to win it included the secret and illegal bombing of Cambodia, which raised opposition at home to a new peak, but ultimately it was simpler to abandon the original goals in the name of "peace with honor". Perceptions differ as to whether the end came in 1972 – when Henry Kissinger and Le Duc Tho were awarded the Nobel Peace Prize for negotiating a treaty, and Tho at least had the grace to decline – or in 1975, when the Americans finally withdrew from Saigon.

During Nixon's first term, many of the disparate individuals politicized during the 1960s coalesced into **activist groupings**. Feminists united to campaign for abortion rights and an Equal Rights Amendment; gay men in New York's *Stonewall* bar fought back after one police raid too many; Native Americans formed the American Indian Movement; and even prisoners attempted to organize themselves, resulting in such bloody debacles as the storming of Attica prison in 1971. Nixon directed

1945	1954	1955
President Truman's decision to drop atomic bombs on Hiroshima and Nagasaki marks the end of World War II	The Supreme Court declares racial segregation in schools to be unconstitutional	Black seamstress Rosa Parks refuses to change her seat on a bus in Montgomery, Alabama

various federal agencies to monitor the new radicalism, but his real bugbear was the antiwar protesters. Increasingly ludicrous covert operations against real and potential opponents culminated in a botched attempt to burgle Democratic National Headquarters in the **Watergate** complex in 1972. It took two years of investigation for Nixon's role in the subsequent cover-up to be proved, but in 1974 he **resigned**, one step ahead of impeachment by the Senate, to be succeeded by **Gerald Ford**, his own appointee as vice president.

With the Republicans momentarily discredited, former Georgia governor **Jimmy Carter** was elected president as a clean-handed outsider in the bicentennial year of 1976. However, Carter's enthusiastic attempts to put his Baptist principles into practice on such issues as global human rights were soon perceived as naive, if not un-American. Misfortune followed misfortune. He had to break the news that the nation was facing an **energy crisis**, while after the Shah of Iran was overthrown, staff at the US embassy in Tehran were taken hostage by Islamic revolutionaries. Carter's failed attempts to arrange their release all but destroyed his hopes of winning re-election in 1980. Instead he was replaced by a very different figure, the former movie actor **Ronald Reagan**.

From Reagan to Clinton

Reagan was a new kind of president. Unlike his workaholic predecessor, he made a virtue of his hands-off approach to the job, joking that "they say hard work never killed anybody, but I figured why take the risk?" That laissez-faire attitude was especially apparent in his domestic economic policies, under which the rich were left to get as rich as they could. The common perception that Reagan was barely aware of what went on around him allowed his popularity to remain undented by scandals that included the labyrinthine **Iran-Contra** affair.

Reagan's most enduring achievement came during his second term, when his impeccable credentials as a Cold Warrior enabled him to negotiate **arms-control** agreements with **Mikhail Gorbachev**, the new leader of what he had previously called the "Evil Empire". His War on Drugs, on the other hand, proved to have equally as impactful consequences, starting a movement towards mass incarceration and devastating African American communities in urban centres like Detroit and Chicago for years to come.

In 1988, **George H.W. Bush** became the first vice president in 150 years to be immediately elected to the presidency. Despite his unusually broad experience in foreign policy, Bush did little more than sit back and watch in amazement as the domino theory suddenly went into reverse. One by one, the Communist regimes of eastern Europe collapsed, until finally even the Soviet Union crumbled away. Bush was also president when **Operation Desert Storm** drove the Iraqis out of Kuwait in 1991, an undertaking that lasted one hundred hours and in which virtually no American lives were lost.

However, the much-anticipated "**peace dividend**" – the dramatic injection of cash into the economy that voters expected to follow the end of the arms race – never materialized. With the 1992 campaign focusing on domestic affairs rather than what was happening overseas, twelve years of Republican government were ended by the election of Arkansas Governor **Bill Clinton**. Clinton was a rare candidate; while

1962	**1963**	**1968**
John Glenn becomes the first US astronaut to go into orbit; President Kennedy faces down the Russians in the Cuban Missile Crisis	Rev Martin Luther King, Jr. delivers "I Have a Dream" speech; President Kennedy is assassinated	With the nation polarized by war in Vietnam, Rev Martin Luther King, Jr, and Robert Kennedy are assassinated

his campaign promises were economically liberal and favorable to Democrats, his commitment to be "tough on crime" as both Reagan and Bush had promised in their campaigns proved decisive.

Although Clinton's initial failure to deliver on specific promises – most obviously, the attempt, spearheaded by his wife Hillary, to reform the healthcare system – enabled the Republicans to capture control of Congress in 1994, the "Comeback Kid" was nonetheless elected to a second term. Holding on to office proved more of a challenge in the face of humiliating sexual indiscretions, but the Senate ultimately failed to convict him in **impeachment** proceedings.

The twenty-first century

When Clinton left the presidency, the economy was **booming**. His former vice president, however, **Al Gore**, contrived to throw away the 2000 presidential election, a tussle for the centre ground that ended in a **tie** with his Republican opponent, **George W. Bush**. With the final conclusion depending on a mandatory re-count in Florida, the impasse was decided in Bush's favour by the conservative **Supreme Court**. At the time, the charge that he had "stolen" the election was expected to overshadow his presidency, while the authority of the Supreme Court was also threatened by the perception of its ruling as partisan.

Within a year, however, the atrocity of **September 11, 2001** drove such concerns into the background, inflicting a devastating blow to both the nation's economy and its pride. More than three thousand people were killed in the worst terrorist attack in US history, when hijacked passenger planes were flown into the World Trade Center in New York City and the Pentagon. The attacks were quickly linked to the al-Qaeda network of Osama bin Laden, and within weeks President Bush declared an open-ended "War on Terror".

Confronting a changed world, Bush set about rewriting the traditional rule-book of international law. In 2002, he declared that the USA had a right to launch pre-emptive attacks: "If we wait for threats to fully materialize, we will have waited too long…We must take the battle to the enemy, disrupt his plans, and confront the worst threats before they emerge."

A US-led invasion of **Afghanistan** in 2001 was followed by a similar incursion into **Iraq** in 2003, ostensibly on the grounds that Iraqi dictator Saddam Hussein was developing "weapons of mass destruction". Saddam was deposed and executed, and no such weapons proved to exist; yet,Iraq degenerated into civil war.

Despite a wave of financial scandals, spearheaded by the collapse of the mighty energy firm Enron, Bush was elected to a second term in 2004. The country remained polarized, however, and the Bush administration was lambasted for its appallingly inadequate response when **Hurricane Katrina** devastated New Orleans and the Gulf Coast in 2005.

President Obama

That the Democrats regained control of both Senate and House in 2006 was due largely to the deteriorating situation in Iraq. Similarly, the meteoric rise of Illinois

1969	1974	1980
Neil Armstrong becomes the first man to walk on the moon	Embroiled in the Watergate scandal, Richard Nixon resigns	With Iranian students holding the US embassy in Tehran, Ronald Reagan defeats President Jimmy Carter

Senator **Barack Obama** owed much to his being almost unique among national politicians in his consistent opposition to the Iraq war. However, while Obama's message of change and optimism, coupled with his oratorical gifts and embrace of new technologies, resonated with young and minority voters, his ultimate triumph over John McCain in that year's presidential election was triggered by a new **recession**. After bankers Lehman Brothers filed for bankruptcy in 2008 – the largest bankruptcy in US history – no element of the economy appeared safe from the consequences of reckless "subprime" mortgage lending.

The exhilaration over Obama's becoming the first black US president soon faded. Despite managing to introduce a universal system of healthcare, which became known as **Obamacare**, he was seen as failing to deliver on many campaign pledges. In particular, he never closed the detention camp at Guantanamo Bay, while his Middle East initiatives had little impact. Although US forces killed Osama bin Laden in 2011, Obama was wrong-footed when the so-called "Arab Spring" toppled governments in Tunisia, Egypt and Libya that same year, and the death of the US ambassador to Libya when terrorists attacked **Benghazi** in 2012 damaged both his credibility and that of his Secretary of State, Hillary Clinton. Above all, the war in Afghanistan dragged on to become the longest conflict in US history.

President Obama's comfortable re-election in 2012 owed much to the role of the Tea Party in drawing the Republican Party ever further to the right. The Republican majority in the House of Representatives, however, continued to impede his agenda, precipitating a two-week **government shutdown** in 2013, and refusing to confirm any nominee to the Supreme Court. During his second term, Obama attempted to govern without Republican support, launching such initiatives as a rapprochement with Cuba, and a deal with Iran over its nuclear programme. Illusions that his rise to the presidency had marked the start of a new "post-racial" era of reconciliation, however, were punctured when the **Black Lives Matter** movement emerged in response to institutionalized indifference to the killings of young black men like Freddie Grey, Trayvon Martin, and Tamir Rice.

President Trump and beyond

For the presidential election of 2016, the Republican Party confounded expectations by selecting real-estate tycoon **Donald Trump** as its candidate. Derided by many as a boorish buffoon, Trump had burnished his image as a business mogul by hosting the TV show *The Apprentice*, and came to political prominence advocating the "birther" smear that Obama had supposedly been born outside the US. Polls and pundits alike confidently predicted that Trump's Democratic opponent, the vastly more experienced **Hillary Clinton**, would become the first woman president of the United States. She however failed to counter allegations of wrongdoing over her use of a private email server while Secretary of State, and dedicated Democratic states and cities in many regions, particularly in the Rust Belt, flipped to Republican. In a sensational upset, it was Trump who triumphed. Hopes that **President Trump** might put the demagoguery of the campaign trail behind him on assuming power were dashed at his inauguration, when he claimed to see "record crowds" along the visibly depopulated Mall. His term in office saw the US shift towards an isolationist stance,

1987	1991	1995	1998
Speaking in front of the Berlin Wall, Reagan challenges: "Mr. Gorbachev, tear down this wall!"	Following the Iraqi invasion of Kuwait, the Gulf War begins	A truck bomb in Oklahoma City kills 168	President Clinton proclaims "I did not have sexual relations with that woman"

abandoning its commitment to climate-change programmes and withdrawing from the anti-nuclear proliferation agreement with Iran. Although Trump's much-vaunted new Wall along the US-Mexico border was not fully constructed, a ban on immigration from certain Muslim countries was followed by restrictive policies resulting in the forcible separation of migrant families attempting to enter from central America. Constitutional norms were eroded, with minimal dissent from Republicans in Congress; federal agencies placed under the control of anti-government lobbyists; and the courts packed with partisan appointees. Pandering to the hard right, and most at ease addressing rallies of his long-term supporters, Trump survived a first impeachment attempt in 2019 and continued to provoke despair in his opponents as no amount of scandal or blatant "alternative facts" seemed able to bring him down.

However, in early 2020, the worldwide coronavirus (Covid-19) pandemic began to spread across the US. Initially dismissed as a "flu" by Trump that would "miraculously…go away", at the time of writing, the US has suffered the highest Covid-19 death toll in the world, with 910,000 dead and the figure still climbing. Unlike in many countries, stay-at-home orders and social distancing and mask-wearing requirements were made on a state or local level, and orders fluctuated as the country went through and recovered from three successive waves of the virus. By spring 2021, infection numbers were still fairly high and there were fears of a fourth wave, but concurrently, the US was making huge strides in its vaccination programme, with 200 million people already vaccinated.

The Covid-19 pandemic was ultimately a major catalyst for Trump's downfall. His lack of empathy for its victims, perception he wasn't taking the outbreak seriously enough and frequent flouting of safety protocols (as well as suggesting people might inject bleach to "clean" themselves at a press conference, to the horror of his scientific advisors) – combined with the inevitable economic downturn – conspired to ultimately lose him many swing voters, whose lives had been so hugely impacted by the pandemic.

But this was not the only major crisis in 2020. The Black Lives Matter movement exploded around the country and the world after African-American George Floyd was killed by a police officer kneeling on his neck to restrain him for over eight minutes. It was one of several killings of Black Americans by the police, but the collective anger and taking to the streets of BLM supporters in protest, despite pandemic restrictions, had a profound impact that raised awareness of ongoing racial injustice.

After a slow start, the Democrat challenger for the Presidency, Joe Biden, energised the African-American vote with his own support and his selection of Kamala Harris as his running mate, casting his campaign as a "battle for the soul of America". By the time Americans went to the polls in November 2020, the expected result was too close to call. However, Biden prevailed, winning more than 81 million votes, the most ever cast for a candidate in a presidential election, and securing 306 of the electoral college votes to Trump's 232.

President Biden and Vice-President Harris – the first female, African-American and Asian-American to hold the office – had made history. But their win wasn't the last twist in the tale. As Congress gathered to count electoral college votes to formalize Biden's win, ahead of his inauguration, the US Capitol building

2000	2001	2005	2008
The Supreme Court rules George W. Bush to have been elected president	On September 11, more than three thousand people die in the worst terrorist attack in US history	Hurricane Katrina slams into the Gulf Coast, devastating New Orleans	Barack Obama wins election as the first black president

was stormed and occupied by a pro-Trump mob, seeking to overturn the result. Encouraged to gather by Trump himself, who had failed to concede the election and was alleging vast vote fraud that he claimed had stolen millions of votes, the rioters forced terrified politicians to flee and vandalized and looted the building, while the world watched in real time in horror. For Americans, this attack on the heart of their democratic traditions was traumatizing. Trump failed to call in the National Guard or explicitly denounce his supporters' actions, and in the aftermath, he was impeached for a second time for incitement to insurrection, although he was eventually acquitted.

President Biden was inaugurated on January 20, 2021, in a ceremony that looked very different to normal, shorn of crowds due to Covid-19 precautions and with the assembled attendees in face masks. His first 100 days have been witness to a huge economic relief package to aid pandemic recovery, as well as the successful vaccine roll-out and re-joining of the Paris Climate Accord. Significantly, the conviction of George Floyd's killer, former officer Derek Chauvin, on April 20, has marked a step forward in police accountability. The US remains a country deeply riven by its racial inequalities and entrenched political and cultural perspectives, but with a more centrist President, time will tell if these divides can begin to be bridged.

2013	2016	2020	2021
The National Security Agency is revealed to be monitoring all electronic communications in the US	To world astonishment, Donald Trump is elected 45th president of the United States	The global Covid-19 crisis hits the US hard; Trump is ousted as president by Joe Biden	Pro-Trump militants storm the US Capitol building; Kamala Harris makes history as first female Vice-President

Books

The following list is an idiosyncratic selection of books affiliated with Chicago and the Great Lakes that may appeal to interested readers. Those tagged with the ★ symbol are particularly recommended.

HISTORY AND SOCIETY

★ **Eric Larson** *Devil in the White City*. Historical fiction written in a novelistic style intertwining Daniel Burnham's planning and development of the 1893 World's Fair, and H. H. Holmes, a serial killer who used the fair to lure his victims.

BIOGRAPHY AND ORAL HISTORY

Jill Ker Conway (ed) *Written by Herself*. Splendid anthology of women's autobiographies from the mid-1800s onwards, including sections on African Americans, scientists, artists and pioneers.

Tim Davenport and David Walters (eds) Selected Works of Eugene V. Debs. Collection of writing by a controversial figure in American history, documenting Deb's role in the organization of workers and Progressive era in the US.

★ **U.S. Grant** *Personal Memoirs*. Encouraged by Mark Twain, the Union general and subsequent president wrote his autobiography just before his death, in a (successful) bid to recoup his horrendous debts. At first the book feels oddly downbeat, but the man's down-to-earth modesty grows on you.

Mike Rokyo *Boss: Richard J. Daley of Chicago*. Chronicles the career of Daley, 20 year mayor of Chicago and boss of the infamous political machine of the 1950s and 60s.

★ **Malcolm X, with Alex Haley** *The Autobiography of Malcolm X*. Searingly honest and moving account of Malcolm's progress from street hoodlum to political leader, which charts the development of his thinking before and after his split from the Nation of Islam. The conclusion, when he talks about his impending assassination, is extremely painful.

FICTION

Sherwood Anderson *Winesburg, Ohio*. Depicts the coming of age and disillusionment of a young man in his Ohio small town.

★ **Eve Ewing** *1919*. This collection of poetry is based on a report analyzing the Chicago's racial dynamics in the aftermath of the 1919 race riots.

★ **Lorraine Hansberry** *A Raisin in the Sun*. Play influenced by Hansberry's experiences in Hyde Park with segregation, red-lining, and the challenges of upward social mobility for African Americans in northern cities.

Garrison Keillor *Lake Wobegon Days*. Wry, witty tales about a mythical Minnesota small town, poking gentle fun at the rural Midwest.

Upton Sinclair *The Jungle*. Documenting the horrific unsanitary conditions in Chicago's meat-packing industry, Sinclair's compelling Socialist-tract-cum-novel, first serialized in 1905, ranks among the most influential books in US history.

★ **Kurt Vonnegut** *Cat's Cradle*. The famous literary Hoosier's fourth novel is a satirical postmodern read with connections and references to different Indianapolis locales.

★ **Laura Ingalls Wilder** *Little House in the Big Woods*. A fascinating and delightful insight into pioneer life in the wilder-ness of nineteenth-century Wisconsin, the first of a series.

Richard Wright *Native Son*. The harrowing story of Bigger Thomas, a black chauffeur who accidentally kills his employer's daughter. The story develops his relationship with his lawyer, the closest he has ever come to being on an equal footing with a white person.

Film

The list below focuses on key films in certain genres that have helped define the Great Lakes experience – both the light and the dark. Those tagged with the ★ symbol are particularly recommended.

MUSIC/MUSICALS

★**Chicago** (Rob Marshall, 2002) Captivating choreography and Roaring 20s aesthetics depict two women on death row for murder competing for publicity and their lawyer's attention.

The Girl Can't Help It (Frank Tashlin, 1956). Pneumatic, pouting Jayne Mansfield defined the blonde bombshell for the Atomic generation. And Tashlin, who spent years as a mad-cap Looney Tunes animator, knew just how best to display her cartoonish, candy-sweet charms. The rock'n'roll plot delivers some fab musical moments, too, with numbers from Eddie Cochran, Little Richard and the wonderful Julie London.

Dreamgirls (Bill Condon, 2006). Based on the rise of Motown girl groups in the 1960s such as the Supremes, the Shirelles, and the Ronnettes, this film adaptation of the Broadway musical tells the story of a fictitious girl group the Dreams from Chicago.

SILENT ERA

Sunrise (F.W. Murnau, 1927). Among the most beautiful Hollywood productions of any era. *Sunrise*'s German émigré director employed striking lighting effects, complex travelling shots and emotionally compelling performances in a tale of a country boy led astray by a big-city vamp. Americana

A Christmas Story (Bob Clark, 1983). A humorous, nostalgic story set firmly in working class Indiana in the 1950s, this film shows the extreme lengths a young boy will go to get a rifle from his parents for Christmas.

The Blues Brothers (John Landis, 1980). In this musical comedy, two brothers try to get their band back together in order to save the orphanage they were raised in from closing. Starring John Belushi and Dan Aykroyd at the height of their Saturday Night Live fame, with a killer soundtrack and amazing road trip across the Great Lakes.

FILM NOIR AND GANGSTER FILMS

★**Bonnie and Clyde** (Arthur Penn, 1967). Warren Beatty and Faye Dunaway play Depression-era gangsters in a film that did much to destroy Hollywood's censorship code by ushering in an era of open sexuality and unmitigated blood and violence.

ON LOCATION

Although many memorable sights are off-limits to the public or exist only on backlot tours of movie-studio theme parks, countless filmmaking locations are accessible to visitors. This list provides an overview of notable films that were shot around the Great Lakes and in Chicago.

8 Mile (Curtis Hanson, 2002) Detroit, MI

The Avengers (Josh Whedon, 2012) Cleveland, OH

The Blues Brothers (John Landis, 1980) Chicago, IL

Chiraq (Spike Lee, 2015) Chicago, IL

A Christmas Story (Bob Clark, 1983) Cleveland, OH

The Dark Night (Christopher Nolan, 2008) Chicago, IL

Ferris Bueller's Day Off (John Hughes, 1986) Chicago, IL

High Fidelity (Stephen Frears, 2000) Chicago, IL

A League of Their Own (Penny Marshall, 1992) Chicago, IL and Huntingburg and Evansville, IN

Public Enemies (Michael Mann, 2009) multiple locations in Illinois, Indiana, and Wisconsin

Shawshank Redemption (Frank Darabont, 1994), Mansfield, OH

The Road to Perdition, Chicago, IL

The Untouachables, Chicago, IL

Tommy Boy (Peter Segal, 1995) Sandusky and Marblehead, OH

The Trial of the Chicago 7 (Aaron Sorkin, 2020) Chicago, IL

Public Enemies (Michael Mann, 2009). Johnny Depp stars as John Dillinger, infamous gangster and bank robber of the 1930s. The film depicts the FBI's pursuit of him in the 1930s and the end of the road for Dillinger, shot on-location across his Great Lakes haunts.

★ **The Untouchables** (Brian De Palma, 1987). Starring Kevin Costner, Sir Sean Connery, and Robert DeNiro as the feared Al Capone, federal Agent Eliot Ness forms a team of law enforcers to try and tackle the corruption of Chicago's prohibition gangs.

INDEPENDENT AND CULT MOVIES

★ **Fargo** (Joel Coen, 1996). Set amid the snowy landscapes of northern Minnesota and North Dakota, a quirky tale of a scheming car salesman whose plan to kidnap his own wife and keep the ransom money goes terribly wrong.

Ferris Bueller's Day Off (John Hughes, 1986) Showcasing iconic scenes from across the city of Chicago, this classic film about suburban high schooler's playing hooky is still quoted by many Americans today.

Small print and index

A ROUGH GUIDE TO ROUGH GUIDES

Published in 1982, the first Rough Guide – to Greece – was a student scheme that became a publishing phenomenon. Mark Ellingham, a recent graduate in English from Bristol University, had been travelling in Greece the previous summer and couldn't find the right guidebook. With a small group of friends he wrote his own guide, combining a contemporary, journalistic style with a thoroughly practical approach to travellers' needs.

The immediate success of the book spawned a series that rapidly covered dozens of destinations. And, in addition to impecunious backpackers, Rough Guides soon acquired a much broader readership that relished the guides' wit and inquisitiveness as much as their enthusiastic, critical approach and value-for-money ethos. These days, Rough Guides include recommendations from budget to luxury and cover more than 120 destinations around the globe, from Amsterdam to Zanzibar, all regularly updated by our team of roaming writers.

Browse all our latest guides, read inspirational features and book your trip at **roughguides.com**.

Rough Guide credits

Editor: Kate Drynan
Cartography: Carte
Picture editor: Tom Smyth

Layout: Katie Bennett
Head of DTP and Pre-Press: Katie Bennett
Head of Publishing: Kate Drynan

Publishing information

First edition 2022

Distribution

UK, Ireland and Europe
Apa Publications (UK) Ltd; sales@roughguides.com
United States and Canada
Ingram Publisher Services; ips@ingramcontent.com
Australia and New Zealand
Booktopia; retailer@ booktopia.com.au
Worldwide
Apa Publications (UK) Ltd; sales@roughguides.com

Special Sales, Content Licensing and CoPublishing
Rough Guides can be purchased in bulk quantities
at discounted prices. We can create special editions,
personalised jackets and corporate imprints tailored to
your needs. sales@roughguides.com.
roughguides.com

Printed in Spain

A catalogue record for this book is available from the
British Library

The publishers and authors have done their best to ensure
the accuracy and currency of all the information in **The
Rough Guide to The Great Lakes & Chicago**, however,
they can accept no responsibility for any loss, injury, or
inconvenience sustained by any traveller as a result of
information or advice contained in the guide.

Help us update

We've gone to a lot of effort to ensure that this edition
of **The Rough Guide to The Great Lakes & Chicago** is
accurate and up-to-date. However, things change – places
get "discovered", opening hours are notoriously fickle,
restaurants and rooms raise prices or lower standards. If
you feel we've got it wrong or left something out, we'd like
to know, and if you can remember the address, the price,
the hours, the phone number, so much the better.

Please send your comments with the subject line
"Rough Guide The Great Lakes & Chicago Update" to
mail@uk.roughguides.com. We'll credit all contributions
and send a copy of the next edition (or any other Rough
Guide if you prefer) for the very best emails.

Photo credits

(Key: T-top; C-centre; B-bottom; L-left; R-right)

Index

Map symbols

21982320502267

The symbols below are used on maps throughout the book

	International boundary		International airport		Spring		Boat
	State/province boundary		Domestic airport/airfield		National Park		Hindu/Jain temple
	Chapter division boundary		Transport stop		Gate/park entrance		Church (regional maps)
	Interstate highway	P	Parking		State capital		Church (town maps)
41	US highway		Post office		Lighthouse		Cemetery
5	State highway	i	Information centre		Statue		Building
	Pedestrianized road		Hospital/medical centre		Bridge		Stadium
	Path		Cave		Battle site		Park/forest
	Railway		Point of interest		Ski		Beach
	Funicular		Viewpoint/lookout		Mountain range		Native American reservation
	Coastline		Campground		Mountain peak		
	Ferry route		Museum		Swamp/marshland		
	National Parkway		Monument/memorial		Tree		
M	Metro/subway		Fountain/garden		Gorge		
T	Tram/trolleybus		Waterfall		Arch		